Thrive!® - People's Guide To A Thriving Future [For All Forever]

by

Gary "Chris" Christopherson
Founder, *Thrive!*® - Building a Thriving Future for All Forever
Founder, Health*e*People® - Building a Healthy and Thriving Future

Nelson, WI   University Park, MD

Thrive!

DEDICATION

People who help build, achieve and sustain

a surviving and thriving future for all forever.

Irene and Lynn Christopherson, nurturing and inspiring parents.

Dr. Patricia Haeuser, friend and supporter.

About The Author

Gary (Chris) Christopherson continues to work nationally and locally on improving health, reducing vulnerability and building a better future. Currently at **The Thrive! Center** he founded, he develops strategy, management and policy for creating, managing and sustaining large positive change and building a better and thriving future for all forever. www.ThrivingFuture.org He wrote several nonfiction books, including **Thrive! - Building a Thriving Future** available via www.Amazon.com or www.ThrivingFuture.org.

Thrive! draws on his 30+ years experience creating, managing and sustaining large positive change at national and local levels in public and private sectors. He founded HealthePeople (building a healthy and thriving future; www.HealthePeople.com), *via*Future (creating large positive change) and **Vulnerable** (minimizing vulnerability). He served as a senior leader, manager and policymaker responsible for multi-billion dollar policy, programs and budgets and thousands of employees. His public service includes: Principal Deputy Assistant Secretary and Acting Assistant Secretary of Defense for Health Affairs and Senior Advisor, Department of Defense; Associate Director, Presidential Personnel, Executive Office of the President, White House; Senior Fellow, National Academy of Public Administration; Senior Advisor to Chief Operating Officer and Deputy Director for the Quality Improvement Group, Centers for Medicare and Medicaid Services, DHHS; Senior Advisor to Under Secretary, Veterans Health Administration, VA; Senior Fellow and Scholar-In-Residence, Institute of Medicine, National Academy of Sciences; Chief Information Officer, Veterans Health Administration, VA; Director of Health Legislation, House Select Committee on Aging, U.S. House of Representatives; and Deputy Director, Municipal Health Services Program (funded by The Robert Wood Johnson Foundation and based at John Hopkins Medical Institutions).

He is a sculptor of abstract art, focusing on mobile and stabile sculptures and creating over 150 sculptures. GChris Sculpture at www.GChris.com. He wrote science fiction books, including **black box** and the illustrated children's book **Angel, Thriving Creator of Artful Things**. Both are available via www.Amazon.com or www.GChris.com.

He received his bachelor's in political science and his master's in urban and regional planning from the University of Wisconsin – Madison, and did doctoral work in health policy and management at John Hopkins University School of Public Health.

Table of Contents

Thrive!® - People's Guide To A Thriving Future [For All Forever].......i

About The Author...iv

Table of Contents..v

Summary..vii

Quick Guide To A Thriving Future 1

Chapter 1: How to use this People's Guide. 3

Chapter 2: What a thriving future will be. 7

Chapter 3: Why care about a thriving future. 11

Chapter 4: How you and your family and friends can thrive. 17

Chapter 5: How you and your community can thrive........................29

Chapter 6: How you and your country can thrive.............................43

Chapter 7: How our world can thrive. 57

Chapter 8: Thrive! System© (TS). Achieve thriving people and
communities with highest levels of thriving for all everywhere. 71

Chapter 9: How the *Thrive!* Endeavor, you and all of us together, builds a
thriving future. 95

Example and Worksheets 103

Complete Guide To A Thriving Future...1

Chapter 1: How to use this People's Guide. 3

Chapter 2: What a thriving future will be. 7

Chapter 3: Why care about a thriving future. 11

Chapter 4: How you and your family and friends can thrive. 15

Chapter 5: How you and your community can thrive........................47

Chapter 6: How you and your country can thrive.............................91

Chapter 7: How our world can thrive. 129

Chapter 8: Thrive! System© (TS). Achieve thriving people and
communities with highest levels of thriving for all everywhere. 165

Chapter 9: How the *Thrive!* Endeavor, you and all of us together, builds a
thriving future. 189

Appendix: *Thrive!* Next Generation Toolkit 197

Brief Summary

This **People's Guide To A Thriving Future [For All Forever]**, in both "Quick Guide" and "Complete Guide" versions, is provided to help you and your family and friends, community, country and world survive and thrive.[1] It shows how to build a thriving future using *Thrive!* **Strategy and Action Plans**. The "Quick Guide" quickly takes you through the basics of building a thriving future. The "Complete Guide" takes you through the basics of building a thriving future but in addition provides detailed examples, the required worksheets, and the detailed *Thrive!* **Next Generation Toolkit**.[2]

For our selves, our future generations and the Earth on which we depend, you and we must, can and will achieve a surviving and thriving future for all forever. This future is *Thrive!* and is a bold vision and mission. This Guide describes what your life and your world will be in a thriving future where all survive and thrive forever, to the maximum extent possible. It lays out why you and we must care about a surviving and thriving future for you, your friends and family, your community, your country and our world. You and we all want and need that future because of our endangered future and our human need to survive and desire to thrive. The Guide shows you and all of us how to build, achieve and sustain a surviving and thriving future for you and your friends and family, your community, your country and our world. And yes, we can as we are now the most able in human history. To help achieve this better future, the *Thrive!* **Next Generation Toolkit** provides next generation strategy and tools. Finally, this guide shows how the *Thrive!* **Endeavor**, you and all of us together, builds, achieves and sustains a thriving future for all forever.

---

[1] This **People's Guide**, including larger, fillable worksheets, can be downloaded free from www.ThrivingFuture.org

[2] You might also want to use *Thrive!* **- Building a Thriving Future** - a manual providing greater depth on strategy and tools and which is available via www.Amazon.com or as free download from www.ThrivingFuture.org.

Summary

This **<u>Quick Guide To A Thriving Future</u>** shows how to build a thriving future using *Thrive!* **Strategy and Action Plans**. [3] The "Quick Guide" quickly takes you through the basics of building a thriving future. [4]

How to use this Guide. (Chapter 1) This Guide helps you and your family and friends, community, country and world survive and thrive. For our selves, our future generations and our Earth on which we depend, you and all of us must, can and will achieve a surviving and thriving future. This Guide describes what your life and world will be in a thriving future where all survive and thrive forever, to the maximum extent possible. It lays out why you and all of us must care about a surviving and thriving future. All of us want and need that future because of our endangered future and our human need to survive and desire to thrive. This Guide shows you how to build, achieve and sustain a surviving and thriving future for you and your friends and family, community, country and world. We can as we are now the most able in human history. To help achieve this better future, the *Thrive!* **Next Generation Toolkit** provides next generation strategy and tools.   Finally, this guide shows how the *Thrive!* **Endeavor**, you and all of us together, builds, achieves and sustains <u>a thriving future</u> <u>for all</u> <u>forever</u>.

What a thriving future will be. (Chapter 2) This Guide describes what your life and our world will be in a thriving future where all survive and thrive forever, to the maximum extent possible. This future is *Thrive!* and is a bold vision and mission. It is different and better than anything tried or achieved in human history. It is a <u>thriving</u> future, not just getting by or achieving a surviving future. It is a thriving future for <u>all people and all future generations</u>, a "50+ generation" strategy. Not just for some people or just for the current or next generation. It is a thriving future <u>forever</u>, a 1000+ year strategy. Not just for today or just 100 years. It is also for <u>the Earth on which we live and depend</u>, not just for people.

Why you and all of us must care about a thriving future. (Chapter 3) This Guides lays out why you and all of us must care about a surviving and thriving future for you, your friends and family, your community, your <u>country and our world</u>. <u>You and</u> all of us want and need that future

---

[3] This **<u>Quick Guide</u>** and the more comprehensive **<u>People's Guide</u>**, including larger, fillable worksheets, can be downloaded free from www.ThrivingFuture.org

[4] You might also want to use *<u>Thrive!</u>* **- <u>Building a Thriving Future</u>** - a manual providing greater depth on strategy and tools and which is available via www.Amazon.com or as free download from www.ThrivingFuture.org.

because of our endangered future and our human need to survive and desire to thrive. What drives us is that a person and a people need to survive and desire to thrive in the current world and a sustainable future world. Further, because it is people who broke much of the world and endangered its future, it is people who must fix what is broken and build a survivable and thriving future for all forever.

How you and all of us can build a surviving and thriving future for you, all of us and those we care about. (Guide Chapters 4 through 7) Can we? Keep in mind that we are more able than any time in human history. We can build a thriving future by effectively and collaboratively using all available knowledge and tools, including next generation *Thrive!* strategy and tools. Next generation *Thrive!* is different and better than anything in human history. It is <u>achieving</u> a thriving future at each level. It understands that <u>people's behavior</u>, including yours, makes (or breaks) a thriving future. It helps you and all of us achieve the behavior that in turn achieves a thriving future at each level and for all forever.

How can we do it for you and those you care about? Chapter 4 shows you how to build, achieve and sustain that future for <u>you and your friends and family</u>. Chapter 5 shows you how to build, achieve and sustain that future for <u>you and your community</u>. Chapter 6 shows you how to build, achieve and sustain that future for <u>you and your country</u>. Chapter 7 shows you how to build, achieve and sustain that future for <u>our world</u>. Each chapter includes how to build a *Thrive!* **Strategy and Action Plan**. Chapter 8 shows you **Thrive! Systems**, how to use such a system to build, achieve and sustain a thriving future for <u>you and your community</u>.

How the *Thrive!* Endeavor, you and all of us together, builds a thriving future. (Chapter 9) <u>All of us together</u>, <u>including you</u>, must and can build a thriving future for all forever via the *Thrive!* **Endeavor**. It is only people that can and must fix what is broken and build a survivable and thriving future. It will take all of us. For these reasons, *Thrive!* is and requires a vast, sustained people endeavor building and sustaining a surviving and thriving future for all forever. Creating and sustaining this vast *Thrive!* **Endeavor** and a surviving and thriving future for all forever is the driving purpose of this **Guide**.[5]

---

[5] You might also want to use <u>***Thrive!* - Building a Thriving Future**</u> - a manual providing greater depth on strategy and tools and which is available via <u>www.Amazon.com</u> or as free download from <u>www.ThrivingFuture.org</u>.

Thrive!

Thrive!® - People's Guide

To A Thriving Future

[For All Forever]

<u>Quick Guide</u> To A Thriving Future

Chapter 1: How to use this <u>People's Guide</u>.

How to use this **<u>People's Guide</u>** to help you and your family and friends, community, country and world survive and thrive forever.

This **<u>People's Guide To A Thriving Future [For All Forever]</u>** is provided to help you and your family and friends, community, country and world survive and thrive forever.[6] For our selves, our future generations and the Earth on which we depend, you and we must, can and will achieve a surviving and thriving future for all forever.[7] This future is *Thrive!*, a bold vision and mission.

In this Guide, the term *Thrive!* [®] has several meanings:[8]

- *Thrive!* is the <u>vision</u> of a thriving and surviving future forever for all (our selves, family and friends, communities, countries and world).
- *Thrive!* is the <u>human aspiration</u> to build, achieve and sustain a surviving and thriving future for all forever.
- *Thrive!* is the <u>mission</u> to create and sustain large, positive and timely change that builds and achieves a surviving and thriving future for all forever.

---

[6] This **People's Guide**, including fillable worksheets, can be downloaded free from www.ThrivingFuture.org

[7] Whenever the term "thriving future" is used, it means "a thriving future for all forever, to the maximum extent possible". For example, while an individual person may not survive (live) and thrive forever, people (human race) may survive and thrive forever, whether on Earth or another inhabitable planet.

[8] The *Thrive!* trademark is registered to Gary Christopherson.

- ***Thrive!*** is the <u>call to action and rallying cry</u> to build, achieve and sustain a surviving and thriving future for all forever.
- ***Thrive!*** is the vast ***Thrive!* Endeavor** by all of us to build, achieve and sustain a surviving and thriving future for all forever.

This Guide describes what your life and your world will be in a thriving future where all survive and thrive forever, to the maximum extent possible. It lays out why you and we must care about a surviving and thriving future for you, your friends and family, your community, your country and our world. You and all of us want and need that future because of our endangered future and our human need to survive and desire to thrive. This Guide shows you how to build, achieve and sustain a surviving and thriving future for you, your friends and family, your community, your country and our world. And yes, we can as we are now the most able in human history. To help, ***Thrive!*** provides next generation strategy and tools.   Finally, this guide shows how the ***Thrive!* Endeavor**, you and all of us together, builds, achieves and sustains <u>a surviving and thriving future</u> <u>for all</u> <u>forever</u>.

More specifically, this Guide describes what your life and your world will be in a thriving future where all survive and thrive forever, to the maximum extent possible. ***Thrive!*** is different and arguably better than anything tried or achieved in human history. It is a <u>thriving</u> future. Not just getting by or achieving a surviving future. A surviving future is necessary but not sufficient. It is a thriving future for <u>all people and all future generations</u>, a "50+ generation" strategy. Not just for some people or just for the current and next generation. It is a thriving future <u>forever</u>, a 1000+ year strategy. Not just for today or just 100 years. It is also for <u>Earth on</u> <u>which we live and depend</u>, not just for people.

So, the first question to ask yourself is whether or not this surviving and thriving future is the future you want? Regardless of how you answer for yourself, then follow other questions. Is this the future your family and friends want? Your community wants? Your country wants? Our world wants?   The answer for each of these may be yes, no or not sure.

If you are not sure or do not want this surviving and thriving future, you should read just a bit further. To convince you, this Guide lays out why you and all of us must care about a surviving and thriving future for you, your friends and family, your community, your country and our world. First, you and all of us want and need that future because our future is endangered if we continue our current path. Second, you and all of us want and need that future because we as humans need to survive and strongly desire to thrive in the current world and a sustainable future world. Third, we have an obligation. Because it is people who broke much of the world and endangered its future, it is people who must fix what is broken and build a survivable and thriving future.

But, if you do not want a surviving and thriving future, this Guide has failed in its mission and is probably not for you. Hopefully, you might change your mind in the future.

If you want this future or if you are not sure, you are going to ask if you and we <u>can</u> build, achieve and sustain a surviving and thriving future. You are going to ask <u>how</u>. Chapters 4 through 7 lay out why you and all of us can and how to do it.

You and all of us <u>can</u> because we are more capable than any time in human history. We can build a thriving future by effectively and collaboratively using all available knowledge and tools, including next generation *Thrive!* strategy and tools. Next generation *Thrive!* is different and better than anything in human history. It is <u>achieving</u> a thriving future at each level. It understands that <u>people's behavior</u>, including yours, makes (or breaks) a thriving future. Its knowledge and tools help people, including you, achieve the behavior that in turn achieves a thriving future at each level (family and friends, community, country, world).

<u>How</u> to build and achieve a thriving future for any or all of those you and we care about is laid out as follows.[9]

- Chapter 4 shows you how to build, achieve and sustain that future for <u>you and your friends and family</u>.
- Chapter 5 shows you how to build, achieve and sustain that future for <u>you and your community</u>.
- Chapter 6 shows you how to build, achieve and sustain that future for <u>you and your country</u>.
- Most ambitiously, Chapter 7 shows you how to build, achieve and sustain that future for <u>our world</u>.
- Chapter 8 shows you **Thrive! Systems**, how to use such a system to build, achieve and sustain a thriving future for <u>you and your community</u>.

This Guide argues <u>why you and all of us should</u> build, achieve and sustain a surviving and thriving future. It argues <u>why we can</u> do it. It walks through <u>how to</u> do it for you and those you and all of us care about. But it will take more than just knowledge and tools and more than just each of us individually. It will take <u>all of us together, including you</u>.

Together, you and all of us must and can build, to the maximum extent possible, a thriving future for all forever via the *Thrive!* **Endeavor**. It is only people that can and must fix what is broken and build a survivable and thriving future. This mission to achieve a thriving future is greater than any in human history and must be sustained for as long as humans exist. To succeed in this mission, it will take all of us working together. For these reasons, *Thrive!* is and requires a vast, sustained endeavor that builds, achieves and sustains a surviving and thriving future for all forever. Creating and sustaining the *Thrive!* **Endeavor** is the driving purpose of this **People's Guide**.[10]

---

[9] In order to make each "how-to" chapter self-sufficient, there is some necessary repetition. The intent is that each chapter stands on its own depending on who and what are your priorities (family and friends, community, country, world).

[10] You might also want to use *Thrive!* **- Building a Thriving Future** - a manual providing greater depth on strategy and tools and which is available via <u>www.Amazon.com</u> or as free download from <u>www.ThrivingFuture.org</u>.

Chapter 2: What a thriving future will be.

What your life and your world will be in a thriving future where all survive and thrive forever, to the maximum extent possible.

This Guide describes what your life and your world will be in a thriving future where all survive and thrive forever, to the maximum extent possible. This future is *Thrive!* and is a bold vision and mission.

For you and your family and friends, a thriving future is a better life now and for the near and long term future for all of you and for future generations.

For you and your community, a thriving future is a better life now and for the near and long term future for the whole community and for all of the community's people.

For you and your country, a thriving future is a better life now and for the near and long term future for the whole country and for all of the country's people.

For our world, a thriving future is a better life now and for the near and long term future for the whole world (people and Earth) and for all of the world's people and the Earth itself.

For you and all that you and we care about, it is a much better life and future with less vulnerability, with surviving and with sustained thriving.

Thrive!

When a surviving and thriving future is achieved, you, families and friends, communities, states, countries and the world will be:
- Performing well,
- Well-off (financially),
- Well nourished,
- Well housed,
- Well protected (exposures, crime),
- Well educated,
- Physically and mentally well (people),
- Growing/developing well,
- Living within good habitat,
- Physically well (Earth, plants, animals, environment),
- Not vulnerable,
- Producing personal and public goods,
- Living within a stable, positive climate, and
- Sustained.

When achieved, we will have helped you, families and friends, communities, states, countries and the world move up from:
- Performing poorly or badly,
- Being poor (financially),
- Being poorly nourished,
- Being poorly housed,
- Being poorly protected (exposures, crime),
- Being poorly educated,
- Being physically or mentally ill (people),
- Growing and developing poorly or badly,
- Not doing well "physically" (Earth, plants, animals, environment),
- Living within poor or bad habitat,
- Being excessively vulnerable,
- Living in an unstable, destructive climate, and
- Not being sustained.

Thrive!

When achieved, we will have fulfilled the hope of all, and especially:

- Vulnerable individual people (persons),
- Vulnerable families and friends,
- Vulnerable communities (including neighborhoods, villages, towns, cities, counties, regions),
- Vulnerable states,
- Vulnerable countries, and
- A vulnerable world.

When achieved, we will have:

- Thriving individual people (persons),
- Thriving families and friends,
- Thriving communities (including neighborhoods, villages, towns, cities, counties, states, regions),
- Thriving countries, and
- A thriving world.

Thrive!, a thriving future, is different and arguably better than anything tried or achieved in human history. Not just getting by or achieving a surviving future. A surviving future is necessary but not sufficient. It is a thriving future for <u>all people and all future generations</u>, a "50+ generation" strategy. Not just for some people or just for the current and next generation. It is a thriving future <u>forever</u>, a 1000+ year strategy. Not just for today or just 100 years. It is also for <u>Earth on which we live and depend</u>, not just for people.

Helping achieve this surviving and thriving future is ***Thrive!*** - a vast human endeavor of you and all of us together striving for a surviving and thriving future. ***Thrive!*** strives for and envisions a surviving and thriving future, to the maximum extent possible, forever for all (you, family and friends, communities, countries and the world (including the Earth on which it depends).

Chapter 3: Why care about a thriving future.

Why you and we must care about a surviving and thriving future for you. Your friends and family. Your community. Your country. Our world.

This Guides lays out why you and we must care about a surviving and thriving future for you and your friends and family, your community, your country and our world. You and all of us want and need that future because of our endangered future and our human need to survive and desire to thrive. What drives us is that a person and a people <u>need to survive</u> and <u>desire to thrive</u> in the current world and a sustainable future world.

Our needing and desiring a surviving and thriving future is driven by a natural human force - "a person needs to survive and desires to thrive." To truly satisfy this need and desire, we need the following:

1) we, as a person <u>and</u> a people, need to survive and desire to thrive,
2) we depend on <u>other persons</u> (a people) for survival and thriving, especially in the long term,
3) our need and desire applies to both the current <u>and</u> future world,
4) our <u>future</u> survival and thriving depends on there being a <u>future world</u>, and
5) our future world must be <u>sustainable</u> and <u>sustained</u> to fully meet our need and desire.

For these reasons, building, achieving and sustaining a thriving future forever (to the maximum extent possible) for you, your family and friends, your community, your country and our world is <u>the</u> human endeavor and <u>the</u> ideal.

This is why you and we care about a thriving future. But let's be a bit more specific.

What future must you and we build, achieve and sustain? You, your family and friends, your community, your country and our world want to and must <u>build, achieve and sustain a surviving and thriving future</u>.

All of us, almost without exception, want to <u>thrive</u>. Thriving means:
- Performing well,
- Being well-off (financially),
- Being well nourished,
- Being well housed,
- Being well protected (exposures, crime),
- Being well educated,
- Being physically and mentally well (people),
- Growing/developing well,
- Living within good habitat,
- Being physically well (Earth, plants, animals, environment),
- Not being vulnerable,
- Producing personal and public goods,
- Living within a stable, positive climate, and
- Being sustained.

This is the best future for you, your family and friends, your community, your country and our world (including the Earth on which we depend).

All of us, almost without exception, want to and must <u>survive</u>. Surviving means at least:
- Performing at a minimal level,
- Having the minimum levels of resources, food, housing, protection, education, physical and mental health (people), personal growth and development, and habitat,
- Surviving "physically" (Earth, plants, animals, environment),
- Not being excessively vulnerable,
- Producing minimum levels of personal and public goods,
- Being in an humanly survivable climate, and
- Being sustained at a minimal survival level.

This is not the best future but it is far better than not surviving.

What future must we avoid? You, your family and friends, your community, your country and our world want to and must <u>avoid a bad or endangered future</u>. A bad future means:
- Performing poorly or badly,
- Being poor (financially),
- Being poorly nourished,
- Being poorly housed,
- Being poorly protected (exposures, crime),
- Being poorly educated,
- Not being physically or mentally well (people),
- Not growing and developing well,
- Not doing well "physically" (Earth, plants, animals, environment),
- Living within poor or bad habitat,
- Being excessively vulnerable,
- Living in an unstable, destructive climate, and/or
- Not being sustained.

In an endangered future, there is the risk of any or all of these. No one wants to risk this bad future let alone live this bad future.

A bad future also means not fixing what we already know is broken and likely to stay broken.

As we look around us at the people and the world which we care about, much of what is important to us is already broken or is endangered, much of it unnecessarily so. This is probably true for you and your family. This is true for your community, your country and our world.

For example, in the United States, our financial systems' failure did and still could bring down countries' and the world's financial system. Housing bubbles have burst and lifetime savings lost. While some of our housing markets improve, many people cannot buy homes (lack resources, can't get loans, job insecurity) or they own homes they cannot afford or sell. Even with the Affordable Care Act, our health care remains inaccessible, unaffordable and of poor quality for many people. Our education systems leave children behind and fail to educate children to their full potential. Our economic system rewards many people far beyond their contribution, holds many far below their potential contribution, and keeps many in or near poverty. Our environment is under more stress than it can handle in the decades and centuries to come. On energy, our future was bet on non-renewable energy sources and we have yet to turn to conservation and renewable energy at a level commensurate with long term energy needs and supply.

For some countries, the situation is better. For some, it is worse. All countries and the world as a whole are and will continue to be broken to some greater or lesser extent.

But these are only individual broken pieces for us to fix. In the real world, fixing the future means fixing these broken pieces together with fixing related broken pieces, e.g. health with the economy, education with food, energy with the environment, and housing with protection. Fixing these together is more likely to achieve a surviving and thriving future. Fixing all of these together is the most likely to achieve a thriving future.

Because it is people who have broken much of the world and endangered its future, it is people who must care about and must fix what is broken and build a survivable and thriving future. Because it is only people who can change our future, it is people who must build, achieve and sustain a surviving and thriving future.

All of this is why you and we care about a surviving and thriving future.

Chapter 4: How <u>you and your family and friends</u> can thrive.

How to build, achieve and sustain a surviving and thriving future for you and your family and friends.

Why you and your family and friends <u>can</u>.

You and your family and friends <u>can</u> have a surviving and thriving future. To get to that future, keep in mind that each of them is different with a different future already beginning. Each and all of them <u>can</u> do better whether that future appears bad or good. To build a better future, *Thrive!* strategy and tools have been used successfully at the personal level and on larger scales (community, country). They can work for you and the people closest to you. As they have for others, *Thrive!* can help you and your people build, achieve and sustain a surviving and thriving future.

Thrive!
Keep in mind that we are more capable than any time in human history. We can build a thriving future by effectively and collaboratively using all available knowledge and tools, including next generation *Thrive!* strategy and tools. Next generation *Thrive!* is different and better than anything in human history. It is <u>achieving</u> a thriving future at each level. It understands that <u>people's behavior</u>, including yours, makes (or breaks) a thriving future. It helps people, including you, achieve the behavior that in turn achieves a thriving future at each level and for all forever.

Why you and your family and friends <u>must</u>.

You and your family and friends <u>must</u> have a surviving and thriving future. Each and all of your people <u>must</u> do better whether that future appears bad or good. Why? Even those that have a good future are not fully thriving, are not likely to be fully thriving in the future, and are still facing uncertainties about the long term future. You and your people all want and need that future because your and their future is endangered and because of your and their need to survive and desire to thrive. What drives each of them is their need to survive and desire to thrive in the current world and a sustainable future world. Further, because some or all of them have broken some part of their world and endangered its future, you and your people must help fix what is broken and help build a survivable and thriving future.

How to build, achieve, and sustain a surviving and thriving future for you and your family and friends.[11]

To build a surviving and thriving future for you and your family and friends, they should be partners in this endeavor from the beginning and through each step. A collaborative approach where they jointly provide leadership, vision, motivation, strategy and successful execution probably has the greater potential to create <u>and</u> sustain large, positive change and a surviving and thriving future. Key to success is the strong desire to move current vulnerabilities through and beyond surviving to a sustained thriving future. *Thrive!* can be helpful to you and is laid out in the following steps.

---

[11] The following strategy is adapted from the *Thrive!* **Next Generation Toolkit** contained in the Appendix. It is customized to help you and your people build, achieve and sustain a surviving and thriving future. More is available in *Thrive! -* **Building a Thriving Future** - a manual providing greater depth on strategy and tools and is available via www.Amazon.com or free download from www.ThrivingFuture.org.

Step 1.

Step 1. Current state of you and your family and friends. The first major step is to understand the current state of you and your family and friends. This "how-to" works whether it is you alone, you and your immediate family, you and a more extended family, and/or you and your friends. In this chapter, the short-hand term "your people" is used and lets you decide on whom (you alone, you and your immediate family, you and a more extended family, and/or you and your friends) you want to focus your efforts.

a. Who are your people? Let's first go through who are you and your people currently. Who are your people? Use Table 4.1 (end of Quick Guide) to describe each of your people.[12] For each person, have the person independently do a one-paragraph description in her/his own words. If the person can't, do one for the person as best you can. Who is the person with respect to working and living? Financial situation? Eating and drinking? Housing? Protection? Education? Physical and mental health? Personal growth and development? Habitat (living environment)? Producing what? Climate? With this information on individuals and as best you can, do a summary of your people as a whole.

b. How well are they? How well (surviving and thriving) are your people? Use Table 4.2a (end of Quick Guide) to describe how well is each person.[13] How well is each person in terms of performing well? Being well-off (financially)? Being well nourished (food and drink)? Being well housed? Being well protected (exposures, crime)? Being well educated? Being physically and mentally well? Personally growing/developing well? Living within good habitat? Not being vulnerable? Producing personal and public goods? Living within a stable, positive climate? Being sustained? With this information and as best you can, create a summary for your people as a whole. Use Table 4.2b (end of Quick Guide) to describe how well are your people as a whole.[14]

---

[12] Free download of larger, fillable worksheets at www.ThrivingFuture.org

[13] Free download of larger, fillable worksheets at www.ThrivingFuture.org

Answering "yes" to all indicates current surviving and thriving. Though the "yes" answers are good, there is still future work to make sure this continues. "No" answers are bad and mean there is current <u>and</u> future work to be done.

c. What positively or negatively impacts them? What positively or negatively impacts or is likely to impact you and your people's surviving and thriving? Use Table 4.2a (individuals) and 4.2b (summary of your people) to describe all of the following impacts (positive and negative; current and future). What impacts your people's performing well? Being well-off (financially)? Being well nourished (food and drink)? Being well housed? Being well protected (exposures, crime)? Being well educated? Being physically and mentally well? Personally growing/developing well? Living within good habitat? Not being vulnerable? Producing personal and public goods? Living within a stable, positive climate? Being sustained?

Good impacts improve and/or sustain surviving and thriving. If they will continue, you probably can focus on other things. If they may or may not continue, your action is needed to make them continue and/or to develop other things to compensate. Bad impacts prevent or limit surviving and thriving. If they will not continue, you probably can focus on other things. If they may or may not continue, your action is needed to stop them or to avoid or minimize their impact.

Optional. Want more on your people's future and behavior? At this point, you have to go to Step 2 and develop strategy for you and your people. If you want to develop strategy and actions further, you may use the *Thrive!* **Next Generation Toolkit** and optional Sections d-e in the full and Complete Guide versions of the **People's Guide**.

---

[14] Free download of larger, fillable worksheets at www.ThrivingFuture.org

Step 2.

Step 2. Strategy to achieve you and your family and friends' surviving and thriving future. The next major step is to develop the strategy that will help your people build and achieve a surviving and thriving future.

a. Who will your people be in the future? Who will be your future people? If there are any changes to your people that are desired or likely, take them into account. You may want to leave out persons that should not or will not be one of your people. You may want to include future persons that should or will become one of your people (for example, new children, spouse, friend).

For each new person and as you did in Step 1, briefly describe the person to the extent possible. Use Table 4.1 to describe your future people individually and as a whole. What will this person do working and living? Financial situation? Eating and drinking? Housing? Protection? Education? Physical and mental health? Personal growth and development? Quality of habitat (living environment)? Producing what? Climate? If there are likely to be changes on these characteristics with existing members of your people in the future, make these changes as best you can. Also in Table 4.1, do a summary of your people as a whole. This should provide a full picture of your future people (individually and as a whole) as it will be and as desired.

b. How well should your people be in the near and long term future? How well should your people as a whole be in the future? Overall, they should be <u>surviving and thriving</u>. With this as a guide, you and your people choose the surviving and thriving future your people want to build and achieve. The "*Thrive!* strategy" will help you accomplish that.

Use Table 4.3a/b (end of Quick Guide) to describe how well your people should be.[15] Table 4.3a is the simpler version. Table 4.3b is the more detailed and powerful version.

From you and your people's view and to be surviving and thriving, indicate to what extent your people should be performing well. Be well-off (financially). Be well nourished (food and drink). Be well housed. Be well protected (exposures, crime). Be well educated. Be physically and mentally well. Be personally growing/developing well. Be living within good habitat. Not be vulnerable. Be producing personal and public goods. Be living within a stable, positive climate. Be sustained. Again, your people should be surviving and thriving.

c. What has to change externally and internally to achieve your people's thriving future? What has to change externally (outside your people) and internally (within your people) to progress from your people's current status to achieve your desired surviving and thriving status? In Step 1, you identified what positively and negatively impacts or is likely to impact your people. Update those, taking into account any changes to who are your people in the future.

Given those, what has to change externally and internally to achieve a surviving and thriving future? Use Table 4.3a/b to describe all that has to change for the following. To achieve performing well? Being well-off (financially)? Being well nourished (food and drink)? Being well housed? Being well protected (exposures, crime)? Being well educated? Being physically and mentally well? Personally growing/developing well? Living within good habitat? Not being vulnerable? Producing personal and public goods? Living within a stable, positive climate? Being sustained?

Good changes improve and/or sustain surviving and thriving. Bad changes prevent and/or limit surviving and thriving.

d. What actions by your people are needed to achieve their thriving future? What internal actions (by you and your people) and external actions (by others) are needed to bring about the needed external and internal changes (identified in "c") that improve your

---

people's current status enough to achieve the desired surviving and thriving status? [See Figure 4.1] [16]

External actions by others. There are very important <u>external</u> actions that are needed to support the *Thrive!* strategy. You already identified what has to change externally to achieve your people's surviving and thriving future. What external actions by others will bring about the needed changes?

Use Table 4.3a/b to describe all the external actions to be taken.

Identify external actions by others that support <u>good</u> changes that will help improve and/or sustain surviving and thriving. If good changes are likely to occur, together with others support them. If good changes are not likely to occur, together with others support them and develop other good changes to compensate.

Identify external actions by others that stop <u>bad</u> changes that prevent or limit surviving and thriving. If bad changes are not likely to occur, together with others ensure that they do not. If bad changes are likely to occur, together with others change them, stop them or avoid/reduce their impact.

Internal actions by your people. There are very important <u>internal</u> actions by you and your people that support the *Thrive!* strategy. Individual members and your people as a whole should support your strategy to ensure your people (individually and as a whole) are performing well. Being well-off (financially). Being well nourished (food and drink). Being well housed. Being well protected (exposures, crime). Being well educated. Being physically and mentally well. Personally growing/developing well. Living within good habitat. Not being vulnerable. Producing personal and public goods. Living within a stable, positive climate. Being sustained.

Use Table 4.3a/b to describe all the internal actions to be taken.

---

[16] An action is defined as "who will do what to/with whom, where, when, and with what result."

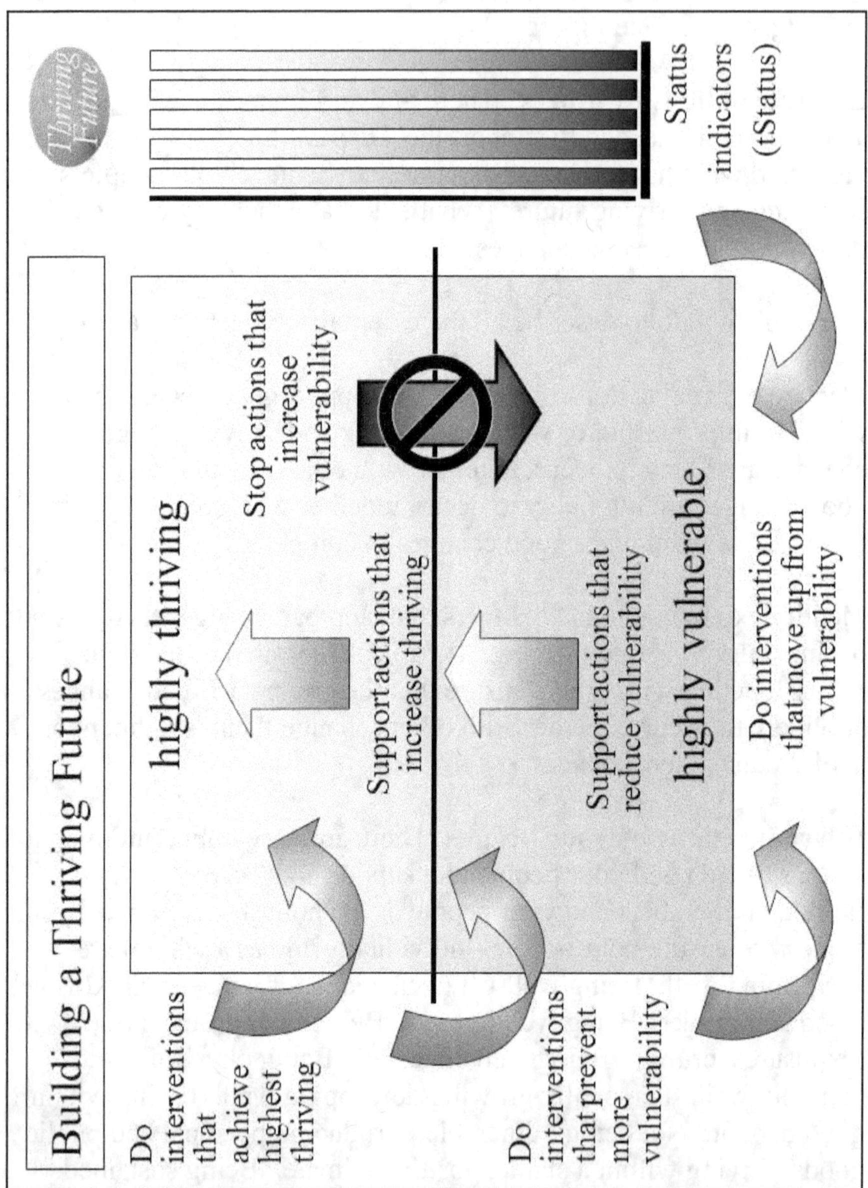

Figure 4.1. Building a Thriving Future.

Identify internal actions by your people that support <u>good</u> changes that will help improve and/or sustain surviving and thriving. If good changes are likely to occur, support them. If good changes are not likely to occur, support them and develop other good changes to compensate. [Use Table 4.3a/b]

Identify internal actions by your people that stop <u>bad</u> changes that prevent or limit surviving and thriving. If bad changes are not likely to occur, ensure that they do not. If bad changes are likely to occur, change them, stop them or avoid/reduce their impact.

e. Overall *Thrive!* strategy and actions. Your overall *Thrive!* strategy and actions need to be documented and agreed to by your people. Different members of your people will take on different responsibilities. For each action, designate who of your people will do what to/with whom, where, when, and with what result. Use Table 4.3a/b to document these actions and responsibilities. [See example table at end of Quick Guide.]

This is your *Thrive!* **Strategy and Action Plan**. As the strategy is executed, you strategy, actions and results should be updated.

Periodically, you and your people should assess your strategies/actions near and long term impact on near and long term surviving and thriving.

When a) your strategies and actions are not building and sustaining a thriving future and/or b) there are changes in the external world and in your people, you and your people should adjust your overall *Thrive!* **Strategy and Action Plan**.

The key is to successfully execute your strategy and actions and to build a near and long term surviving and thriving future.[17] Each and

---

[17] At this point, you should have enough good information to execute you and your people's *Thrive!* Strategy and Action Plan. If you want to develop your strategy and actions further, you may want to use more of the tools and models already mentioned and the *Thrive!* **Next Generation Toolkit**.

The full *Thrive!* **Next Generation Toolkit** includes strategy, policy and tools for creating and sustaining large, positive change and building a thriving future. You might also want to use *Thrive!* **- Building a Thriving Future** - a manual providing greater depth on strategy and tools and available via www.Amazon.com

all must successfully carry out the assigned action. That is, each/all must successfully do what is required to/with whoever is required, where required, when required, and with what needed/desired result.

A *Thrive!* **Strategy and Action Plan** is only as good as its successful execution and successful achievement of the desired outcome - a surviving and thriving future. *[Following is an example of a stronger **Thrive! Strategy and Action Plan** for you and your family's surviving <u>and</u> thriving future.]*

Example of you and your family surviving <u>and</u> thriving. *To build, achieve and sustain a surviving <u>and</u> thriving future, the **Thrive! Strategy and Action Plan** for you and your family and friends should be more like the following example: [Who will do what to/with whom, where, when, and with what result?]*

Starting immediately, you and your family and friends build, achieve, and sustain a surviving and thriving future, including:

- Performing well. *Starting immediately, you and your family and friends act to ensure, within the next 10 years, a) all (who are able and not appropriately retired) can work and earn a living income sufficient to survive and thrive and b) all have sufficient resources for and are living, recreating, learning so that they are surviving and thriving to maximum extent feasible.*
- Being well-off (financially). *Starting immediately, you and your family and friends act to ensure, within the next 10 years, a) all have sufficient income/resources to survive and thrive.*
- Being well nourished (food and drink). *Starting immediately, you and your family and friends act to ensure, within the next 5 years, that all have access to, be able to afford and consume healthy foods enough to survive and thrive.*
- Being well housed. *Starting immediately, you and your family and friends act to ensure, within the next 10 years, all have access to, be able to afford and live in adequate and preferably high performing housing that supports surviving and thriving.*

or as a free download from www.ThrivingFuture.org.

- Being well protected (exposures, crime). *Starting immediately, you and your family and friends act to ensure, within the next 5 years, environmental exposures in home, workplace and elsewhere are minimized so as to not prevent surviving and thriving.*
- Being well educated. *Starting immediately, you and your family and friends act to ensure, within the next 10 years, all are educated to the full extent of their abilities, needs and desires and to support their surviving and thriving.*
- Being physically and mentally well. *Starting immediately, you and your family and friends act to ensure, within the next 5 years, a) all receive the optimal health support to ensure, within the next 20 years, surviving and thriving and b) physical and mental health is optimized to best ensure surviving and thriving.*
- Personally growing/developing well. *Starting immediately, you and your family and friends act to ensure, within the next 10 years, all people are personally growing and developing to best ensure surviving and thriving.*
- Living within good habitat. *Starting immediately, you and your family and friends act to ensure, within next 20 years, a) all have access to habitat that best supports their surviving and thriving.*
- Not being vulnerable. *Starting immediately, you and your family and friends act to ensure, within the next 20 years, all, if vulnerable, are vulnerable only to the minimum extent feasible.*
- Producing personal and public goods. *Starting immediately, you and your family and friends act to ensure, within the next 10 years, all produce personal and public goods (including personal income/resources, housing, food and drink, energy, education, health, protection, personal growth and development, and habitat) so as to support surviving and thriving for all.*
- Living within a stable, positive climate. *Starting immediately, you and your family and friends act to ensure, within the next 2years, all behave so as to avoid negative impacts and support positive impacts so as to help ensure a stable, positive climate.*
- Being sustained. *Starting immediately, you and your family and friends act to ensure, within the next 5 years, all behave so as to ensure the sustainability of you and your family and friends.*

Chapter 5: How <u>you and your community</u> can thrive.

How to build, achieve and sustain a surviving and thriving future for you and your community.

Why you and your community <u>can</u>.

You and your community <u>can</u> have a surviving and thriving future. To get to that future, keep in mind that each community is different with a different future already beginning.[18] Whether that future appears bad or good, each community can do better. To build a better future, the *Thrive!* strategy and tools has been used successfully at the personal level and on larger scales (community, country). They can work for you and the community you care about. As they have for others, this strategy and these tools can help you and your community build, achieve and sustain a surviving and thriving future.

> *Thrive!*
> Keep in mind that we are more capable than any time in human history. We can build a thriving future by effectively and collaboratively using all available knowledge and tools, including "next generation" *Thrive!* strategy and tools. Next generation *Thrive!* is different and better than anything in human history. It is <u>achieving</u> a thriving future at each level. It understands that <u>people's behavior</u>, including yours, makes (or breaks) a thriving future. It helps people, including you, achieve the behavior that in turn achieves a thriving future at each level and for all forever.

---

[18] A community can be defined by geography (for example, a neighborhood, a region), by political boundaries (for example, a village, town, city, county, state), or by common population characteristics (e.g. racial/ethnic, gender, economics, political view, similar mission, religion, labor, profession, business).

Why you and your community <u>must</u>.

You and your community <u>must</u> have a surviving and thriving future. Each community <u>must</u> do better whether that future appears bad or good. Why? Even those communities that have a good future are not fully thriving, are not likely to be fully thriving in the future, and are still facing uncertainties about the long term future. You and your community want and need a surviving and thriving future because your community's future is endangered and because of our human need to survive and desire to thrive. What drives a community and its people is our human need to survive and desire to thrive now and in a sustainable future. Further, because your community's people (past and present) have broken some part of your community and endangered its future, you and your community's people (present and future) must help fix what is broken and build a survivable and thriving future for your community.

Why we all must and can do it together.

To build this better future, your community's people and leaders should be partners in this endeavor from the beginning and through each step. Success is dependent on positive and effective leadership from your community's leaders and people. How that leadership comes about is the subject of some debate. Some people argue for a leader driven approach where the leader creates the vision and motivation and the people join and/or follow. Some argue for bottom-up or self-organizing approaches where the people lead and the traditional leaders may or may not join and/or follow. Some argue for a collaborative approach where the traditional leaders and the people (also serving as leaders) jointly provide leadership, vision, motivation, strategy and successful execution. In general, the latter approach probably has the greater potential to create <u>and</u> sustain large, positive change and a surviving and thriving community.

Some communities will be geographic communities (including villages, towns, cities, counties and states). When feasible and when your community's governments are a positive force, governments should be part of the leadership and be partners in building a surviving and thriving community. However, it is not sufficient for governments to be the only leaders in this endeavor. Non-governmental organizations need to be leaders. Private businesses need to be leaders. Individual people need to be leaders. To be successful, this needs to be a whole community (people and leaders) endeavor.

Key to success is the strong desire by you and your community to move your community from its current vulnerabilities through and beyond surviving to a sustained thriving future.

How to build, achieve, and sustain a surviving and thriving future for you and your community.

To build a surviving and thriving future for you and your community, ***Thrive!*** can be helpful to you and is laid out in the following "how-to".[19] The following "how-to" is a relatively basic "how-to". The underlying principles and the strategy, models and tools apply to communities from small size and low complexity to very large size and very high complexity.

It is adapted from the ***Thrive!*** **Next Generation Toolkit**. It is customized to help you and your people build, achieve and sustain a surviving and thriving future. More is available in the full **People's Guide** and in ***Thrive!* - Building a Thriving Future** - a manual providing greater depth on strategy and tools and available via www.Amazon.com or free download from www.ThrivingFuture.org.

---

[19] Note that Using ***Thrive!*** for a community is very similar to using it for a country. If your primary interest is in a whole country, you may want to skip to the next chapter. A country is handled separately because of likely increased size and likely increased complexity and diversity of its people, its politics, its geography, its resources and its habitat.

Step 1.

Step 1. Current state of you and your community. The first major step is to understand the current state of your community.

a. What is your community? Let's first go through what is your community today. A community can be defined by geography (for example, a neighborhood, a region), by political boundaries (for example, a village, town, city, county, state), or by common population characteristics (e.g. racial/ethnic, gender, economics, political view, similar mission, religion, labor, profession, business). It can be a combination of these.

For your community, what are its geographic boundaries and characteristics? Use Table 5.1 (end of Quick Guide) to describe all of the following for your community.[20] Its gender, age, racial, ethnic make-up. Lifestyle. Type of work. Financial situation. Food and drink. Housing. Protection (crime, environmental hazards). Education. Physical and mental health. Personal growth and development. Habitat (living environment, neighboring communities, part of what state, country, continent). Producing what. Climate. Sustainability.

b. How well is your community? How well (surviving and thriving) is your community? Use Table 5.2 (end of Quick Guide) to describe how well is your community.[21] How well is your community in terms of performing well? Being well-off (financially)? Being well nourished (food and drink)? Being well housed? Being well protected (exposures, crime)? Being well educated? Being physically and mentally well? Personally growing/developing well? Living within good habitat? Not being vulnerable? Producing personal and public goods? Living within a stable, positive climate? Being sustained?

---

[20] Free download of larger, fillable worksheets at www.ThrivingFuture.org
[21] Free download of larger, fillable worksheets at www.ThrivingFuture.org

Answering "yes" to all indicates current surviving and thriving. Though the "yes" answers are good, there is still future work to make sure this continues. "No" answers are bad and mean there is current <u>and</u> future work to be done.

c. What positively or negatively impacts your community? What positively or negatively impacts or is likely to impact you and your community's surviving and thriving? Use Table 5.2 to describe all of the following impacts (positive and negative; current and future). What impacts your community's performing well? Being well-off (financially)? Being well nourished (food and drink)? Being well housed? Being well protected (exposures, crime)? Being well educated? Being physically and mentally well? Personally growing/developing well? Living within good habitat? Not being vulnerable? Producing personal and public goods? Living within a stable, positive climate? Being sustained?

Positive impacts improve and/or sustain surviving and thriving. If they will continue, you probably can focus on other things. If they may or may not continue, your action is needed to make them continue and/or to develop other things to compensate. Bad impacts prevent or limit surviving and thriving. If they will not continue, you probably can focus on other things. If they may or may not continue, your action is needed to stop them or to avoid or minimize their impact.

d. What is near and long term future behavior of your community? How is your community likely to behave in the near and long term future. For example, will it behave (individual behavior; group behavior, overall community behavior) so as to protect/improve public services, help each other survive/thrive, protect/increase jobs, maintain/improve community environment, and/or sustain the community near and long term.

Use Table 5.2 to describe all of the following behaviors. How will your community behave with respect to performing well? Being well-off (financially). Being well nourished (food and drink)? Being well housed? Being well protected (exposures, crime)?

Being well educated? Being physically and mentally well?
Personally growing/developing well? Living within good habitat?
Not being vulnerable? Producing personal and public goods?
Living within a stable, positive climate? Being sustained?

e. Want more on your community's future and behavior? At this
point, you have a baseline with which to measure progress for your
community. You have enough information to move to Step 2 and to
develop strategy for you and your community. If you want more
information before moving to strategy, you may want to use more of
the tools and models already mentioned and the *Thrive!* **Next
Generation Toolkit.**[22]

Step 2.

**Step 2. Strategy to achieve you and your community's surviving
and thriving future.** The next major step is to develop the strategy
that will help you and your community build and achieve a surviving
and thriving future.

a. What will your community be in the future? What will be your
desired and/or likely future community? Use Table 5.3 (end of
Quick Guide) to describe the likely future.[23] If there are any changes
to your community that are desired or likely, take them into account.
You may want to leave out parts of the community that should not or
will not be part of your community. You may want to include future
additions that should or will be part of the community (for example,
the next neighborhood, the next village/town/city, the surrounding
area, another interest group, another population).

---

[22] Using the full *Thrive!* **Next Generation Toolkit** is recommended because it
includes more strategy, policy and tools for creating and sustaining large, positive
change and building a surviving and thriving future. You might also want to use
Thrive! **- Building a Thriving Future** - a manual providing greater depth on
strategy and tools and available via www.Amazon.com or as free download from
www.ThrivingFuture.org.

[23] Free download of larger, fillable worksheets at www.ThrivingFuture.org

With this updated information, what will be your community's geographic boundaries and characteristics? Type of work/how people live. Financial situation. Food and drink. Housing. Protection (crime, environmental hazards). Education. Physical and mental health. Personal growth and development. Habitat (living environment, neighboring communities, part of what state, country, continent). Producing what. Climate. Sustainability. Update Table 5.3 with this information.

b. How well should your community be in the near and long term future? How well should your community as a whole be in the future? Overall, it should be <u>surviving and thriving</u>. With this as a guide, you and your community choose the surviving and thriving future your community wants to build and achieve. The "*Thrive!* strategy" will help you accomplish that.

Use Table 5.4 (end of Quick Guide) to describe how well your community should be.[24] From you and your community's view and to be surviving and thriving, indicate to what extent your community should be performing well. Be well-off (financially). Be well nourished (food and drink). Be well housed. Be well protected (exposures, crime). Be well educated. Be physically and mentally well. Be personally growing/developing well. Be living within good habitat. Not be vulnerable. Be producing personal and public goods. Be living within a stable, positive climate. Be sustained. Again, your community should be surviving and thriving.

c. What has to change externally and internally to achieve your community's thriving future? What has to change externally (outside your community) and internally (within your community) to progress from your community's current status to achieve your desired surviving and thriving status? In Step 1, you identified what positively and negatively impacts or is likely to impact your community. Update those, including any changes to your future community from Step 2a.

---

[24] Free download of larger, fillable worksheets at <u>www.ThrivingFuture.org</u>

Given those, what has to change to achieve a surviving and thriving future? Use Table 5.4 to describe all that has to change externally and internally for the following. To achieve performing well? Being well-off (financially)? Being well nourished (food and drink)? Being well housed? Being well protected (exposures, crime)? Being well educated? Being physically and mentally well? Personally growing/developing well? Living within good habitat? Not being vulnerable? Producing personal and public goods? Living within a stable, positive climate? Being sustained?

Good changes improve and/or sustain surviving and thriving. Bad changes prevent and/or limit surviving and thriving.

d. What actions by your community are needed to achieve its thriving future? What internal actions (by you and your community) and external actions (by others) are needed to bring about the needed external and internal changes (identified in "c") that improve your community's current status enough to achieve the desired surviving and thriving status? [See Figure 5.1] [25]

External actions by others. There are very important external actions that are needed to support the *Thrive!* strategy. You already identified what has to change externally to achieve your community's surviving and thriving future. What external actions by others will bring about the needed changes?

Use Table 5.4 to describe all the external actions to be taken.

Identify external actions by others that support good changes that will help improve and/or sustain surviving and thriving. If good changes are likely to occur, together with others support them. If good changes are not likely to occur, together with others support them and develop other good changes to compensate.

---

[25] An action is defined as "who will do what to/with whom, where, when, and with what result."

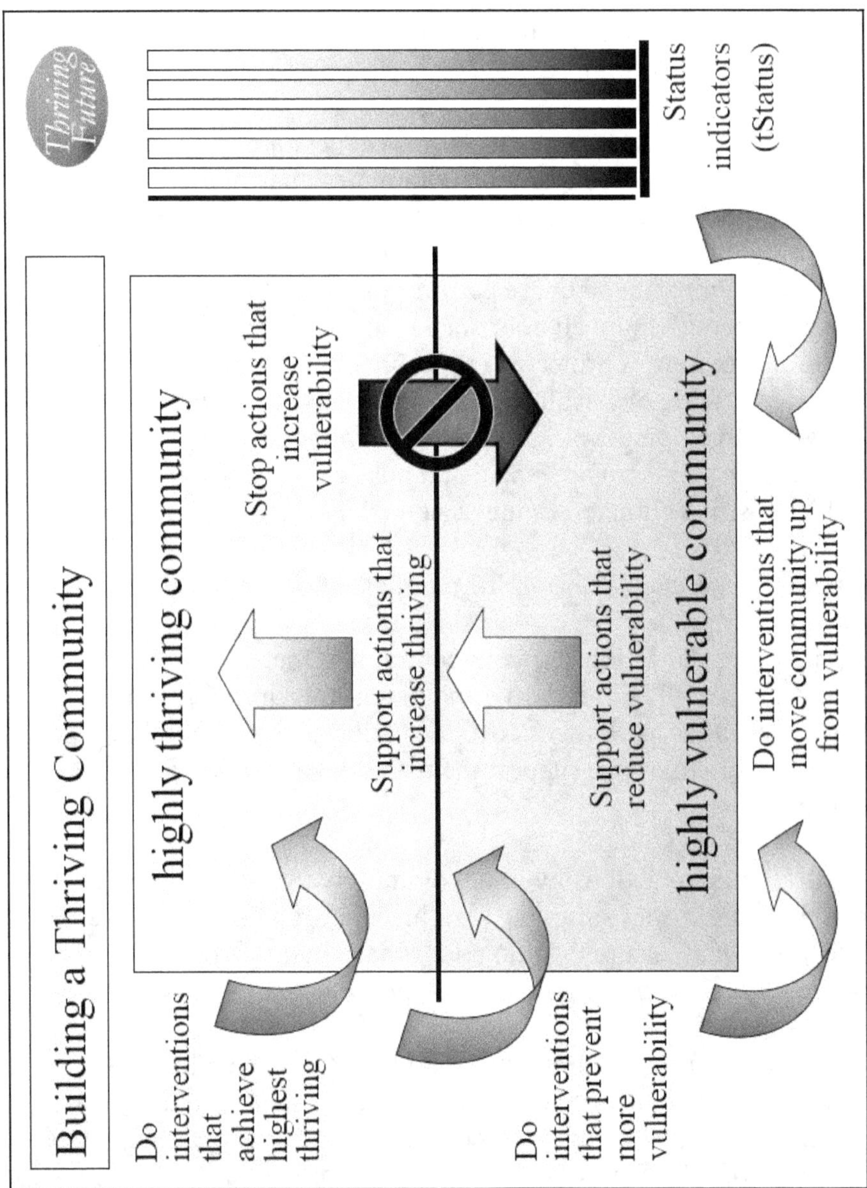

Figure 5.1. Building a Thriving Community.

Identify external actions by others that stop <u>bad</u> changes that prevent or limit surviving and thriving. If bad changes are not likely to occur, together with others ensure they do not. If bad changes are likely to occur, together with others change them, stop them or avoid/reduce their impact.

Internal actions by your community. There are very important internal actions by you and your community that support the *Thrive!* strategy. Individual community members and your community as a whole should support your strategy to ensure your community and each community member are performing well. Being well-off (financially). Being well nourished (food and drink). Being well housed. Being well protected (exposures, crime). Being well educated. Being physically and mentally well. Personally growing/developing well. Living within good habitat. Not being vulnerable. Producing personal and public goods. Living within a stable, positive climate. Being sustained.

Use Table 5.4 to describe all the internal actions to be taken.

Identify internal actions by your community that support <u>good</u> changes that will help improve and/or sustain surviving and thriving. If good changes are likely to occur, support them. If good changes are not likely to occur, support them and develop other good changes to compensate.

Identify internal actions by your community that stop <u>bad</u> changes that prevent or limit surviving and thriving. If bad changes are not likely to occur, ensure they do not. If bad changes are likely to occur, change them, stop them or avoid/reduce their impact.

e. Overall *Thrive!* strategy and actions. Your overall *Thrive!* strategy and actions need to be documented and agreed to by your community. This will be your community's *Thrive!* **Strategy and Action Plan.** Different members of your community will take on different responsibilities. For each action, designate who of your community will do what to/with whom, where, when, and with what result. Use Table 5.4 to document these actions and responsibilities. [See example table at end of Quick Guide.] Make sure you have all the actions that are needed to build, achieve and sustain a surviving and thriving community.

As the strategy is executed, you strategy, actions and results should be updated in your *Thrive!* **Strategy and Action Plan**.

Periodically, you and your community should do an evaluation - assessing your strategies/actions near and long term impact on near and long term surviving and thriving. When a) your strategies and actions are not building and sustaining a thriving future and/or b) there are changes in the external world and in your community, you and your community should adjust your overall *Thrive!* **Strategy and Action Plan**.

The key is to successfully execute your community's *Thrive!* **Strategy and Action Plan** and to build a near and long term surviving and thriving future.[26] Each and all must successfully carry out the assigned action. That is, each/all must successfully do what is required to/with whoever is required, where required, when required, and with what needed/desired result. A *Thrive!* **Strategy and Action Plan** is only as good as its successful execution and successful achievement of the desired outcome - a surviving and thriving future. *[Following is an example of a stronger **Thrive!** **Strategy and Action Plan** for you and your community's surviving <u>and</u> thriving future.]*

---

[26] At this point, you may have enough good information to execute you and your country's *Thrive!* strategy and actions. If you want to develop your strategy and actions further, you may want to use more of the tools and models already mentioned and the *Thrive!* **Next Generation Toolkit**.

The full *Thrive!* **Next Generation Toolkit** (Appendix) includes strategy, policy and tools for creating and sustaining large, positive change and building a thriving future. Your community might also want to use ***Thrive! - Building a Thriving Future*** - a manual providing greater depth on strategy and tools and available via <u>www.Amazon.com</u> or free download from <u>www.ThrivingFuture.org</u>.

Example of you and your community surviving and thriving. *To build, achieve and sustain a surviving and thriving future, the* **Thrive! Strategy and Action Plan** *for you and your community should be more like the following example: [Who will do what to/with whom, where, when, and with what result?]*

Starting immediately for you and your community, people, business/industry, private organizations (local, country), governments (local, country) and international organizations) build, achieve, and sustain a surviving and thriving future for you and your community, including:[27]

- Performing well. *Starting immediately for you and your community, people, business/industry, private organizations (local, country), governments (local, country) and international organizations act to ensure, within the next 10 years, a) all (who are able and not appropriately retired) can work and earn a living income sufficient to survive and thrive and b) all have sufficient resources for and are living, recreating, learning so that they are surviving and thriving to maximum extent feasible.*
- Being well-off (financially). *Starting immediately for you and your community, people, business/industry, private organizations (local, country), governments (local, country) and international organizations act to ensure, within the next 10 years, a) all have sufficient income/resources to survive and thrive and b) all governments have sufficient resources to provide needed (supporting surviving) and desired (supporting thriving) public programs and policies.*
- Being well nourished (food and drink). *Starting immediately for you and your community, people, business/industry, private organizations (local, country), governments (local, country) and international organizations act to ensure, within the next 10 years, that all have access to, be able to afford and consume healthy foods enough to survive and thrive.*
- Being well housed. *Starting immediately for you and your community, people, business/industry, private organizations (local,*

---

[27] International organizations could be a major resource, especially if the community extends beyond a single country's boundaries.

country), governments (local, country) and international organizations act to ensure, within the next 20 years, all have access to, be able to afford and live in adequate and preferably high performing housing that supports surviving and thriving.

- Being well protected (exposures, crime). *Starting immediately for you and your community, people, business/industry, private organizations (local, country), governments (local, country) and international organizations act to ensure, within the next 10 years, a) environmental exposures in home, workplace and elsewhere are minimized so as to not prevent surviving and thriving and b) crimes are minimized to the extent feasible in terms of frequency and impact so as to not prevent surviving and thriving.*

- Being well educated. *Starting immediately for you and your community, people, business/industry, private organizations (local, country), governments (local, country) and international organizations act to ensure, within the next 20 years, all are educated to the full extent of their abilities, needs and desires and to support their surviving and thriving.*

- Being physically and mentally well. *Starting immediately for you and your community, people, business/industry, private organizations (local, country), governments (local, country) and international organizations act to ensure, within the next 20 years, a) all receive the optimal health support to ensure, within the next 10 years, surviving and thriving and b) physical and mental health is optimized to best ensure surviving and thriving.*

- Personally growing/developing well. *Starting immediately for you and your community, people, business/industry, private organizations (local, country), governments (local, country) and international organizations act to ensure, within the next 10 years, all are personally growing and developing to best ensure surviving and thriving.*

- Living within good habitat. *Starting immediately for you and your community, people, business/industry, private organizations (local, country), governments (local, country) and international organizations act to ensure, within the next 10 years, a) all have access to habitat that best supports their surviving and thriving and b) your community has the optimal mix, quantity and quality of habitat to best support its inhabitants' surviving and thriving.*

- Not being vulnerable. *Starting immediately for you and your community, people, business/industry, private organizations (local, country), governments (local, country) and international organizations act to ensure, within the next 10 years, that all, if vulnerable, are vulnerable only to the minimum extent feasible.*

- Producing personal and public goods. *Starting immediately for you and your community, people, business/industry, private organizations (local, country), governments (local, country) and international organizations act to ensure, within the next 10 years, your community produces personal and public goods (including personal income/resources, housing, food and drink, energy, education, health, protection, personal growth and development, and habitat) so as to support surviving and thriving for all.*

- Living within a stable, positive climate. *Starting immediately for you and your community, people, business/industry, private organizations (local, country), governments (local, country) and international organizations act to ensure, within the next 10 years, all behave so as to avoid negative impacts and support positive impacts so as to help ensure a stable, positive climate.*

- Being sustained. *Starting immediately for you and your community, people, business/industry, private organizations (local, country), governments (local, country) and international organizations act to ensure, within the next 5 years, all people behave so as to ensure the sustainability of your community and its people.*

Chapter 6: How <u>you and your country</u> can thrive.

How to build, achieve and sustain a surviving and thriving future for you and your country.

Why you and your country <u>can.</u>

You and your country can have a surviving and thriving future. To get to that future, keep in mind that each country is different with a different future already beginning. Whether that future appears bad or good, each country can do better. To build a better future, the *Thrive!* strategy and tools has been used successfully at the personal level and on larger scales (community, country). They can work for you and the country you care about. As they have for others, this strategy and these tools can help you and your country build, achieve and sustain a surviving and thriving future.

Thrive!
Keep in mind that we are more capable than any time in human history. We can build a thriving future by effectively and collaboratively using all available knowledge and tools, including "next generation" *Thrive!* strategy and tools. Next generation *Thrive!* is different and better than anything in human history. It is <u>achieving</u> a thriving future at each level. It understands that <u>people's behavior,</u> including yours, makes (or breaks) a thriving future. It helps people, including you, achieve the behavior that in turn achieves a thriving future at each level and for all forever.

Why you and your country <u>must</u>.

You and your country <u>must</u> have a surviving and thriving future. Each country <u>must</u> do better whether that future appears bad or good. Why? Even those countries that have a good future are not fully thriving, are not likely to be fully thriving in the future, and are still facing uncertainties about the long term future.   You and your country want and need a surviving and thriving future because your country's future is endangered and because of our human need to survive and desire to thrive. What drives your country and its people is our human need to survive and desire to thrive now and in a sustainable future. Further, because your country's people (past and present) have broken some part of your country and endangered its future, you and your country's people (present and future) must help fix what is broken and build a survivable and thriving future for your country.

Why we all must and can do it together.

To build this better future, your country's people and leadership should be partners in this endeavor from the beginning and through each step. Success is dependent on positive leadership from the country's people and leaders. How that leadership comes about is the subject of some debate. Some people argue for a leader driven approach where the leader creates the vision and motivation and the people join and/or follow. Some argue for bottom-up or self-organizing approaches where the people lead and the traditional leaders may or may not join and/or follow. Some argue for a collaborative approach where the traditional leaders and the people (also serving as leaders) jointly provide leadership, vision, motivation, strategy and successful execution. In general, the latter approach probably has the greater potential to create <u>and</u> sustain large, positive change and a surviving and thriving country.

When feasible and when your country's national, state and local governments are a positive force, your governments should be part of the leadership and be partners in building a surviving and thriving country. However, it is not sufficient for government to be the only leader in this endeavor. Non-governmental organizations need to be leaders. Private businesses need to be leaders. Individual people need to be leaders. To be successful, this needs to be a whole country (people and leaders) endeavor.

Key to success is the strong desire by you and your country's people to move your country from its current vulnerabilities through and beyond surviving to a sustained thriving future.

How to build, achieve, and sustain a surviving and thriving future for you and your country.

To build a surviving and thriving future for you and your country, *Thrive!* can be helpful to you and is laid out in the following "how-to".[28] The strategy, models and tools apply to countries from small size and low complexity to very large size and very high complexity.

The following "how-to", by design, is simple but powerful. It is a relatively basic how-to providing the framework if not necessarily all the details for doing "your country" strategy.

This "your country" how-to is adapted from the *Thrive!* **Next Generation Toolkit**. More is available in the full **People's Guide** and in *Thrive!* **- Building a Thriving Future** - a manual providing greater depth on strategy and tools and available via www.Amazon.com or free download from www.ThrivingFuture.org. The optimal approach is to use the following how-to framework and also use the strategies, models and tools in the full **People's Guide** and in *Thrive!* **- Building a Thriving Future**.

---

[28] Note that using *Thrive!* for a country is very similar to using it for a community. In many ways, a country is a community. Here a country is handled separately because of the likely increased size, larger number of governments, and the likely increased complexity and diversity of its people, its politics, its geography, its resources and its habitat.

Step 1.

Step 1. Current state of you and your country. The first major step is to understand the current state of your country.

a. What is your country? Let's first go through what is your country today. A country is defined by its geography, political boundaries, or population characteristics (e.g. racial/ethnic, gender, economics, political view, similar mission, religion, labor, profession, business).

For your country, what are its geographic boundaries and characteristics? Use Table 6.1 (end of Quick Guide) to describe all of the following for your country.[29] Its gender, age, racial, ethnic make-up. Lifestyle. Type of work. Financial situation. Food and drink. Housing. Protection (crime, environmental hazards). Education. Physical and mental health. Personal growth and development. Habitat (living environment, neighboring communities, part of what state, country, continent). Producing what. Climate. Sustainability.

b. How well is your country? How well (surviving and thriving) is your country? Use Table 6.2 (end of Quick Guide) to describe how well is your country.[30] How well is your country in terms of performing well? Being well-off (financially)? Being well nourished (food and drink)? Being well housed? Being well protected (exposures, crime)? Being well educated? Being physically and mentally well? Personally growing/developing well? Living within good habitat? Not being vulnerable? Producing personal and public goods? Living within a stable, positive climate? Being sustained?

Answering "yes" to all indicates current surviving and thriving. Though the "yes" answers are good, there is still future work to

---

[29] Free download of larger, fillable worksheets at www.ThrivingFuture.org
[30] Free download of larger, fillable worksheets at www.ThrivingFuture.org

make sure this continues. "No" answers are bad and mean there is current and future work to be done.

c. What positively or negatively impacts your country? What positively or negatively impacts or is likely to impact you and your country's surviving and thriving? Use Table 6.2 to describe all of the following impacts (positive and negative; current and future). What impacts your country's performing well? Being well-off (financially)? Being well nourished (food and drink)? Being well housed? Being well protected (exposures, crime)? Being well educated? Being physically and mentally well? Personally growing/developing well? Living within good habitat? Not being vulnerable? Producing personal and public goods? Living within a stable, positive climate? Being sustained?

Positive impacts improve and/or sustain surviving and thriving. If they will continue, you probably can focus on other things. If they may or may not continue, your action is needed to make them continue and/or to develop other things to compensate. Bad impacts prevent or limit surviving and thriving. If they will not continue, you probably can focus on other things. If they may or may not continue, your action is needed to stop them or to avoid or minimize their impact.

d. What is near and long term future behavior of your country? How is your country likely to behave in the near and long term future. For example, will it behave (individual behavior; group behavior, overall country behavior) so as to protect/improve public services, help each other survive/thrive, protect/increase jobs, maintain/improve country's environment, and/or sustain the country near and long term.

Use Table 6.2 to describe all of the following behaviors. How will your country behave with respect to performing well? Being well-off (financially). Being well nourished (food and drink)? Being well housed? Being well protected (exposures, crime)? Being well educated? Being physically and mentally well? Personally growing/developing well? Living within good habitat? Not being vulnerable? Producing personal and public goods? Living within a stable, positive climate? Being sustained?

e. Want more on your country's future and behavior? At this point, you have a basic baseline with which to measure progress for your country. Your country may have enough good information to move to Step 2 and to develop strategy for you and your country. If your country wants more information before moving to strategy, your country may want to use more of the tools and models already mentioned and the *Thrive!* **Next Generation Toolkit**. This is encouraged and may be necessary for very large, complex countries.

Using the full *Thrive!* **Next Generation Toolkit** is recommended because it includes more strategy, policy and tools for creating and sustaining large, positive change and building a surviving and thriving future. Using the manual ***Thrive!* - Building a Thriving Future** is recommended because it provides even greater depth on strategy and tools. It is available via www.Amazon.com or free download from www.ThrivingFuture.org.

Step 2.

Step 2. Strategy to achieve you and your country's surviving and thriving future. The next major step is to develop the strategy that will help you and your country build and achieve a surviving and thriving future.

a. What will your country be in the future? What will be your likely future country? Use Table 6.3 (end of Quick Guide) to describe the likely future.[31] If there are any changes to your country that are desired or likely, take them into account. What will be its characteristics? Type of work/how people live. Financial situation. Food and drink. Housing. Protection (crime, environmental hazards). Education. Physical and mental health. Personal growth and development. Habitat (living environment, neighboring

---

[31] Free download of larger, fillable worksheets at www.ThrivingFuture.org

communities, part of what state, country, continent). Producing what. Climate. Sustainability.

b. How well should your country be in the near and long term future? How well should your country as a whole be in the future? Overall, it should be <u>surviving and thriving</u>. With this as a guide, you and your country choose the surviving and thriving future your community wants to build and achieve. The "*Thrive!* strategy" will help you accomplish that.

Use Table 6.4 (end of Quick Guide) to describe how well your country should be.[32] From you and your country's view and to be surviving and thriving, indicate to what extent your country should be performing well. Be well-off (financially). Be well nourished (food and drink). Be well housed. Be well protected (exposures, crime). Be well educated. Be physically and mentally well. Be personally growing/developing well. Be living within good habitat. Not be vulnerable. Be producing personal and public goods. Be living within a stable, positive climate. Be sustained. Again, your country should be surviving and thriving.

c. What has to change externally and internally to achieve your country's thriving future? What has to change externally (outside your country) and internally (within your country) to progress from your country's current status to achieve your desired surviving and thriving status? In Step 1, you identified what positively and negatively impacts or is likely to impact your country. Update those, including any changes to your future country.

Given those, what has to change externally and internally to achieve a surviving and thriving future? Use Table 6.4 to describe all that has to change for the following. To achieve performing well? Being well-off (financially)? Being well nourished (food and drink)? Being well housed? Being well protected (exposures, crime)? Being well educated? Being physically and mentally well? Personally growing/developing well? Living within good habitat?

---

[32] Free download of larger, fillable worksheets at <u>www.ThrivingFuture.org</u>

Not being vulnerable? Producing personal and public goods? Living within a stable, positive climate? Being sustained?

Good changes improve and/or sustain surviving and thriving. Bad changes prevent and/or limit surviving and thriving.

d. What actions by your country are needed to achieve its thriving future? What internal actions (by you and your country) and external actions (by others) are needed to bring about the needed external and internal changes (identified in "c") that improve your country's current status enough to achieve the desired surviving and thriving status? [Figure 6.1] [33]

External actions by others. There are very important <u>external</u> actions that are needed to support the *Thrive!* strategy. You already identified what has to change externally to achieve your country's surviving and thriving future. What external actions by others will bring about the needed changes?

Use Table 6.4 to describe all the external actions to be taken.

Identify external actions by others that support <u>good</u> changes that will help improve and/or sustain surviving and thriving. If good changes are likely to occur, together with others support them. If good changes are not likely to occur, together with others support them and develop other good changes to compensate. [Use Table 6.4]

Identify external actions by others that stop <u>bad</u> changes that prevent or limit surviving and thriving. If bad changes are not likely to occur, together with others ensure they do not. If bad changes are likely to occur, together with others change them, stop them or avoid/reduce their impact.

---

[33] An action is defined as "who will do what to/with whom, where, when, and with what result."

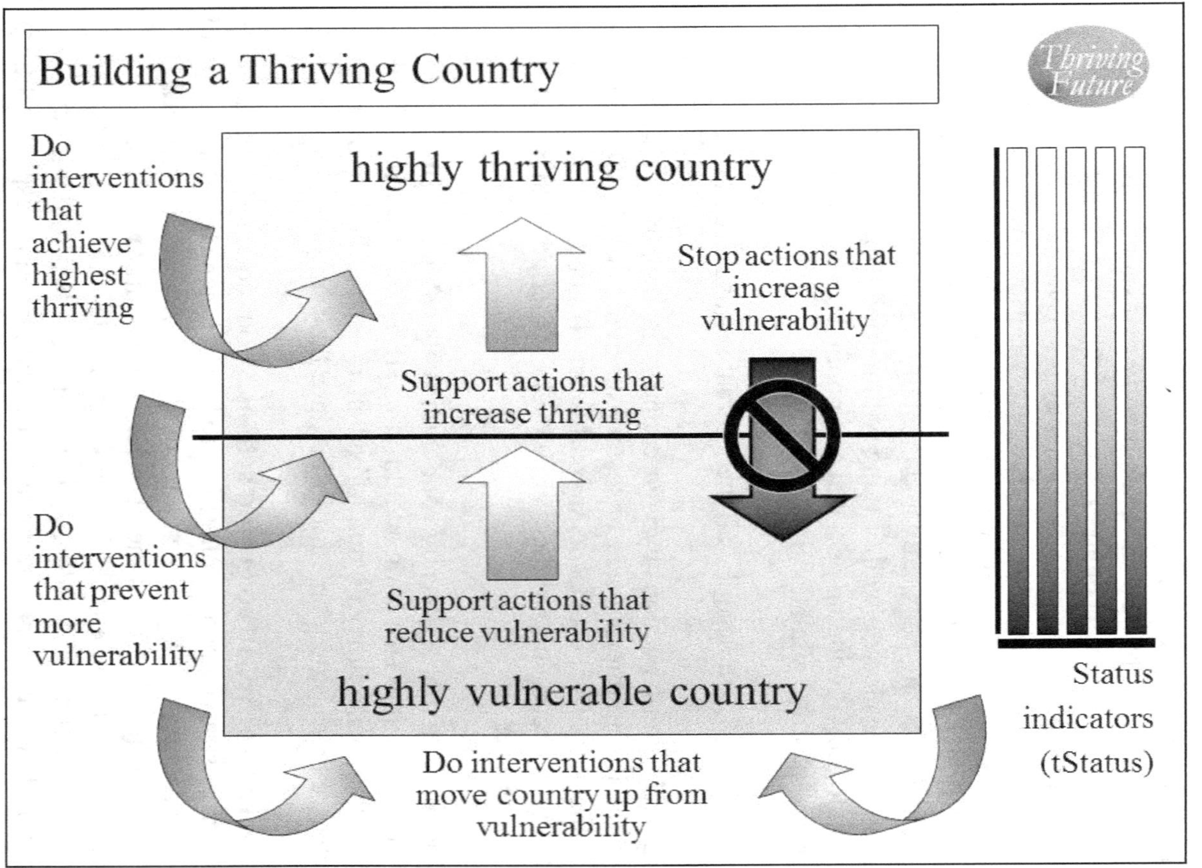

Figure 6.1. Building a Thriving Country.

Internal actions by your country. There are very important <u>internal</u> actions by you and your country that support the *Thrive!* strategy. Individual country members and your country as a whole should support your country's strategy to ensure your country and each country member are performing well. Being well-off (financially). Being well nourished (food and drink). Being well housed. Being well protected (exposures, crime). Being well educated. Being physically and mentally well. Personally growing/developing well. Living within good habitat. Not being vulnerable. Producing personal and public goods. Living within a stable, positive climate. Being sustained.

Use Table 6.4 to describe all the internal actions to be taken.

Identify internal actions by your country that support <u>good</u> changes that will help improve and/or sustain surviving and thriving. If good changes are likely to occur, support them. If good changes are not likely to occur, support them and develop other good changes to compensate.

Identify internal actions by your country that stop <u>bad</u> changes that prevent or limit surviving and thriving. If bad changes are not likely to occur, ensure they do not. If bad changes are likely to occur, change them, stop them or avoid/reduce their impact.

Overall *Thrive!* strategy and actions. Your country's overall *Thrive!* strategy and actions need to be documented and agreed to by your country. This will be your country's ***Thrive!* Strategy and Action Plan**. Different members of your country will take on different responsibilities. For each action, designate who of your country will do what to/with whom, where, when, and with what result. Use Table 6.4 to document these actions and responsibilities. [See example table at end of Quick Guide.] Make sure your country has all the actions that are needed to build, achieve and sustain a surviving and thriving country.

As the strategy is executed, your country's strategy, actions and results should be updated in your *Thrive!* **Strategy and Action Plan**.

Periodically, you and your country should do an evaluation - assessing your country's strategies/actions near and long term impact on near and long term surviving and thriving. When a) your country's strategies and actions are not building and sustaining a thriving future and/or b) there are changes in the external world and in your country, you and your country should adjust your overall *Thrive!* strategy and actions.

The key is to successfully execute your country's *Thrive!* **Strategy and Action Plan** and to build a near and long term surviving and thriving future.[34] Each and all must successfully carry out the assigned action. That is, each/all must successfully do what is required to/with whoever is required, where required, when required, and with what needed/desired result. A *Thrive!* **Strategy and Action Plan** is only as good as its successful execution and successful achievement of the desired outcome - a surviving and thriving future. *[Following is an example of a stronger Thrive! Strategy and Action Plan for you and your country's surviving <u>and</u> thriving future.]*

---

[34] At this point, you and your country should have enough good information to execute you and your country's *Thrive!* Strategy and Action Plan. If you and your country want to develop strategy and actions further, you and your country may want to use more of the tools and models already mentioned and the *Thrive!* **Next Generation Toolkit.** This is encouraged and may be necessary for very large, complex countries.

As stated earlier, this "how-to", by design, is simple but powerful. It is relatively basic providing the framework for doing "your country" strategy. The optimal approach is to use this how-to framework <u>and</u> use the more extensive strategy, models and tools in a) the *Thrive!* **Next Generation Toolkit** and b) *Thrive!* **- Building a Thriving Future** available via www.Amazon.com or free download from www.ThrivingFuture.org.

Example of you and your country surviving _and_ thriving. *To build, achieve and sustain a surviving _and_ thriving future, the* **Thrive! Strategy and Action Plan** *for you and your country should be more like the following example: [Who will do what to/with whom, where, when, and with what result?]*

Starting immediately for you and your country, people, business/industry, private organizations (local, country), governments (local, country) and international organizations build, achieve, and sustain a surviving and thriving future for you and your country, including:

- Performing well. *Starting immediately for you and your country, people, business/industry, private organizations (local, country), governments (local, country) and international organizations act to ensure, within the next 20 years, a) all (who are able and not appropriately retired) can work and earn a living income sufficient to survive and thrive and b) all have sufficient resources for and are living, recreating, learning so that they are surviving and thriving to maximum extent feasible.*

- Being well-off (financially). *Starting immediately for you and your country, people, business/industry, private organizations (local, country), governments (local, country) and international organizations act to ensure, within the next 20 years, a) all have sufficient income/resources to survive and thrive and b) all governments have sufficient resources to provide needed (supporting surviving) and desired (supporting thriving) public programs and policies.*

- Being well nourished (food and drink). *Starting immediately for you and your country, people, business/industry, private organizations (local, country), governments (local, country) and international organizations act to ensure, within the next 20 years, that all have access to, be able to afford and consume healthy foods enough to survive and thrive.*

- Being well housed. *Starting immediately for you and your country, people, business/industry, private organizations (local, country), governments (local, country) and international organizations act to ensure, within the next 20 years, all have access to, be able to afford and live in adequate and preferably high performing housing that supports surviving and thriving.*

- Being well protected (exposures, crime). *Starting immediately for you and your country, people, business/industry, private organizations (local, country), governments (local, country) and international organizations act to ensure, within the next 20 years, a) environmental exposures in home, workplace and elsewhere are minimized so as to not prevent surviving and thriving and b) crimes are minimized to the extent feasible in terms of frequency and impact so as to not prevent surviving and thriving.*

- Being well educated. *Starting immediately for you and your country, people, business/industry, private organizations (local, country), governments (local, country) and international organizations act to ensure, within the next 20 years, all people are educated to the full extent of their abilities, needs and desires and to support their surviving and thriving.*

- Being physically and mentally well. *Starting immediately for you and your country, people, business/industry, private organizations (local, country), governments (local, country) and international organizations act to ensure, within the next 20 years, a) all receive the optimal health support to ensure, within the next 20 years, surviving and thriving and b) physical and mental health is optimized to best ensure surviving and thriving.*

- Personally growing/developing well. *Starting immediately for you and your country, people, business/industry, private organizations (local, country), governments (local, country) and international organizations act to ensure, within the next 20 years, all are personally growing and developing to best ensure surviving and thriving.*

- Living within good habitat. *Starting immediately for you and your country, people, business/industry, private organizations (local, country), governments (local, country) and international organizations act to ensure, within the next 20 years, a) all have access to habitat that best supports their surviving and thriving and b) your country has the optimal mix, quantity and quality of habitat to best support its inhabitants' surviving and thriving.*

- Not being vulnerable. *Starting immediately for you and your country, people, business/industry, private organizations (local, country), governments (local, country) and international organizations act to ensure, within the next 20 years, your country and all of its people, if vulnerable, are vulnerable only to the minimum extent feasible.*

- Producing personal and public goods. *Starting immediately for you and your country, people, business/industry, private organizations (local, country), governments (local, country) and international organizations act to ensure, within the next 20 years, your country produces personal and public goods (including personal income/resources, housing, food and drink, energy, education, health, protection, personal growth and development, and habitat) so as to support surviving and thriving for all persons and for our world overall.*

- Living within a stable, positive climate. *Starting immediately for you and your country, people, business/industry, private organizations (local, country), governments (local, country) and international organizations act to ensure, within the next 10 years, all behave so as to avoid negative impacts and support positive impacts so as to help ensure a stable, positive climate.*

- Being sustained. *Starting immediately for you and your country, people, business/industry, private organizations (local, country), governments (local, country) and international organizations act to ensure, within the next 5 years, all behave so as to ensure the sustainability of your country and its people.*

Chapter 7: How <u>our world</u> can thrive.

How to build, achieve and sustain a surviving and thriving future for our world. [35,36]

Why our world <u>can</u>.

Our world can have a surviving and thriving future. To get to that future, keep in mind that our world has a future already beginning. Whether that future appears bad or good, our world can do better. To build a better future, the *Thrive!* strategy and tools has been used successfully at the personal level and on larger scales (community, country). They can work for the world we all care about. As they have for others, this strategy and these tools can help our world build, achieve and sustain a surviving and thriving future.

Thrive!

Keep in mind that we are more capable than any time in human history. We can build a thriving future by effectively and collaboratively using all available knowledge and tools, including "next generation" *Thrive!* strategy and tools. Next generation *Thrive!* is different and better than anything in human history. It is <u>achieving</u> a thriving future at each level. It understands that <u>people's behavior</u>, including yours, makes (or breaks) a thriving future. It helps people, including you, achieve the behavior that in turn achieves a thriving future at each level and for all forever.

---

[35] In working through "how our world can thrive", the focus shifts from "you and family, friends, community and country" to "we" and "our world" in keeping with the all inclusive context. Also, in this context, the word "we" means essentially all of us, including future generations, joined together.

[36] We must keep in mind that "our world" is expanding as we explore and move beyond earth to other parts of our universe. For that reason, "a thriving future for all forever" reaches at least as far as we touch or ever hope to touch.

Why our world <u>must</u>.

Our world <u>must</u> have a surviving and thriving future. Our world <u>must</u> do better whether that future appears bad or good. Why? Even if we believe that our world has a good future, we are not fully thriving, are not likely to be fully thriving in the future, and are still facing uncertainties about the long term future. We want and need a surviving and thriving future because our world's future is endangered and because of our human need to survive and desire to thrive. What drives our world and all of us is our human need to survive and desire to thrive now and in a sustainable future. Further, because we (past and present) have broken parts of our world and endangered its future, we (present and future) must help fix what is broken and build a survivable and thriving future for our world.

Why we all must and can do it together.

To build this better future, we (our world's current and future people and leadership) should be partners in this endeavor from the beginning and through each step. Success is dependent on positive leadership from us - our world's people and leaders. How that leadership comes about is the subject of some debate. Some people argue for a leader driven approach where the leader creates the vision and motivation and the people join and/or follow. Some argue for bottom-up or self-organizing approaches where the people lead and the traditional leaders may or may not join and/or follow. Some argue for a collaborative approach where the traditional leaders and the people (also serving as leaders) jointly provide leadership, vision, motivation, strategy and successful execution. In general, the latter approach probably has the greater potential to create <u>and</u> sustain large, positive change and a surviving and thriving world.

For a world or global endeavor, international organizations (e.g. the United Nations, multi-country regional organizations) and country governments should be part of the leadership and be partners in building a surviving and thriving world. However, it is not sufficient for government-based international organizations and country governments to be the only leaders in this endeavor. Non-governmental international and national organizations need to be leaders. Private businesses need to be leaders. Individual people need to be leaders. To be successful, this needs to be a whole world (people and leaders) endeavor.

Key to success is the strong desire by all of us (our world's leaders and people) to move our world from its current vulnerabilities through and beyond surviving to a sustained thriving future.

How to build, achieve, and sustain a surviving and thriving future for our world.

To build a surviving and thriving future for our world, *Thrive!* can be helpful and is laid out in the following "how-to".[37]

The following "how-to", by design, is simple but powerful. It is a relatively basic how-to providing the framework, but not all the details, for doing "our world" strategy.

This "our world" how-to is adapted from the *Thrive!* **Next Generation Toolkit**. More is available in the full **People's Guide** and in *Thrive! -* **Building a Thriving Future** - a manual providing greater depth on strategy and tools and available via www.Amazon.com or free download from www.ThrivingFuture.org. The optimal approach is to use the following how-to framework and also use the strategies, models and tools in the full **People's Guide** and in *Thrive! -* **Building a Thriving Future**.

---

[37] Note that using *Thrive!* for our world has some similarities to using it for your community or your country. Our world has some of the characteristics of a community and a country but is much, much larger in terms of land/water, people, and governments and is much, much more complex and diverse in terms of its people, its politics, its geography, its resources and its habitat.

Step 1.

Step 1. Current state of our world. The first major step for us is to understand the current state of our world.

a. What is our world? We first define and understand what our world is today. Our world is defined by its geography, political boundaries, and population characteristics (including racial/ethnic, gender, economics, political view, religion, labor, profession, business).

We need to understand our world's geographic boundaries and characteristics. Use Table 7.1 (end of Quick Guide) to describe all of the following for our world.[38] Its gender, age, racial, ethnic make-up. Lifestyle. Type of work. Financial situation. Food and drink. Housing. Protection (crime, environmental hazards). Education. Physical and mental health. Personal growth and development. Habitat (living environment). Producing what. Climate. Sustainability.

b. How well is our world? How well (surviving and thriving) is our world? How well is our world in terms of performing well? Being well-off (financially)? Being well nourished (food and drink)? Being well housed? Being well protected (exposures, crime)? Being well educated? Being physically and mentally well? Personally growing/developing well? Living within good habitat? Not being vulnerable? Producing personal and public goods? Living within a stable, positive climate? Being sustained?

Answering "yes" indicates current surviving and thriving. Though the "yes" answers are good, there is still future work to make sure this continues. "No" answers are bad and mean there is current and future work to be done.

For our world, there are relatively few "yes" answers when it comes to thriving and very many no answers when it comes to surviving.

---

[38] Free download of larger, fillable worksheets at www.ThrivingFuture.org

Use Table 7.2 (end of Quick Guide) to more specifically describe how well is our world.[39]

c. What positively or negatively impacts our world? What positively or negatively impacts or is likely to impact our world's surviving and thriving? Use Table 7.2 to describe all of the following impacts (positive and negative; current and future). What impacts our world's performing well? Being well-off (financially)? Being well nourished (food and drink)? Being well housed? Being well protected (exposures, crime)? Being well educated? Being physically and mentally well? Personally growing/developing well? Living within good habitat? Not being vulnerable? Producing personal and public goods? Living within a stable, positive climate? Being sustained?

Positive impacts improve and/or sustain surviving and thriving. If they will continue, we probably can focus on other things. If they may or may not continue, our action is needed to make them continue and/or to develop other things to compensate. Bad impacts prevent or limit surviving and thriving. If they will not continue, we probably can focus on other things. If they may or may not continue, our action is needed to stop them or to avoid or minimize their impact.

d. What is near and long term future behavior of our world? How is our world (including international and country organizations, countries, business/industry, people) likely to behave in the near and long term future. For example, will it behave (individual behavior; group behavior, country behavior, overall world behavior) so as to protect/improve public services, help each other survive/thrive, protect/increase jobs, maintain/improve world's environment, and/or sustain the world near and long term.

Use Table 7.2 to describe all of the following behaviors. How will our world behave with respect to performing well? Being well-off

---

[39] Free download of larger, fillable worksheets at <u>www.ThrivingFuture.org</u>

(financially). Being well nourished (food and drink)? Being well housed? Being well protected (exposures, crime)? Being well educated? Being physically and mentally well? Personally growing/developing well? Living within good habitat? Not being vulnerable? Producing personal and public goods? Living within a stable, positive climate? Being sustained?

e. More on our world's future and behavior? At this point, we have a basic baseline with which to measure progress for our world. We may have enough good information to move to Step 2 and to develop strategy for our world. But using more of the tools and models already mentioned would greatly improve our chances of success and our outcome in terms of surviving and thriving.

Using the full *Thrive!* **Next Generation Toolkit** is very highly recommended because it includes more strategy, policy and tools for creating and sustaining large, positive change and building a surviving and thriving future. Using ***Thrive!* - Building a Thriving Future** is very highly recommended because it provides much greater depth on strategy and. It is available via www.Amazon.com or free download from www.ThrivingFuture.org.

Step 2.

Step 2. Strategy to achieve our world's surviving and thriving future. The next major step is to develop the strategy that will help us build and achieve a surviving and thriving future.

a. What will our world be in the future? What will be our likely future world? Population characteristics. Type of work/how people live. Financial situation. Food and drink. Housing. Protection (crime, environmental hazards). Education. Physical and mental health. Personal growth and development. Habitat (living environment, neighboring communities, part of what state, country, continent). Producing what. Climate. Sustainability.

If there are any changes to our world that are desired or likely, take them into account. Use Table 7.3 (end of Quick Guide) to describe the likely future.[40]

b. How well should our world be in the near and long term future? How well should our world as a whole be in the future? Overall, it should be <u>surviving and thriving</u>. The "*Thrive!* strategy" will help us accomplish that.

Use Table 7.4 (end of Quick Guide) to describe how well our world should be.[41] From our world's view and to be surviving and thriving, indicate to what extent our world should be performing well. Be well-off (financially). Be well nourished (food and drink). Be well housed. Be well protected (exposures, crime). Be well educated. Be physically and mentally well. Be personally growing/developing well. Be living within good habitat. Not be vulnerable. Be producing personal and public goods. Be living within a stable, positive climate. Be sustained. Again, our world should be surviving and thriving.

c. What has to change to achieve our world's thriving future? What has to change to progress from our world's current status to achieve our desired surviving and thriving status? In Step 1, we identified what positively and negatively impacts or is likely to impact our world. We include any changes to our future world.

Given those, what has to change to achieve a surviving and thriving future? To achieve performing well? Being well-off (financially)? Being well nourished (food and drink)? Being well housed? Being well protected (exposures, crime)? Being well educated? Being physically and mentally well? Personally growing/developing well? Living within good habitat? Not being vulnerable? Producing personal and public goods? Living within a stable, positive climate? Being sustained?

---

[40] Free download of larger, fillable worksheets at www.ThrivingFuture.org
[41] Free download of larger, fillable worksheets at www.ThrivingFuture.org

Good changes improve and/or sustain surviving and thriving. Bad changes prevent and/or limit surviving and thriving.

These should be the overarching changes:
- Our world and our people should be performing (living, working, recreating, learning) well enough to survive and thrive.
- Our world and our people should be well-off (financially) enough to survive and thrive.
- Our world and our people should be well nourished (food and drink) enough to survive and thrive.
- Our world and our people should be well housed enough to survive and thrive.
- Our world and our people should be well protected (exposures, crime) enough to survive and thrive.
- Our world and our people should be well educated enough to survive and thrive.
- Our world and our people should be physically and mentally well enough to survive and thrive.
- Our world and our people should be personally growing/developing well enough to survive and thrive.
- Our world should be good habitat enough to survive and thrive.
- Our world and our people should not be vulnerable.
- Our world and our people should be producing personal and public goods enough to survive and thrive.
- Our world should have a stable, positive climate.
- Our world and our people should be sustained.

Based on these overarching changes, use Table 7.4 to describe more specifically what all that has to change to progress from our world's current status to achieve our desired surviving and thriving status.

d. What actions are needed to achieve its thriving future? What actions are needed to bring about the needed changes (identified in "c") that improve our world's current status enough to achieve the desired surviving and thriving status? [Figure 7.1] [42]

Being well-off (financially). Being well nourished (food and drink).
Being well housed. Being well protected (exposures, crime). Being
well educated. Being physically and mentally well. Personally
growing/developing well. Living within good habitat. Not being
vulnerable. Producing personal and public goods. Living within a
stable, positive climate. Being sustained.

We identify actions that support <u>good</u> changes that will help improve
and/or sustain surviving and thriving. If good changes are likely to
occur, together we support them. If good changes are not likely to
occur, together we support them and develop other good changes to
compensate.

Use Table 7.4 to describe all the actions to be taken.

We identify actions that stop <u>bad</u> changes that prevent or limit
surviving and thriving. If bad changes are not likely to occur,
together we ensure they do not. If bad changes are likely to occur,
together we change them, stop them or avoid/reduce their impact.
As individual people, private business, interest groups/organizations,
countries and international organizations, together we should support
our jointly developed strategy and successfully take the actions to
ensure our world and each person in our world are performing well.

Overall *Thrive!* strategy and actions. Our overall *Thrive!* strategy
and actions need to be documented and agreed to by all of us - our
world's people and leaders. This will be our world's ***Thrive!***
Strategy and Action Plan.

---

[42] An action is defined as "who will do what to/with whom, where, when, and with
what result."

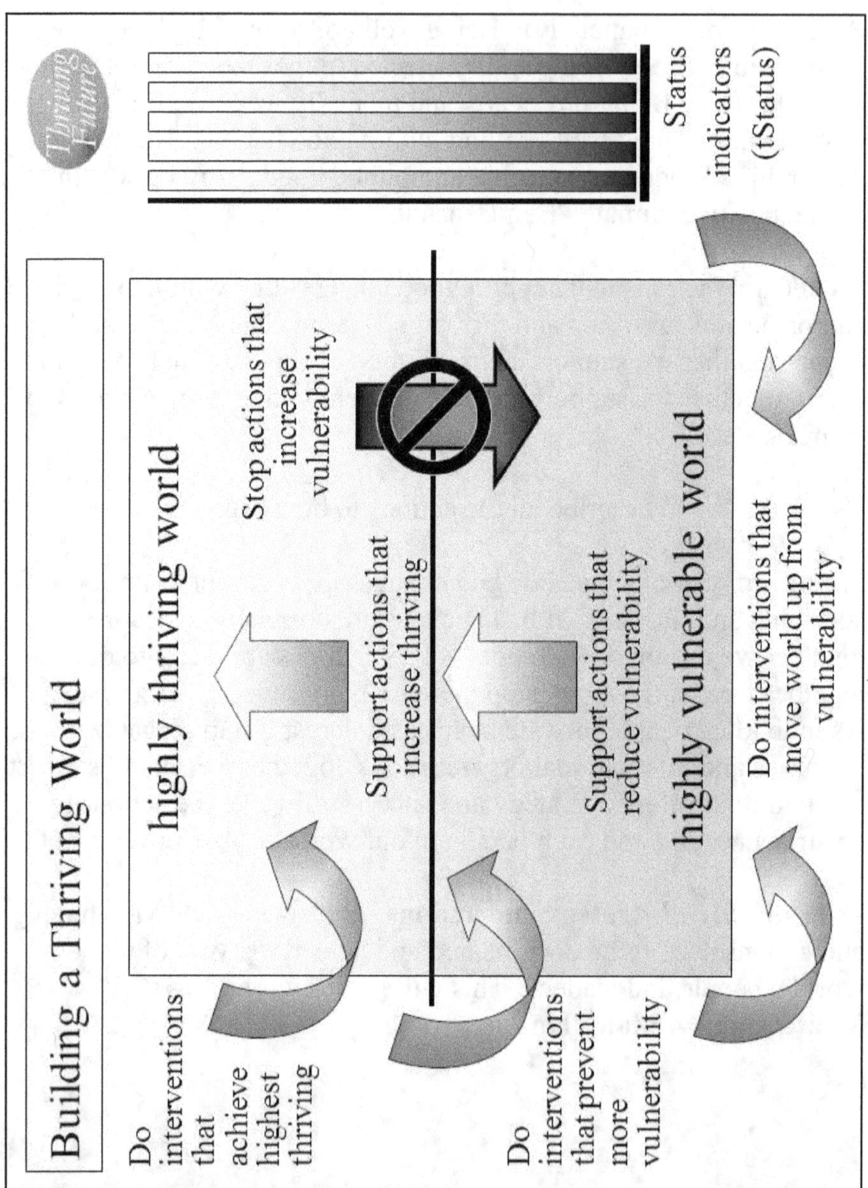

Figure 7.1. Building a Thriving World.

Different individual people, interest groups/organizations, countries and international organizations will take on different responsibilities. For each action, we designate who will do what to/with whom, where, when, and with what result. Use Table 7.4 to document these actions and responsibilities. We make sure we have all the actions that are needed to build, achieve and sustain our surviving and thriving world.

As the strategy is executed, our strategy, actions and results should be updated in our *Thrive!* **Strategy and Action Plan**.

Periodically, we should do an evaluation that assesses our world's strategies/actions near and long term impact on near and long term surviving and thriving. When a) our world's strategies and actions are not building and sustaining a thriving future and/or b) there are changes in our world, we should adjust our overall *Thrive!* strategy and actions.

The key is to successfully execute our world's *Thrive!* **Strategy and Action Plan** and to build a near and long term surviving and thriving future.[43] *[Following is an example of a stronger **Thrive! Strategy and Action Plan** for our world's surviving <u>and</u> thriving future.]*

---

[43] At this point, we have good information to execute our world's *Thrive!* Strategy and Action Plan. We can make progress. But, if feasible, we should develop our strategy and actions further using more of the tools and models already mentioned. This is very highly encouraged and is necessary because of our very, very complex world.

   As stated earlier, this "how-to", by design, is simple but powerful. It is relatively basic providing the framework for doing "our world" strategy. The optimal approach is to use this how-to framework <u>and</u> use the more extensive strategy, models and tools in a) the *Thrive!* **Next Generation Toolkit** contained in the full **People's Guide** and b) *Thrive! -* **Building a Thriving Future** available via <u>www.Amazon.com</u> or free download from <u>www.ThrivingFuture.org</u>.

Example of our world surviving _and_ thriving. *To build, achieve and sustain a surviving _and_ thriving future, the **Thrive! Strategy and Action Plan** for our world should be more like the following example: [Who will do what to/with whom, where, when, and with what result?]*

Starting immediately, we (people, business/industry, private organizations (local, country), governments (local, country) and international organizations) build, achieve, and sustain a surviving and thriving future for our world and for all forever, including:

- Performing well. *Starting immediately, people, business/industry, private organizations (local, country), governments (local, country) and international organizations act to ensure, within the next 20 years, a) all (who are able and not appropriately retired) can work and earn a living income sufficient to survive and thrive and b) all have sufficient resources for and are living, recreating, learning so that they are surviving and thriving to maximum extent feasible.*
- Being well-off (financially). *Starting immediately, people, business/industry, private organizations (local, country), governments (local, country) and international organizations act to ensure, within the next 20 years, a) all have sufficient income/resources to survive and thrive and b) all governments have sufficient resources to provide needed (supporting surviving) and desired (supporting thriving) public programs and policies.*
- Being well nourished (food and drink). *Starting immediately, people, business/industry, private organizations (local, country), governments (local, country) and international organizations act to ensure, within the next 20 years, that all people have access to, be able to afford and consume healthy foods enough to survive and thrive.*
- Being well housed. *Starting immediately, people, business/industry, private organizations (local, country), governments (local, country) and international organizations act to ensure, within the next 20 years, all have access to, be able to afford and live in adequate and preferably high performing housing that supports surviving and thriving.*
- Being well protected (exposures, crime). *Starting immediately,*

people, business/industry, private organizations (local, country), governments (local, country) and international organizations act to ensure, within the next 20 years, a) environmental exposures in home, workplace and elsewhere are minimized so as to not prevent surviving and thriving and b) crimes are minimized to the extent feasible in terms of frequency and impact so as to not prevent surviving and thriving.

- Being well educated. *Starting immediately, people, business/industry, private organizations (local, country), governments (local, country) and international organizations act to ensure, within the next 20 years, all people are educated to the full extent of their abilities, needs and desires and to support their surviving and thriving.*

- Being physically and mentally well. *Starting immediately, people, business/industry, private organizations (local, country), governments (local, country) and international organizations act to ensure, within the next 20 years, a) all people receive the optimal health support to ensure, within the next 20 years, surviving and thriving and b) all people's physical and mental health is optimized to best ensure surviving and thriving.*

- Personally growing/developing well. *Starting immediately, people, business/industry, private organizations (local, country), governments (local, country) and international organizations act to ensure, within the next 20 years, all people are personally growing and developing to best ensure surviving and thriving.*

- Living within good habitat. *Starting immediately, people, business/industry, private organizations (local, country), governments (local, country) and international organizations act to ensure, within the next 20 years, a) all people have access to habitat that best supports their surviving and thriving and b) our world has the optimal mix, quantity and quality of habitat to best support our world and its inhabitants' surviving and thriving.*

- Not being vulnerable. *Starting immediately, people, business/industry, private organizations (local, country), governments (local, country) and international organizations act to ensure, within the next 20 years, our world and all of its people, if vulnerable, are vulnerable only to the minimum extent feasible.*

- Producing personal and public goods. *Starting immediately, people, business/industry, private organizations (local, country), governments (local, country) and international organizations act to ensure, within the next 20 years, our people produce personal and public goods (including personal income/resources, housing, food and drink, energy, education, health, protection, personal growth and development, and habitat) so as to support surviving and thriving for all persons and for our world overall.*

- Living within a stable, positive climate. *Starting immediately, people, business/industry, private organizations (local, country), governments (local, country) and international organizations act to ensure, within the next 10 years, all people behave so as to avoid negative impacts and support positive impacts so as to help ensure a stable, positive climate.*

- Being sustained. *Starting immediately, people, business/industry, private organizations (local, country), governments (local, country) and international organizations act to ensure, within the next 5 years, all people behave so as to ensure the sustainability of our world <u>and</u> its people.*

Chapter 8: Thrive! System© (TS). Achieve thriving people and communities with highest levels of thriving for all everywhere.

How Thrive! Systems help builds, achieves and sustains <u>a thriving future</u> <u>for people and communities.</u>

In the 1970s, inner city Milwaukee (WI) suffered from a severe shortage of health and related support for its low- and middle-income people. The author, serving as Director of Special Projects for the Milwaukee Health Department, designed and implemented a four-site personal support system providing support to inner city people. It was a rudimentary first instance of a Thrive! System. Bringing together a wide range of public and private organizations, a wide range of personal support was provided together in several sites. They included preventive health, public health, medical care, dental care, mental health care, social services, and financial assistance. This personal support was coordinated for persons by Nurse Coordinators in each site. The community was actively involved and supportive. The system was funded through a collaboration of the City, County, private hospitals, the dental school, The Robert Wood Johnson Foundation, Community Development Funds and waiver from the Medicare and Medicaid programs. This effort operated successfully for decades. While far short of what is described here as a Thrive! System, this effort served as a foundation for Thrive! Systems proposed here.

In previous chapters, vision and strategy for achieving thriving people and communities has been laid out. Also laid out has been the rationale for **Thrive! Systems (TS),** ideal systems that can help achieve that vision.

In our lives, if we survive birth, only two things are sure about our lives. We are born. We die. Everything else varies from person to person and over a person's lifetime.

Better than our current incomplete and inadequate personal support, a Thrive! System (TS) gives us our best chance to survive and thrive throughout our lifetime.[44] Our having a TS for our community ensures we are more thriving people in a more thriving community. (Table 8.1. Thrive! System – Helping Ensure Thriving for All)

A TS has persons and their communities at the center-. At the center with persons are their Primary Personal Support (PPS) surrounded by all needed and wanted Personal Support (PS). A TS adjusts when locations, time, person, and community change. It takes into account all of personal and community characteristics and all of health and well-being. It understands personal and community environment and its impact on thriving. It understands and uses the full range of thriving support to improve and sustain thriving. It connects all of these, with information and other support, into a fully integrated and supportive system for persons and their communities. (Figure 8.1. Thrive! Systems Ensure More Thriving People)

---

[44] Thrive! Systems (TS) are comprehensive systems that can be of almost any size and for any type of community. Community includes legal communities (e.g., village, town, city, county, State, nation), geographic areas (e.g., regions), groups (e.g. families, ethnic groups, affinity groups), and worlds.

Thrive! System – Helping Ensure Thriving For All [1]

Vision	Thriving people and communities with highest levels of thriving for all everywhere.
Mission	Achieve thriving people and communities with highest levels of thriving for all everywhere.
System	<ul><li>Ensures accessible, affordable and high quality Personal Support for everyone in community.</li><li>Supports whole person and whole community's thriving rather than disconnected or partially connected support or supporting only parts of a person (e.g. only health) and a community.</li><li>Operates in partnership with the person and their family and community.</li><li>Provides a person-centered Primary Personal Support as the primary partner with the person to access and coordinate all needed Personal Support to achieve highest levels of thriving.</li><li>Provides a personal support system for persons and their Primary Personal Support.</li><li>Provides directly or indirectly the full range of Personal Support.</li><li>Provides directly and provides collaboratively via affiliations the full range of Personal Support to ensure accessibility for the person and the community.</li><li>Utilizes all payers (public, private and person) and optimizes costs to ensure affordability of Primary Personal Support and Personal Support for the person and the community.</li><li>Utilizes effective quality assurance collaboratively by Thrive! Systems and affiliated organizations to ensure high quality Primary Personal Support and Personal Support.</li><li>Ensures that all people, other creatures and Earth survive and thrive to maximum extent feasible.</li></ul>

[1] Thrive! System is the updated, upgraded and more comprehensive and complete version of system created for and implemented in inner city Milwaukee (WI) in late 1970s and which operated successfully for decades.

Table 8.1. Thrive! System – Helping Ensure Thriving for All.

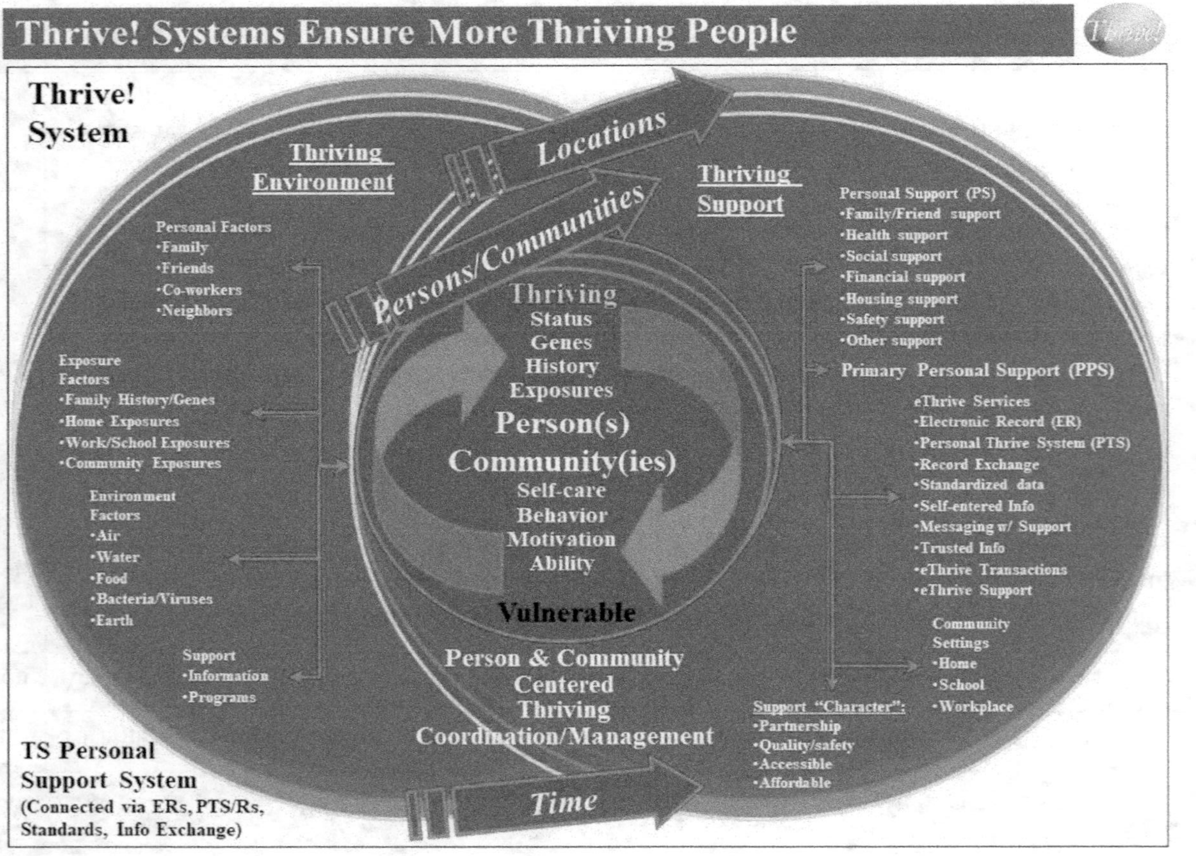

Figure 8.1. Thrive! Systems Ensure More Thriving People.

Thrive!

We want to thrive as much as possible over our lifetime.

We are born. If we live long enough, we are a child, an adult, and an older adult. Then we die. Over our lifetime and depending on how long we live, we may go through early development, may learn, may work, may expand our family, and may have post-work time. Then we die.

If we are fortunate, we live many years through all of these stages until we die a quick and painless death. If we are truly fortunate, we thrive through all of these stages. Very few of us will be that fortunate under the current incomplete and inadequate system.

During our lives after we are born, we may thrive and/or we may be vulnerable. Then we die.

We should want to thrive for as much of our lives as possible. We should do everything reasonable and possible to thrive. While we may be able and willing to do much by ourselves, we will be more successful with truly good partners (Primary Personal Support (PPS)) with all needed and wanted Personal Support (PS) in a truly good system (a Thrive! System (TS)). (Figure 8.2. Persons & Our Lifetime.)

What does it mean for us to thrive?

Very simply, we thrive when we do well throughout our lives. When our families and friends do well throughout their lives. When our communities do well now and for the long term. When our world does well now and for the long term.

More specifically, we, our families and friends, our communities and our world thrive when we are:
- Performing well,
- Well-off (financially),
- Well nourished,
- Well housed,
- Well protected (exposures, crime),
- Well educated,
- Physically and mentally well (people),
- Growing/developing well,
- Living within good habitat,

- Physically well (Earth, plants, animals, environment),
- Not vulnerable,
- Producing personal and public goods,
- Living within a stable, positive climate, and
- Sustained.

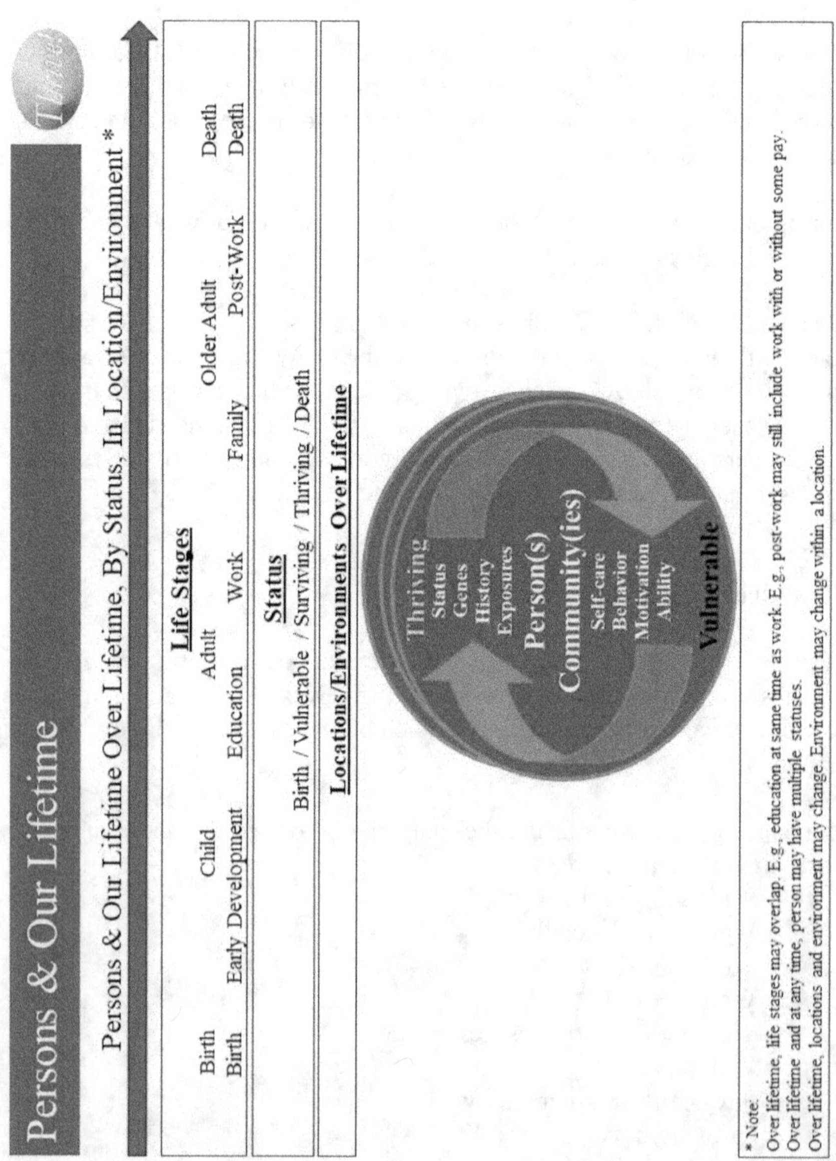

Figure 8.2. Persons & Our Lifetime.

We are more likely to thrive in a Thrive! System© (TS).

The U.S. Institute of Medicine (IOM) [now the National Academy of Medicine] provides a way of viewing a health system's performance through our eyes. What we want from a health system is that we are "staying healthy", "getting better", "living with illness or disability" and/or "coping with the end of life." Only considering health, this is a health system we want and need. This health system, a Thriving Health System, is described in **HealthePeople® - Achieving Health People, Communities & World Via Thrive!®**.

Going beyond health and taking this one more major positive step via a Thrive! System (TS), we "start and stay thriving", "get better (from vulnerable to thriving) faster", "live as well as possible with illness or disability" and/or "cope as well as possible with end of life." Some of us may experience more than one of these at the same time. IOM's quality reports have six aims for a high performing health system. They stress it should be safe, effective, person/patient-centered, timely, efficient, and equitable. Going further, a Thrive! System should be safe, effective, person- and community-centered, efficient and equitable, and should help achieve thriving for both a person and a community.

Building on and going beyond the IOM work, a TS should perform well from the person's perspective and a community's perspective. As depicted in the attached figure, a TS would "check all the boxes." (Figure 8.3. Thrive! System's Six Aims & Person's and Community's Perspective on Thriving) As suggested earlier, a TS can, should and will do much better.

To get to the personal support we truly want and need, we need a TS that has us and our Primary Personal Support (PPS) at the center. Together as partners from birth to death, we access whatever other support is needed to help us start and stay thriving, help us get better (from vulnerable to thriving) faster, help us live as well as possible with illness or disability, and help us cope as well as possible with end of life.

Six Aims & Person/Community's Perspective on Thriving

Supportive of Institute of Medicine principles and aims, a Thrive! System supports persons, communities and their Primary Personal Support, and the rest of Personal Support in continuing to innovate and find better ways to achieve thriving.

Person & Community's Perspective on Needs	Aims for Personal Support Performance/Quality. Achieve Thriving for Both Person and Community.					
	Safe	Effective	Person & Community centered	Timely	Efficient	Equitable
Start & stay thriving	+	+	+	+	+	+
Get better (from vulnerable to thriving) faster	+	+	+	+	+	+
Live as well as possible with illness or disability	+	+	+	+	+	+
Cope as well as possible with end of life	+	+	+	+	+	+

Figure 8.3. Six Aims & Person's and Community's Perspective on Thriving.

Can we transform what we have into TS? Yes, but not easily. Most of the elements exist in our current communities. But they are poorly organized, poorly connected and poorly communicating. The first step is to put in place the Primary Personal Supports (PPS) and connect them to us and the rest of Personal Support (PS). We need to improve and organize the existing PS elements so they better provide and coordinate personal support. We need a lifetime electronic personal support system that tracks and appropriately shares both our interactions with our PPS and all other PS and appropriately and carefully tracks our own personal needs, wants, behaviors and conditions. We need our PPS and ourselves to appropriately share our information carefully and accurately only with whom we want when we want and how we want.

We are more likely to thrive in a Thrive! System© (TS) that addresses the whole person and the whole community.

A Thrive! System (TS) is very different from what we have today. TS addresses the whole person, not just piecemeal parts of the person. TS addresses the whole community, not just piecemeal parts of the community.

What we have today is a piecemeal approach to persons. It is more problem by problem oriented than effectively dealing with the <u>full range</u> of problems experienced by persons at a point in time or over their lifetime. Health is generally addressed separately from housing. Housing from income. Work from school. Public safety from environmental protection. Etc. The same is generally true for a community.

What we have today is more oriented toward solving individual problems rather than being oriented toward solving <u>all</u> problems that a person experiences. The same is generally true for a community.

What we have today is more oriented toward solving problems than <u>helping the whole person thrive</u>. The same is generally true for a community

What we have today is a non-system in which different parts of personal support are poorly coordinated, are disconnected and communicate poorly.

What we have today is a non-system where persons are essentially on their own when it comes to addressing the whole set of factors that reduce vulnerability and increase thriving. Not only is the person not well served but the community is not well served.

Very differently and much more effectively, a TS has a PPS for each person who partners with the person to address all factors that reduce vulnerability and increase thriving.

Very differently and much more effectively, a TS is fully coordinated, is fully connected and communicates well among persons, their Primary Personal Support (PPS), and their total Personal Support (PS). A TS addresses all the factors in a person's life that reduce vulnerability and increase thriving. A TS addresses all the factors in a community that reduce vulnerability and increase thriving.

We are more likely to thrive with a Primary Personal Support (PPS) partner in a Thrive! System© (TS).
A Primary Personal Support (PPS) functions as a partner with us within our community. A partner who brings more knowledge about how to reduce vulnerability and increase thriving than we have and who supports our efforts to thrive. This partner would preferably be a person with specific training and experience to be a PPS. This partner must be well trained and may come from a range of professions, including a social worker or a nurse.

On our behalf, a PPS partners with the rest of Primary Support (PS) across as many life stages and as much of our life as is appropriate and feasible.

Our PPS partner knows us, knows our key thriving and vulnerability factors, knows our needs and wants, knows our behaviors, knows our living and work environment, and provides continuity over as much of our lifetime as possible. Our PPS partner helps us start and stay thriving, helps us get better (from vulnerable to thriving) faster, helps us live as well as possible with illness or disability, and helps us cope as well as possible with end of life. (Figure 8.4. Persons & Our Personal Support)

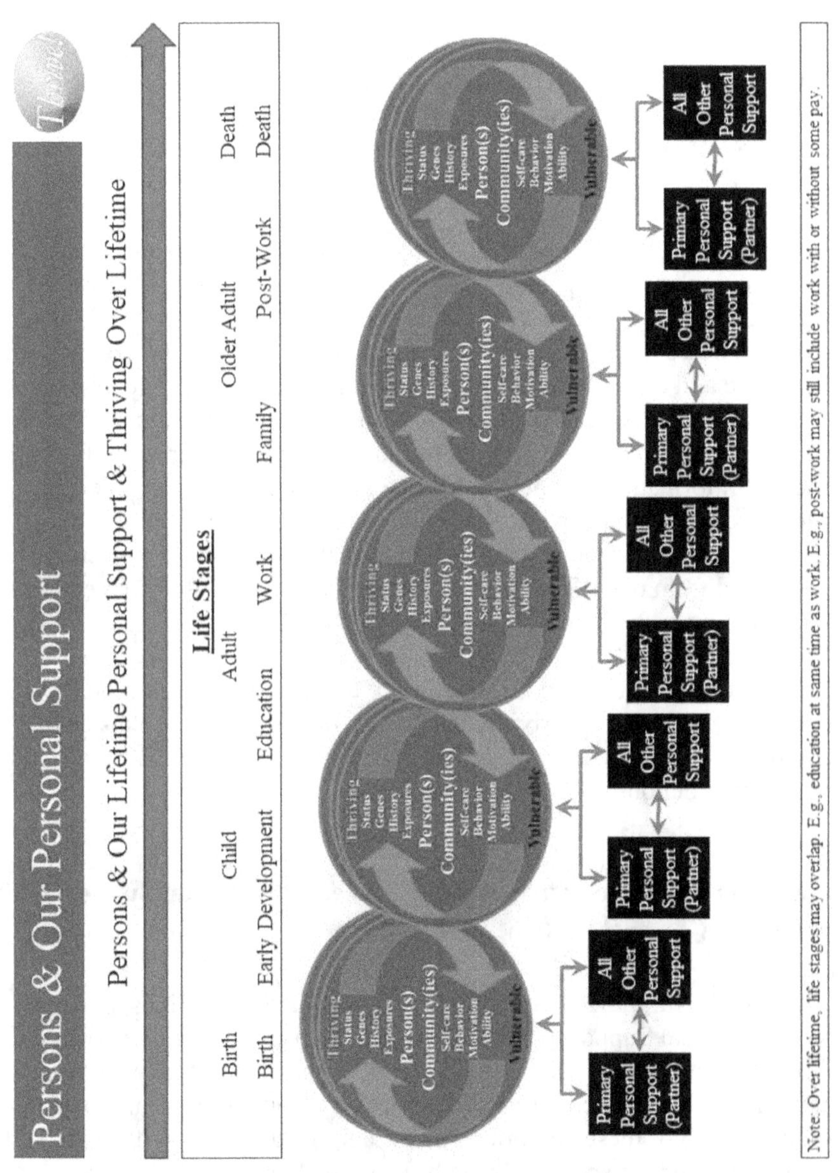

Figure 8.4. Persons & Our Personal Support.

**We are more likely to thrive by having and using Thrive! System©
(TS) personal support systems for persons and their Primary Personal
Support (PPS). [45]**

---

[45] The TS personal support system is also known as a "Thrive! System", a

As is increasingly the case with respect to health, persons and their Primary Personal Support (PPS) need personal support systems to help them collect and store personal information, access electronic support resources (information and tools), and decide and adjust the best path and actions to reduce vulnerability and increase thriving.

These Thrive! System (TS) personal support systems collect and hold the personal information on persons that relate to vulnerability and thriving. They help persons and their PPS assess the current status and develop and adjust the strategy that will achieve the most thriving. They utilize artificial intelligence and other decision support mechanisms to support decision-making. They track progress toward reducing vulnerability and increasing thriving. They help connect to and use the full range of internet and other electronic information and personal support resources. They enable communication and information sharing between persons and their PPS and with any other needed Personal Support (PS). They enable information to be moved from one PPS to a subsequent PPS. They enable connecting information on and for members of a family.

When persons want or need information or to take an action to reduce vulnerability or increase thriving, the TS personal support systems enable them to get the information, make better decisions, and effectively take the best action or actions.

We are more likely to thrive by using all needed Personal Support (PS) partners in a Thrive! System© (TS).

To address the full range of conditions we may face in our lives, our Primary Personal Support (PPS) and we both need all needed Personal Support (PS) as partners. We need partners to help successfully address conditions such as an acute illness or injury, a chronic illness and/or a disability. Each of these conditions often require additional skills and knowledge. Maybe a specialist or subspecialist. Maybe rehabilitation people. Maybe a therapist of one kind or another. Maybe home care or community care people. Maybe a palliative or hospice care team.

---

subsystem of the overall TS.

Thrive!

PS may include family and friends. It may include public social services and financial assistance. May include spiritual healers, public health, and personal assistants. May include schools and employers. May include public safety people. May include food and nutrition people.

PS may be any one of the full range of personal support that can and should be provided when needed. Many different types of people and organizations will have the skills and knowledge to be partners and help address conditions. Depending on our need, any of these people may have an important role as partners in helping us start and stay thriving, helping us get better (from vulnerable to thriving) faster, helping us live as well as possible with illness or disability, and helping us cope as well as possible with end of life.

Our having full "Personal Support (PS)" is more and better than what supports us today.

To keep ourselves thriving, traditional personal support is not enough. While traditional support has a very important role to play, we need more and better support. Full Personal Support (PS) is more complete and is the full range of people, goods and services that can help us thrive as much as possible. This includes the partners described above. But it also includes electronic support (e.g. internet information, apps and devices, messaging, our personal record) and devices, sensors, computers, smartphones, tablets and many more support tools yet to come. A Thrive! System (TS) has the types of personal support we have today plus other important personal support and plus future personal support yet to be available or even developed.

At the center of a TS are persons and their Primary Personal Support (PPS). Together, they access whatever PS is wanted or needed. Traditional PS services may include health care and social services. When needed for a severe or terminal illness, PS may also include hospice and palliative care. When a person has a disability, PS may include personal assistance or home care. When a person has multiple issues, the Primary Personal Support (PPS) is especially important.

In the following figure, many more of the potential PS are detailed. But even this is not a complete PS list. (Figure 8.5. Thrive! Systems – Person and Primary and Other Personal Support.)

- Support For Thriving
- Support Against Vulnerability
- Community Support
- Family/Friends Support
- Financial/Income Support
- Health Support
- Food/Nutrition Support
- Disability Support
- End of Life Support
- Education/Training Support
- Supportive Environment/Habitat
- Housing Support
- Internet Info & Services
- Protection from Crime
- Protection from Exposures
- Growth & Development Support

There are many other types of personal support that are part of a TS. There is information that is provided through understanding a person's history, family history, environmental history, education history, work history and genetic makeup.

There is also indirect support, support that may never touch the person directly but that helps reduce vulnerability and increase thriving for the person. Examples of indirect support include advocacy, government executive and legislative branches, environmental protection, workplace protection, health-related research, food production, regulation, and standards setting.

In a TS, personal support is whatever support a person wants and needs that will improve or maintain thriving or will help a person who is vulnerable with a disability and/or with a terminal illness or injury. The PPS partners with a person to make best use of any or all available personal support.

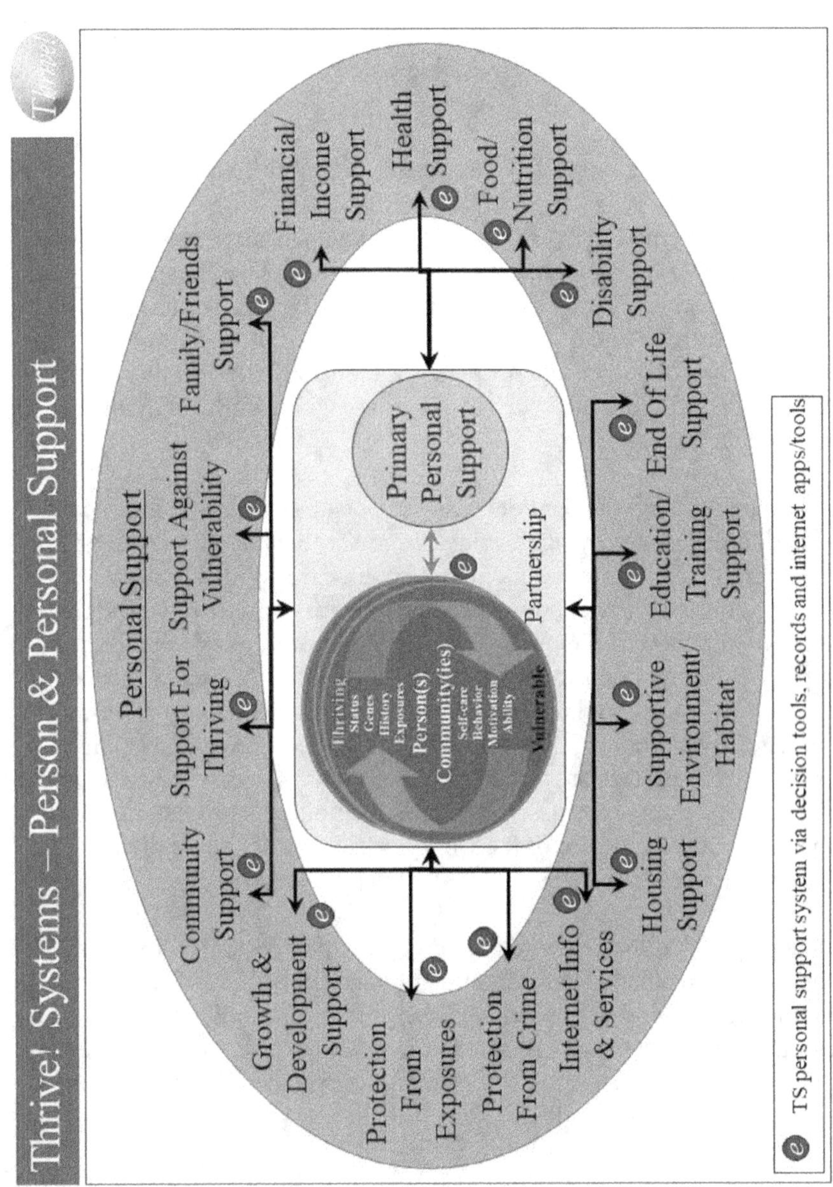

Figure 8.5. Thrive! Systems – Person and Primary and Other Personal Support.

Together in a TS, all of this personal support best supports persons and their PPS as they partner to help start and stay thriving, get better (from vulnerable to thriving) faster, live as well as possible with illness or disability, and cope as well as possible with end of life.

How is a Thrive! System© (TS) best organized to help us?

A Thrive! System (TS) for a community may provide personal support via a fully integrated TS (single organization with Primary Personal Support (PPS) at the center) and/or partially-integrated TS (well-connected multiple organizations with one or more Primary Personal Support at one or more centers). They both can support persons, their PPS and all other Personal Support (PS). (Figure 8.6. Thrive! Systems – Person & Community Centered Organizations.)

Public and private organizations provide personal support that is key to maintaining and improving thriving. Together, they should include PPS and other Personal Support, including health care, skilled nursing home, long term nursing home, home care, personal assistance, rehabilitation, illness/injury specific support, public health, nutrition, emotional support, hospice, palliative, and holistic therapies. They should include social service, food/nutrition, housing, income support, financial services, payment for health care, personal security, justice, education/training, environmental protection, regulation, roads, parks, waste disposal, utilities, libraries, and emergency assistance. Some employers provide personal support in- and/or outside of the workplace. Some schools provide personal support. The Federal government provides national security.

Connecting all of this PS with persons and their PPS are TS personal support systems that can and should hold and process information to be shared carefully and only when needed, appropriate and authorized. They must be able to exchange information in a standardized way that supports effective decision-making for the person, for a person's PPS and for a person and community's PS.

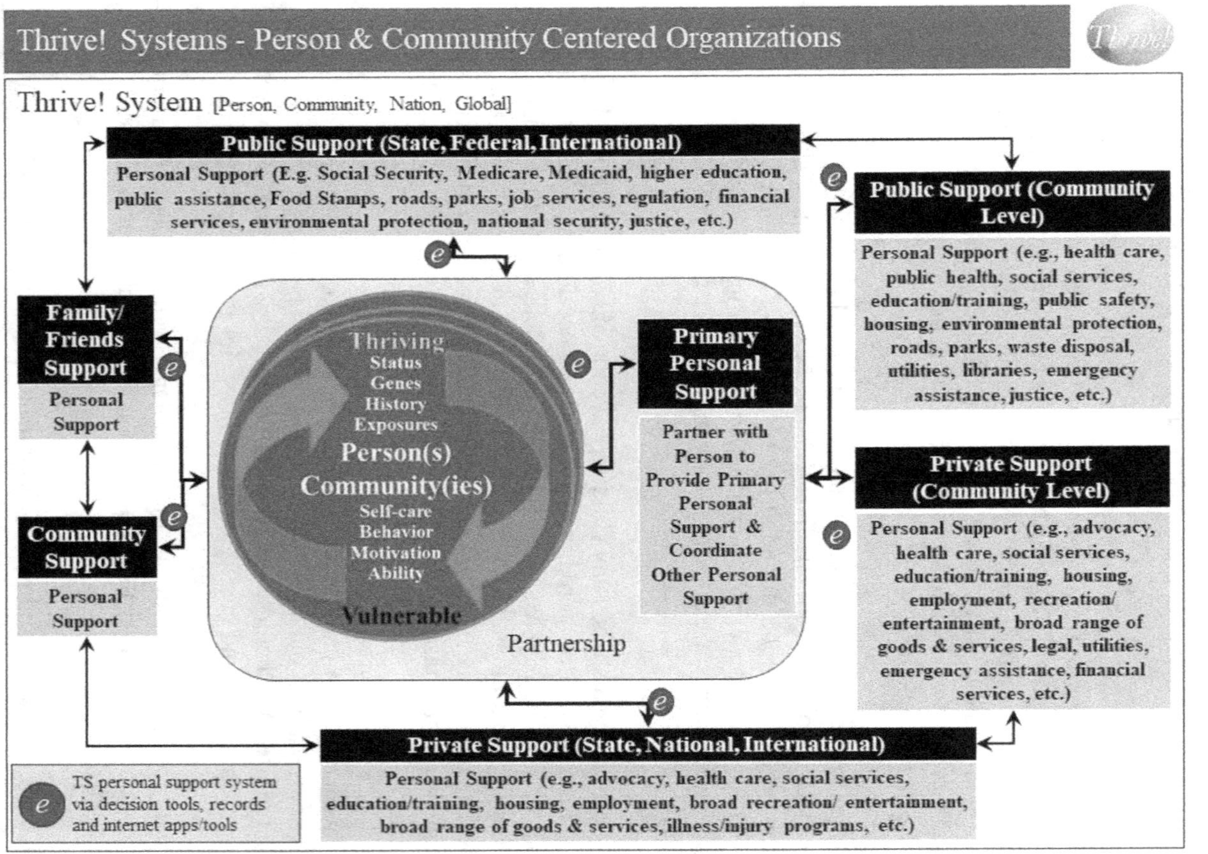

Figure 8.6. Thrive! Systems - Person & Community Centered Organizations.

How does a Thrive! System© (TS) support a person and a community?

A Thrive! System (TS) supports a person or persons from beginning to end. Prior to birth, we, via our family, are partnered with a Primary Personal Support (PPS). Starting with our birth and through childhood, we have a PPS partner. The PPS partners with us as individuals or with us and our family and helps us access all other Personal Support (PS). As children and as we grow, we take an increasing part in our own pursuit of thriving. The more the better.

When we become an adult, we may change our PPS partner. Our respective roles are similar. Our PPS may be one with more skills and knowledge to support our adult lives. As an adult and to the extent we can, we take on a stronger role in our pursuit of thriving. The more the better. If we have a family, we and our family may partner with a PPS as a family unit.

In our later years when any children have moved on to their own lives and we may experience more illness or disabling conditions, we may change our PPS to one who has more skills and knowledge with illness and/or disabling conditions. We and our PPS will need to access the PS that can best help us manage illnesses or disabling conditions. To the extent we are able, we should take a strong role in our pursuit of thriving. The more the better.

If we have a terminal illness or are just nearing the end of our lives as part of normal aging, our PPS may be one who can best help us best cope with end of life. We should live this part of our lives as independently and with as much dignity and quality of life as possible. The more the better.

At any point in our lives, we may experience a major illness or disabling condition that requires us to partner with a PPS with that skill and knowledge.

In a TS, all wanted and needed PS must be physically accessible. This is particularly challenging in rural areas but more doable today with internet and other communication resources. Special provisions must be made for people with physical or cognitive limitations.

Even if all this PS is available, interconnected and accessible, financial access must be ensured. PS must be affordable for all payers, including the person. Today, this is through private support, public support, charity and self-pay. There are possibly better ways a TS can ensure financial access. In a TS, no person fails to receive wanted and needed PS due to financial limitations or inability.

What will our lives be like in a Thrive! System© (TS)?

Starting with our birth and through childhood, we and our families and our Primary Personal Support (PPS) focus on how to increase and sustain thriving in the way we live our daily lives. Eat and drink healthier. Exercise better. Avoid or minimize environmental risks. Get age-appropriate health and well-being exams. Treat illnesses and injuries early and well. Obtain education and training. Track our personal vulnerability and thriving. Use effective Personal Support (PS) partners. Take responsibility for our and our family's thriving and for our community's thriving. Together, these actions help us reduce vulnerability and increase thriving.

When we become an adult, we take more responsibility for our own vulnerability and thriving. But we still do so in partnership with our PPS. We continue to eat and drink healthier. Exercise better. Avoid or minimize environmental risks. Get age-appropriate health and well-being exams. Treat illnesses and injuries early and well. Continue to learn and develop. Ensure our food and housing. Ensure our financial viability now and through the end of our lives. Ensure our personal safety. Track our personal vulnerability and thriving. Learn more about our specific risks from family history, genetic make-up, environmental risks, and how we live our lives. Together, these actions help us reduce vulnerability and increase thriving, help us deal with vulnerabilities earlier and better, and help us reduce vulnerability and increase thriving.

In our later years when any children have moved on to their own lives and we may experience more illness or disabling conditions, we continue with our PPS and with what we have been doing throughout our adulthood. But now we may be experiencing even more vulnerability, more illnesses, more disabling conditions, more of these at the same time and more severe versions of these. Together, we and our PPS help us reduce vulnerability, prevent illness and injury, help us deal with vulnerabilities earlier and better, help us reduce the severity of these, help us better deal with simultaneous vulnerabilities, help us better cope with a chronic or disabling condition, help us better deal with simultaneous and different PS, and help us reduce vulnerability and increase thriving.

If we have a terminal illness or are just nearing the end of our lives as part of normal aging, our PPS may be one who can best help us best cope with end of life. We still try to thrive as best we can given that we are nearing the end. Managing pain better. Prioritizing what PS are done or not done. Addressing emotional issues better for ourselves and our family and friends. Making sure we have our final arrangements in order. Handling the end of our lives as we want and with dignity.

Across and throughout our lives, we effectively use effective PS partners. We take responsibility for our and our family's health and well-being and for our community's health and well-being.

We want our "status" to improve from "worst thriving (highly vulnerable)" to "best thriving (highly thriving)" status. (Figure 8.7. Thriving Status – Move From Vulnerable To Thriving.)

It is worst when we are highly vulnerable and experience low personal and support ability, low personal and support motivation, unsupportive "environment", poor prevention outcomes, poor treatment and intervention outcomes, high risk for adverse events, high morbidity, low quality of life, high mortality, low life expectancy, and low satisfaction with PPS and PS.

It is best when we are highly thriving and experience high personal and support ability, high personal and support motivation, supportive "environment", good prevention outcomes, good treatment and intervention outcomes, low risk for adverse events, low morbidity, high quality of life, low mortality, high life expectancy, and high satisfaction with PPS and PS.

We need to move each element of our lives from being worst (highly vulnerable) to being best (highly thriving). Move to best outcomes and status. Move to thriving. We do that best in a Thrive! System (TS).

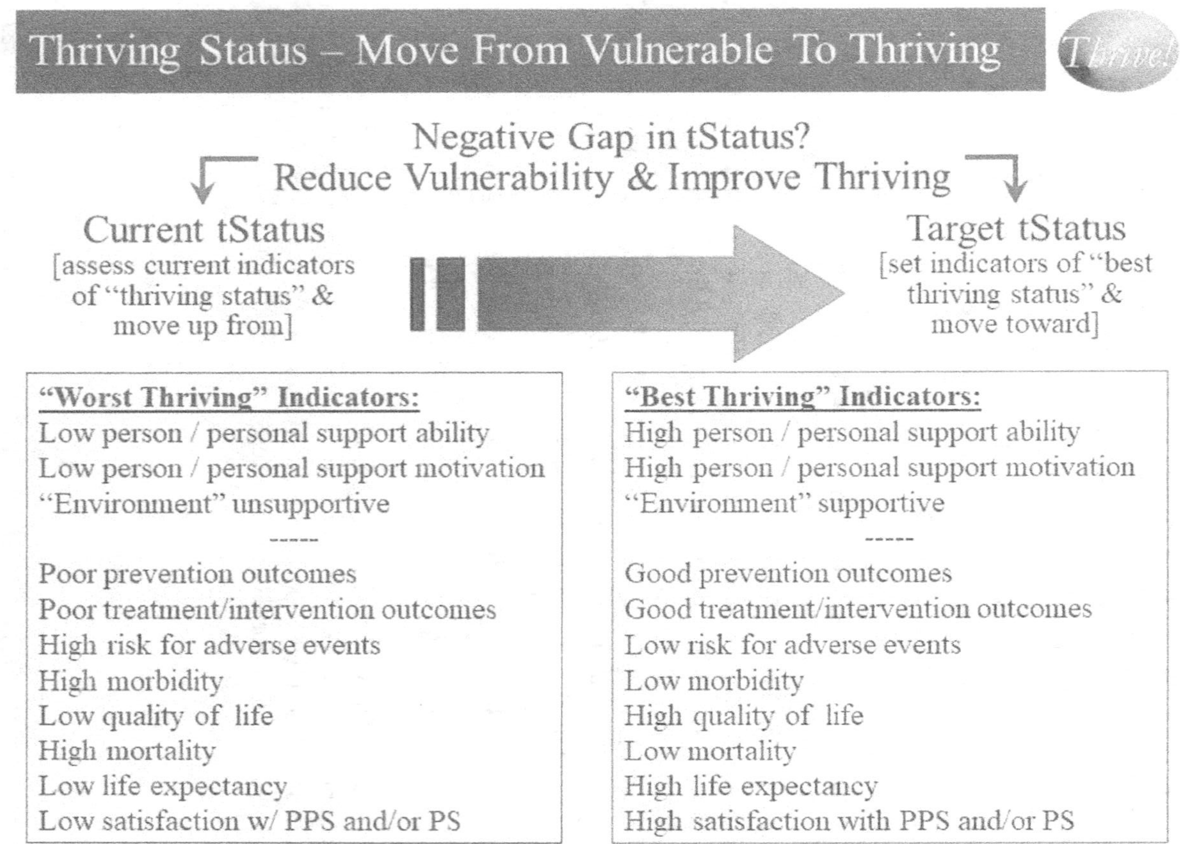

Figure 8.7. Thriving Status – Move From Vulnerable To Thriving.

How will we know when we are successful? When we are thriving? As noted earlier, thriving is when we are: performing well, well-off (financially), well nourished, well housed, well protected (exposures, crime), well educated, physically and mentally well (people), growing/developing well, living within good habitat, physically well (Earth, plants, animals, environment), not vulnerable, producing personal and public goods, living within a stable, positive climate, and sustained.

Our having Thrive! Systems© (TS) can and should achieve thriving people and communities for all everywhere.

Thrive!® and Thrive! Systems (TS) have a vision of thriving people and communities for all everywhere. They have the strategy to achieve that vision. (Figure 8.8. Thrive! Systems – Help Achieve Thriving).

The strategy is for us to thrive as best we can by doing the following:
- Stop actions that increase vulnerability.
- Support actions that increase thriving.
- Support actions that reduce vulnerability.
- Do interventions that best achieve highest thriving.
- Do interventions that best prevent more vulnerability.
- Do interventions that move up from vulnerability.

This is the Thrive!® vision for Thrive! Systems and for us and the communities these systems support.[46] As people, communities, nations and world, we should proceed toward the vision of achieving thriving people and communities for all everywhere.

---

[46] Thrive!® - Vision, mission, strategy and supportive tools help create and sustain large, positive and timely change and build a thriving future for all forever. They help build a thriving and surviving future:
- Vision: All thrive forever. All includes persons, communities, and world.
- Mission: Large, positive, timely change achieving surviving and thriving future for all forever.
- Strategy: A joint Thrive! Endeavor and call to action building a thriving future for all forever.

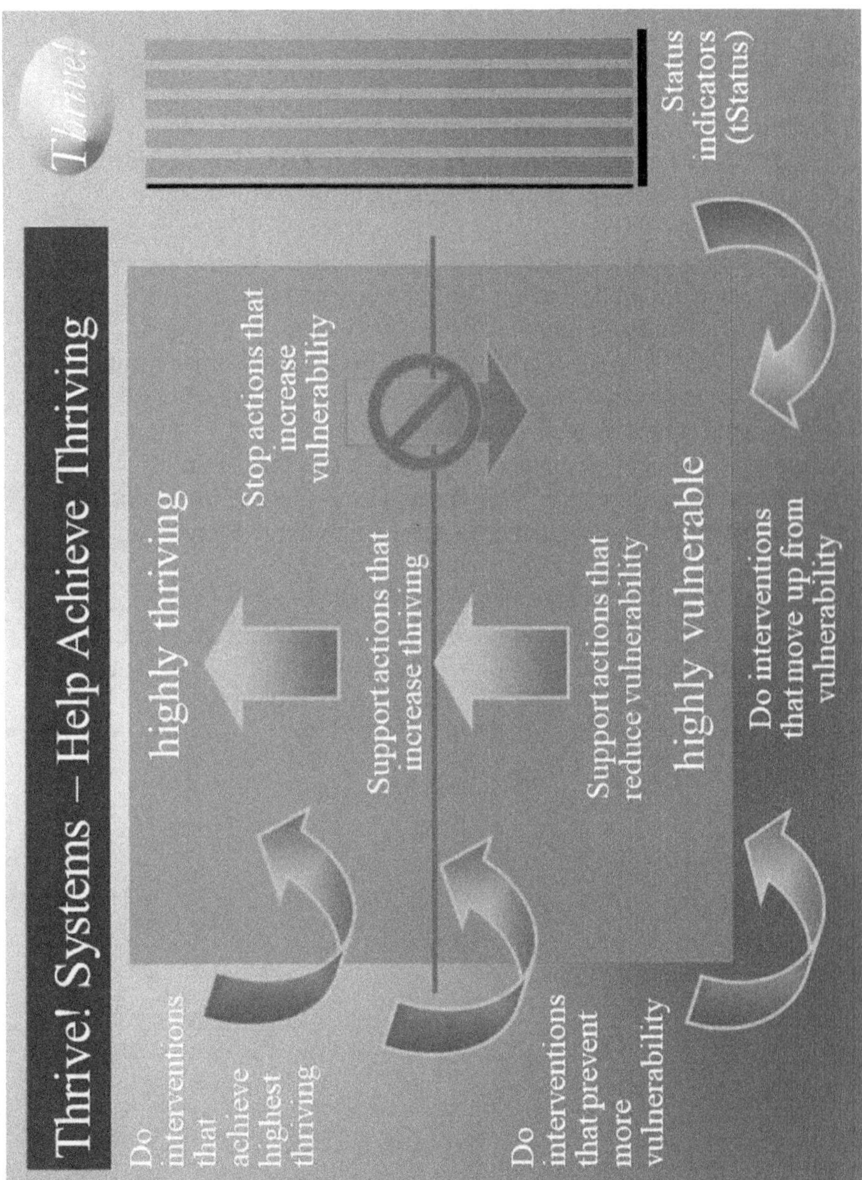

Figure 8.8. Thrive! Systems – Help Achieve Thriving.

We do this via a strategy of TS for all people and communities everywhere. TS are self-perpetuating, very affordable, easily accessible, "e" enabled, person-centered, prevention-oriented, and high quality systems. They produce high outcomes and status (thriving).

Such TS, partly physical and partly virtual and put into place by collaborative private and public partnerships, will greatly improve accessibility, quality and affordability for all people everywhere. They will greatly reduce vulnerability and increase thriving for all people everywhere and for all other creatures and for Earth.

Every community everywhere should have an effective and comprehensive TS. By every community having an effective and comprehensive TS, we can help people and communities thrive everywhere in the world. Every community's TS should effectively connect with every other community's TS. Together, they can best support people as they move amongst the world's communities. Together, they can share valuable resources to most efficiently and effectively support people and their communities. Together, they can best support people, their communities and the world, including the Earth upon which we depend for our continuing existence and thriving.

We can and should build and sustain TS for all people everywhere. We can and should achieve substantially more thriving people, communities, nations and world. We can and should move toward a truly thriving world. All people everywhere deserve and should expect nothing less.

Chapter 9: How the *Thrive!* Endeavor, you and all of us together, builds a thriving future.

How the *Thrive!* **Endeavor**, you and all of us together, builds, achieves and sustains a thriving future for all forever.

Thrive! Survive! Vulnerable! These are the keys to a call for creating and sustaining large, positive and timely change and building a surviving and thriving future. We are all vulnerable to some extent but that can change for the better. *Thrive!* is that call to action and a rallying cry for a better and thriving future. It is a vision and a mission for those wanting to build a better future. To achieve that vision and succeed with the mission, the *Thrive!* **Endeavor**, all of us together, strives to energize and empower people to build a thriving future for our families and friends, communities, countries and world. It strives to build, achieve and sustain a surviving and thriving future for all forever, to the maximum extent possible.[47] This future is *Thrive!* and is a bold vision and mission.

We have laid out why (Chapters 2 and 3) and how (Chapters 4 through 8) to build a surviving and thriving future for you and your family and friends, for you and your community, for you and your country, and for you and our world. But to truly have a thriving future, we need to have it for you and everybody's family and friends and every community and every country and every part of and our entire world. When all this comes together, you and all of us

---

[47] We must keep in mind that "our world" and "all" is expanding as we explore and move beyond earth to other parts of our universe. For that reason, "a thriving future for all forever" reaches as far as we reach or hope to reach.

will have built, achieved and sustained a surviving and thriving future.

How best to do this? We bring all this together with the *Thrive!* **Endeavor** where you and all of us together, build, achieve and sustain <u>a thriving future</u> <u>for all</u> <u>forever</u>. Creating and sustaining this vast human endeavor is the driving purpose and mission of this **Guide**.

Why the *Thrive!* Endeavor?

As laid out in Chapters 2 and 3, you and all of us want and need a surviving and thriving future because of our endangered future and our human need to survive and desire to thrive. And <u>only people</u> can and must fix all that is broken. And <u>only people</u> can and must build, achieve and sustain a survivable and thriving future. And <u>only all of us joined together</u> can succeed due to the scope (all), level (surviving and thriving), duration (forever) of the challenge. For these reasons, building, achieving and sustaining a surviving and thriving future requires a vast, sustained *Thrive!* **Endeavor** of all of us together.

What is the *Thrive!* Endeavor?

The *Thrive!* **Endeavor** is all of us together. It is vision, mission, strategy and call to action. Its vision is a surviving and thriving future for all forever. Its mission is to create and sustain large positive and timely change that builds, achieves and sustains a surviving and thriving future for all forever, to the maximum extent possible. Its strategy is to energize and empower all of us together in the vast, sustained human endeavor building and sustaining a thriving future. Its call for action is to motivate all of us (individual people, groups of people, private sector organizations, governments) to seek a thriving future, to create and sustain the necessary large positive change, and to work together to build, achieve and sustain a surviving and thriving future.

Thrive!

In support of this vision and mission, the Endeavor adopts and embraces "<u>A People's Constitution</u>" - "We the people, in order to form a more perfect union, commit to a thriving future for all forever." [48]

Who is and will be the ***Thrive!*** Endeavor?

The ***Thrive!*** **Endeavor** is <u>all of us together</u> building, achieving and sustaining a surviving and thriving future. "All of us together" include individual people, groups of people, private sector organizations and governments. "All of us together" include <u>current and future generations</u>. "All of us together" include <u>you</u>, and <u>everybody's</u> family and friends, and <u>every</u> community, and <u>every</u> country, and <u>every part of and our entire</u> world.

Who does what and how in the ***Thrive!*** Endeavor?

What the ***Thrive!*** **Endeavor** does and how it does it is different than past and current approaches which have major limitations and defects. The Endeavor is unique and better because it:
- Strives to achieve a thriving and sustainable future for all forever, to the maximum extent possible. But it also helps ensure survival, a necessary but not sufficient step to achieving a thriving future
- Enables the building of a surviving and thriving future for you, your family and friends, your community, your country and our world.
- Joins people of all backgrounds/generations together to achieve a thriving future.
- Is able to address every person, community and issue.
- Uses whole "community" (local, regional, state, country, world/global) strategy for creating and sustaining change and building thriving futures. [No longer should we rely on piecemeal strategies.]

---

[48] The **People's Constitution** should be just this brief, understandable and powerful. It should not replace any country's constitution. The intent is for it to be embraced by and acted upon affirmatively by all people forever.

- Uses whole "person" strategy for creating and sustaining change and building thriving futures. [No longer is the focus only on parts (ill health, hunger, poor education or insufficient income).]
- Uses whole "system" (community, health, education, economy, housing, etc.) strategy for creating and sustaining change and building thriving futures. [No longer should we rely on survival and piecemeal strategies for just parts of a system.]
- Takes an integrated approach to cross-cutting issues.
- Uses an integrated approach to people/environment strategy, change and thriving futures. [No longer is the focus only on people <u>or</u> the environment.]
- Uses a "person-centered" strategic approach that recognizes people's behaviors are the problem and the solution. [No longer should we fail to address "people's behavior".]
- Uses eMedia and social networking to expand communication and joint action and to activate and coordinate a large endeavor in "real time".
- Uses the *Thrive!* **Next Generation Toolkit** [in the full **<u>People's Guide</u>**] of strategy, models and tools to create and sustain change and build thriving futures. [No longer should we rely on past approaches that failed or had limited success.]
- Uses strategic/operational planning and combines it with strategic/operational execution.
- Creates a collaborative strategy with the necessary positive actions to build, achieve and sustain a surviving and thriving future.

To improve our chances of success, the *Thrive!* **Endeavor** recognizes and will positively use tipping points, a critical element in positive change efforts historically.[49] Throughout human history, we see moments when "tipping points" exist. Tipping points can enable negative or positive change. We see moments when a positive action is taken at a tipping point and major positive change occurs. We are now at such a tipping point. We are now at an historical moment when government and the private sector are broken in many ways, when our resources are becoming increasingly limited, when our environment is increasingly and negatively impacted, when our future is endangered, and when a failure to act positively dooms us to a failed, potentially non-survivable future. But, it is also a historical moment when we are the most able to change all that for the better. At this tipping point when our future is most endangered and we are most able, carefully developed and positive actions are more necessary and more likely to be effective and successful.

As laid out above in this Chapter and in Chapters 4 through 8, each and all of us should develop and take as many positive actions as we can. The more positive actions taken, the better for all of us. Each

---

[49] Using tipping points can be very helpful in building a thriving future. However, positive change efforts can also occur without an existing tipping point or without any tipping point. It is just more difficult. Where feasible, we should use current, future and creatable tipping points:
- Use current tipping points.
- Partner with families and friends, communities and countries that are broken and/or with clearly endangered futures.
- Partner with families and friends, communities and countries that are positioned to move up from surviving to thriving.
- Build off issue areas and cross-cutting issue areas that are broken and/or with endangered futures.
- Use breakthroughs in knowledge and technology.
- Partner with new, more capable and more motivated leaders emerge.
- Use eMedia and social networking.
- Use grassroots and self-organizing movements.
- Watch for and use new tipping points as they emerge.
- When necessary, appropriate and doable, create new tipping points that are opportunities to build a thriving future.

and all of us should help build, achieve and sustain a surviving and thriving future for <u>our family and friends</u>. Each and all of us should help build, achieve and sustain a surviving and thriving future for <u>our community</u>. Each and all of us should help build, achieve and sustain a surviving and thriving future for <u>our country</u>. Each and all of us should help build, achieve and sustain a surviving and thriving future for <u>our world</u>, including the Earth on which we depend. Via these actions and the ***Thrive!*** **Endeavor**, <u>each and all of us together</u> should build, achieve and sustain a surviving and thriving future.

What positive actions are needed to bring about the needed changes that improve our current status enough to achieve the desired surviving and thriving status? [Figure 9.1] Each and all of us identify actions that support <u>good</u> changes that will help reduce vulnerability and/or improve and/or sustain surviving and thriving. If good changes are likely to occur, together we support them. If good changes are not likely to occur, together we support them and develop other good changes to compensate.

Each and all of us identify actions that stop <u>bad</u> changes that increase vulnerability and/or prevent or limit surviving and thriving. If bad changes are not likely to occur, together we ensure they do not. If bad changes are likely to occur, together we change them, stop them or avoid/reduce their impact.

Via the Endeavor, all of us together develop our strategy and successfully take the actions to ensure a surviving and thriving future.

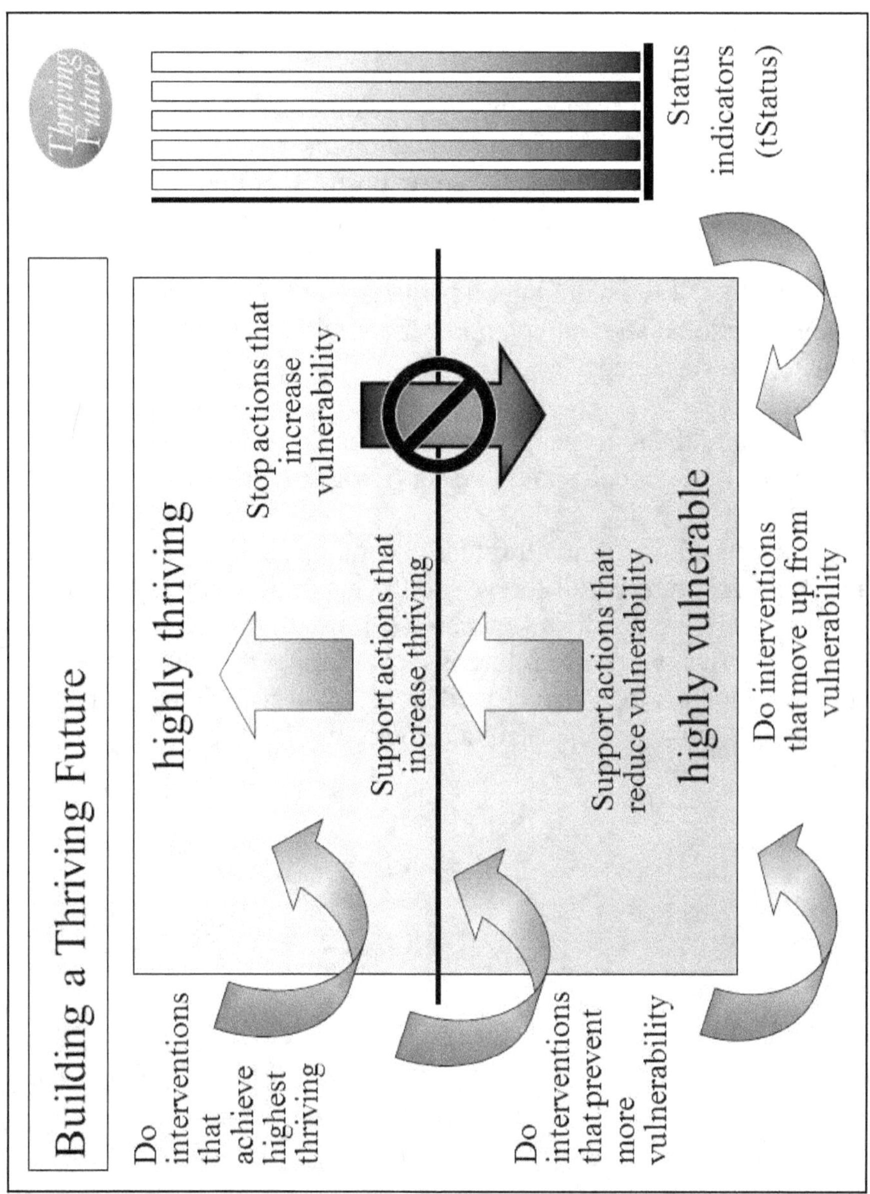

Figure 9.1. Building and Sustaining a Thriving Future.

With what result?

When successful, all of us, current and future, should be performing well. Be well-off (financially). Be well nourished (food and drink). Be well housed. Be well protected (exposures, crime). Be well educated. Be physically and mentally well (people). Personally grow/develop well. Be physically well (Earth, plants, animals, environment). Live within good habitat. Not be vulnerable. Produce personal and public goods. Live within a stable, positive climate. Be sustained.

But it is more than just people surviving and thriving. The Earth upon which we depend should be surviving and thriving.

When successful, we and all future generations achieve the surviving and thriving future for all forever, to the maximum extent possible. At this time in human history when we desire to thrive, when we need to survive, when our future is most endangered, and when we are most capable, the *Thrive!* **Endeavor**, all of us together, can and must build, achieve and sustain a thriving future for all forever.

Example and Worksheets

Example and Worksheets
for
You and Your Family and Friends

Thrive!

***Thrive!* Strategy and Action Plan** (Example of surviving and somewhat thriving).

Thriving and Surviving	How well (surviving/ thriving) should your people as a whole be in near/long term future?	External/internal changes needed to achieve surviving and thriving future	Actions by your people and others Who will do what to/with whom, where, when, and with what result?
Performing (live/work/ play) well?	*Jane has better job with better income, more certainty, pension, health benefits and no occupational exposure. John likes being electrician and continues but with more construction work.*	**External**: *Jane needs employer (current or a new one) to give her job with better income, more certainty, pension, health benefits and no occupational exposure. John needs home and business owners to do more construction and repair.*	**External by others**: *Community has begun seeking new employers with the intent of having 1000 new jobs within 12 months.* **Internal by your people**: *Jane will talk to current employer about higher pay and change in job to avoid exposure. John will approach home and business owners to get more jobs.*
		Internal:	**Internal by your people**: *Jane will more actively seek new job starting next Monday and, if feasible, change jobs to one with better income, more certainty, pension, health benefits and no occupational exposure within 3 months. John likes being electrician and continues but will market himself more and travel more within next two weeks.*
Well-off?	*Jane and John's employers provide better income security.*	**External**: *Need employers to provide better income security.*	**External by others**: *See above* **Internal by your people**: *See above*
		Internal:	**Internal by your people**: *See above*
Well nourished?	*Family has enough food but needs healthier diet, including reduced salt and saturated fat.*	**External**: *Need no-cost nutritionist/ dietician to help buying/preparing healthier diet, including reduced*	**External by others**: *Local grocery agrees to add more healthy food, on trial basis, within 30 days.*

			salt and saturated fat. situation. Need accessible and affordable healthy food source.	**Internal by your people:**
		Internal:	**Internal by your people:** *Family will shop for and help prepare healthier diet, including reduced salt and saturated fat, starting next Saturday. Family will avoid eating out in less healthy restaurants from today forward.*
Well housed	*Family improves home energy efficiency.*	**External**: *Need financial incentives to improve home energy efficiency, especially for heating during cold, harsh winters.*	**External by others**: *State may provide new energy efficiency incentives within 12 months but needs substantial public pressure within next 2 months.*
			Internal by your people:
		Internal:	**Internal by your people**: *Family will work to improve home energy efficiency doing as much as they can themselves and starting immediately.*
Well protected?	*Low crime is in work and home area.*	**External**: *Need police to continue to keep crime low in work and home area.*	**External by others**: *Low crime in work and home area may be enough. Community commits to sufficient funding to sustain effective police protection from this time forward.*
			Internal by your people:
		Internal:	**Internal by your people**: *Family will avoid situations where crime is more likely starting next weekend.*

Well educated?	*Jane and John have improved job skills for new and future jobs.*	**External**: *Need physically and financially accessible training program to improve job skills for new and future jobs.*	**External by others**: *Nearby community college will add re-training programs starting this fall session.* **Internal by your people:**
		Internal:	**Internal by your people**: *Jane and John will go through re-training to improve job skills for new and future jobs within next 6 months.*
Physically/ mentally well?	*Family improves mental health; Jane and John's job improvement helps. Family has improved physical and mental health by eating better, lowering stress, changing jobs, getting health benefits, and seeking better health care for more complex health problems.*	**External**: *Need physically and financially accessible mental health and physical health services that can successfully treat fairly complex problems.*	**External by others**: *Local health provider will add more mental health services within 12 months. More public health insurance programs are available that include physical and mental health services within 6 months.* **Internal by your people:**
		Internal:	**Internal by your people**: *Family will assist and support each other to improve mental health starting immediately. Job change and improvement will help (see above). Family will work together to improve physical and mental health by eating better, lowering stress, changing or improving jobs, getting health benefits, and seeking better health care from better providers for more complex health problems starting immediately.*
Growing/ developing	*Family has improved personal growth and*	**External**: *Need physically and*	**External by others**:

well?	*development at least in job/career.*	*financially accessible re-training programs.*	**Internal by your people:**
		Internal:	**Internal by your people:** *Family will improve personal growth and development, at least in job/career and re-training (see above)*
Living in good habitat?	*Habitat is beautiful and good.*	**External:** *No change needed, except to sustain habitat.*	**External by others:**
			Internal by your people: *Family will do volunteer work on protecting environment.*
		Internal:	**Internal by your people:** *Family will enjoy the beautiful and good habitat starting next weekend.*
Not vulnerable?	*Family minimizes vulnerability to job loss, health problems, low retirement resources. Children's school situation is good.*	**External:** *Need school and counselors to work successfully with Jane, John, Jim and Joan on improving children's school*	**External by others:**
			Internal by your people:
		Internal:	**Internal by your people:** *Jane and John will improve income security (see above). Family will work with school and counselors and with children to improve children's school situation starting with new school year.*
Producing personal/ public goods?	*Family produces thriving family life and high quality work products.*	**External:** *See above*	**External by others:** *School agrees to provide more support to children to produce better learning starting with new school year.*
			Internal by your people:

		Internal:	Internal by your people: *Family will join together to produce thriving family life (see above). Jane and John will produce high quality work products/services (see above).*
Stable, positive climate?	*Family is more energy efficient, especially for heating, to help with harsh, cold winters. Family takes positive advantage of climate. Family may move to more positive climate.*	External: *Need local heating fuel supplier to provide lower price heating fuel.*	External by others: *Local heating fuel supplier provides lower price heating fuel to avoid more competition effective immediately.*
			Internal by your people:
		Internal:	Internal by your people: *Family will be more energy efficient, especially for heating, which will help with harsh, cold winters starting this winter. Family will take better advantage of climate starting immediately. If they don't, they will explore moving to more positive climate within 2 years.*
Sustainable?	*Family ensures sustainability by working though marital issues, working through children's school issues, minimizing family stressors, improve retirement and savings, and improve health.*	External: *Need community, state and Federal social safety programs to receive stronger support and provide more assurance to family within 6 months. Need school and counselors to work successfully with Jane, John, Jim and Joan on improving children's school situation.*	External by others: *Community, state and Federal social safety programs receive stronger support and can provide more assurance to family within 6 months.*
			Internal by your people:

		Internal:	Internal by your people: *Family will ensure sustainability by getting better job situation, working though marital issues, working through children's school issues, minimizing family stressors, improve retirement and savings, and improve health within 12 months.*

Table 4.3b. How well should your future people as a whole be in near/long term future? What external/internal changes are needed to achieve your people's thriving future? To make this happen, what external/internal actions are needed?

Current and Future Persons (name)	For each person, have the person independently do a one-paragraph description in her/his own words. If the person can't, do one for the person. Cover things like work/living/playing, financial situation, eating/drinking, housing, protection, education, physical/mental health, growth/development, habitat, producing what, and climate. Enter the descriptions into this worksheet/table. Do a summary of your people as a whole.
Your current and future people as a whole. [Summary]	

Table 4.1. Who are your current and future people?

Thrive!

Current/Future Person: _________________________ (Do for each person)

Thriving and Surviving	How well (surviving/ thriving) is the person?	What positively/ negatively impacts her/his thriving/ surviving?	[Optional] If no change, what is her/his near/ long term future behavior as to thriving/ surviving?
Performing (live/work/play) well?			
Well-off?			
Well nourished?			
Well housed?			
Well protected?			
Well educated?			
Physically/ mentally well?			
Growing/ developing well?			
Living in good habitat?			
Not vulnerable?			
Producing personal/ public goods?			
Stable, positive climate?			
Sustainable?			

Table 4.2a. How well (surviving/thriving) is the person? What positively/negatively impacts the person? What is her/his near/long term future behavior?

Thriving and Surviving	How well (surviving/ thriving) are your people as a whole?	What positively/ negatively impacts their thriving/ surviving?	[Optional] What is their near/ long term future behavior as to thriving/ surviving?
Performing (live/work/play) well?			
Well-off?			
Well nourished?			
Well housed?			
Well protected?			
Well educated?			
Physically/ mentally well?			
Growing/ developing well?			
Living in good habitat?			
Not vulnerable?			
Producing personal/ public goods?			
Stable, positive climate?			
Sustainable?			

Table 4.2b. How well (surviving/thriving) are your people as a whole? What positively/negatively impacts them? If no change, what is their near/long term future behavior?

Thriving and Surviving	How well (surviving/ thriving) should your people as a whole be in near/long term future?	External/ internal changes needed to achieve thriving/ surviving future	External actions by others - Who externally will do what to/with whom, where, when, and with what result? How to make that happen?	Internal actions by your people - Who of your people will do what to/with whom, where, when, and with what result
Performing (live/work/ play) well?				
Well-off?				
Well nourished?				
Well housed?				
Well protected?				
Well educated?				
Physically/ mentally well?				
Growing/ developing well?				
Living in good habitat?				
Not vulnerable?				
Producing personal/public goods?				
Stable, positive climate?				
Sustainable?				

Table 4.3a. *Thrive!* **Strategy and Action Plan.** How well (surviving/thriving) should your people as a whole be in near/long term future? What external/internal changes are needed to achieve your people's thriving future? To make this happen, what external/internal actions are needed?

Thriving and Surviving	How well (surviving/ thriving) should your people as a whole be in near/long term future?	External/internal changes needed to achieve surviving and thriving future	Actions by your people and others Who will do what to/with whom, where, when, and with what result?
Performing (live/work/ play) well?		External:	External by others:
			Internal by your people:
		Internal:	Internal by your people:
Well-off?		External:	External by others:
			Internal by your people:
		Internal:	Internal by your people:
Well nourished?		External:	External by others:
			Internal by your people:
		Internal:	Internal by your people:
Well housed		External:	External by others:
			Internal by your people:
		Internal:	Internal by your people:
Well protected?		External:	External by others:
			Internal by your people:
		Internal:	Internal by your people:
Well educated?		External:	External by others:
			Internal by your people:
		Internal:	Internal by your people:

Physically/ mentally well?		External:	External by others:
			Internal by your people:
		Internal:	Internal by your people:
Growing/ developing well?		External:	External by others:
			Internal by your people:
		Internal:	Internal by your people:
Living in good habitat?		External:	External by others:
			Internal by your people:
		Internal:	Internal by your people:
Not vulnerable?		External:	External by others:
			Internal by your people:
		Internal:	Internal by your people:
Producing personal/ public goods?		External:	External by others:
			Internal by your people:
		Internal:	Internal by your people:
Stable, positive climate?		External:	External by others:
			Internal by your people:
		Internal:	Internal by your people:
Sustainable?		External:	External by others:
			Internal by your people:
		Internal:	Internal by your people:

Table 4.3b. *Thrive!* **Strategy and Action Plan.** How well should your future people as a whole be in near/long term future? What external/internal changes are needed to achieve your people's thriving future? To make this happen, what external/internal actions are needed?

Example and Worksheets
for
You and Your Community

***Thrive!* Strategy and Action Plan** (Example of surviving and somewhat thriving).

Thriving and Surviving	How well (surviving/ thriving) should your community be in near/long term future?	External/internal changes needed to achieve surviving and thriving future	Actions by your community and others - Who will do what to/with whom, where, when, and with what result?
Performing (live/work/ play) well?	*Community should perform well with close to country's average mix lifestyles for city of its size. Unemployment should be 2 percentage points lower than country; mix of work should be similar to that of country as a whole and continue with a slightly larger percentage of blue collar workers and light industry.*	**External**: *Externally, outside employers should locate new jobs in community.*	**External by others**: *Outside employers locate new jobs in community within 12 months.*
			Internal by your community:
		Internal: *Internally, community should perform better than it has. Internally, community needs to gain more employers to get to 2 percentage points lower than country; community needs to gain more blue collar workers and light industry; internally, community employers should expand and add jobs.*	**Internal by your community**: *Community provides property tax incentives and community support within 12 months to gain more employers to get to 2 percentage points lower than country and to gain more blue collar workers and light industry; community employers expand and add 10% more jobs within 1 year. Community recruits outside 5 new employers to locate new jobs in community within 2 years.*
Well-off?	*Financial condition of community should be generally stable and sufficient to support public services; community should have slightly higher percentage of blue collar workers but who are no longer facing potential outsourcing of jobs and declining*	**External**: *Externally, outside employers should locate new jobs in community. .*	**External by others**: *Outside employers locate new jobs in community within 12 months.*
			Internal by your community: *Community provides incentives to outside employers to locate new jobs in community (see above).*

		Internal	Internal by your community
		Internal: *Internally, financial condition of community should be even better managed to be generally stable and sufficient to support public services; community should gain slightly higher percentage of blue collar workers; employers should avoid outsourcing of jobs and reducing union effectiveness*	**Internal by your community**: *Community better manages financial condition to be generally stable and sufficient to support public services starting next fiscal year; community retains and recruits employers to gain slightly higher percentage of blue collar workers (see above); employers avoid outsourcing of jobs and reducing union effectiveness over next 2 years.*
Well nourished?	*Food and drink should be available and affordable with prices 5% below average for country; community should have sufficient sources of healthy food; low income people should have adequate resources for healthy food and for food generally; community should have sufficient resources to feed very poor.*	**External**: *Externally, retail and wholesale food sources should hold down prices and add more healthy foods; country and state should provide resources to ensure food affordability for low and lower middle income persons.*	**External by others**: *Retail and wholesale food sources hold down prices to 1% increase for next 12 months and add more healthy foods on trial basis starting within 6 months; country and state provide resources this fiscal year to ensure food affordability for low and lower middle income persons.*
			Internal by your community: *Starting immediately, community with other communities presses retail and wholesale food sources to hold down prices and add more healthy foods; starting immediately, community with other communities presses country and state to provide resources to ensure food affordability for low and lower middle income persons.*

		Internal: *Internally, community, grocers and restaurants should make food and drink available and affordable with prices 5% below average for country; community, grocers and restaurants should have sufficient sources of healthy food; community should ensure low income people have adequate resources for healthy food and for food generally; community should add resources to have sufficient resources to feed very poor.*	**Internal by your community**: *Within 12 months, community, grocers and restaurants make food and drink available and affordable with prices 5% below average for country; community, grocers and restaurants provide sufficient sources of healthy food within 12 months; community provides support to low income people to ensure adequate resources for healthy food and for food generally within 12 months; community adds resources to have sufficient resources to feed very poor within 12 months.*
Well housed	*Housing for upper and middle income people should be available and affordable; housing for low and lower middle income people should be affordable, available and adequate.*	**External**: *Externally country and state should provide resources to build affordable housing and resources for lower middle and low income people to rent or buy a house.*	**External by others**: *Country and state provide resources to build affordable housing and resources for lower middle and low income people to rent or buy a house.*
			Internal by your community: *Starting immediately, community presses country and state to provide resources to build affordable housing and resources for lower middle and low income people to rent or buy a house.*

		Internal: *Internally, community should make available housing for low and lower middle income people that is affordable, available and adequate.*	**Internal by your community**: *Within 2 years, community should make available housing for low and lower middle income people that is affordable, available and adequate.*
Well protected?	*Community police force should be in top 10% for country; some neighborhood watch groups should exist but without any significant problems.*	**External**: *Externally, country and state should provide resources to adequately supplement community police resources.*	**External by others**: *Country and state provide resources this fiscal year to adequately supplement community police resources.*
			Internal by your community: *Starting immediately, community presses country and state to provide resources to adequately supplement community police resources.*
		Internal: *Internally, community should provide resources and management to ensure police force should be in top 10% for country; neighborhood watch groups should exercise good management to avoid any significant problems.*	**Internal by your community**: *Community provides resources and management this fiscal year to ensure police force is in top 10% for country; neighborhood watch groups exercise good management to avoid any significant problems starting within 30 days.*
Well educated?	*Education availability and quality should be in the top 10% of cities of its size; community should have slightly higher percentage of college educated.*	**External**: *Externally, country and state should provide resources to adequately supplement community education resources.*	**External by others**: *Country and state provide resources this fiscal year to adequately supplement community education resources.*
			Internal by your community: *Starting immediately, community presses country and state to provide resources to adequately supplement community education resources.*

		Internal: *Internally, community should provide resources and management to ensure education availability and quality in the top 10% of cities of its size; community should work to retain and increase the percentage of college educated.*	**Internal by your community**: *Community provides resources and management this fiscal year to ensure education availability and quality in the top 10% of cities of its size; starting immediately, community works to retain and increase the percentage of college educated.*
Physically/ mentally well?	*Physical and mental health should be in top 10% of cities of its size; community should have substantially less occupationally related illness; private health services should be in top 25% and public health services should be in top 25% of cities of its size.*	**External**: *Externally, country and state should ensure affordability (cost and insurance) of health services.*	**External by others**: *Country and state ensure affordability (cost and insurance) of health services by instituting cost constraints to less than 3% increase and providing affordable health insurance within 12 months.*
			Internal by your community: *Starting immediately, community presses country and state to ensure affordability (cost and insurance) of health services.*

		Internal: *Internally, community and private and public health services should improve services so that physical and mental health should be in top 10% of cities of its size; community and industry should ensure having substantially less occupationally related illness; community and private health services should ensure private health services in top 25% and community should ensure public health services in top 25% of cities of its size.*	Internal by your community: *Within 2 years, community and private and public health services improve services so that physical and mental health should be in top 10% of cities of its size; community and industry ensure having substantially less occupationally related illness within 2 years; community and private health services ensure private health services in top 25% within 2 years; community manages and provides resources this fiscal year to ensure public health services in top 25% of cities of its size.*
Growing/ developing well?	*Personal growth and development should be substantially better than cities of its size and community should have job re-training in top 10% of its size.*	External: *Externally, country and state should provide additional re-training resources to supplement community.*	External by others: *Country and state provide additional re-training resources this fiscal year to supplement community.*
			Internal by your community: *Starting immediately, community presses country and state to provide additional re-training resources to supplement community.*

		Internal: *Internally, community should help ensure personal growth and development is substantially better than cities of its size; community should ensure job re-training is in top 10% of its size.*	**Internal by your community**: *Community helps ensure personal growth and development is substantially better than cities of its size within 18 months; community adds resources this fiscal year to ensure job re-training is in top 10% of its size.*
Living in good habitat?	*Habitat should be very pleasant and very healthy.*	**External**: *Externally, country and state should ensure habitat is very pleasant and very healthy.*	**External by others**: *Country and state ensure habitat is very pleasant and very healthy by adding 25% more funding this fiscal year for public parks and preventive health programs.*
			Internal by your community: *Starting immediately, community presses country and state to ensure habitat is very pleasant and very healthy.*
		Internal: *Internally, community should ensure habitat is very pleasant and very healthy.*	**Internal by your community**: *Within 1 year, community implements policies to ensure habitat is very pleasant and very healthy.*

Not vulnerable?	*Community should have much less vulnerability; community should greatly reduce its vulnerability on job and income loss, affordable and healthy foods, affordable housing, public health services, and community revenues.*	**External**: *Externally, country and state should reduce vulnerability country and state-wide with special efforts (as listed for other areas) to greatly reduce its vulnerability on job and income loss, affordable and healthy foods, affordable housing, public health services, and community revenues.*	**External by others**: *Within 2 years, country and state policies and programs substantially reduce vulnerability country and state-wide with special efforts (as listed for other areas) to greatly reduce its vulnerability on job and income loss, affordable and healthy foods, affordable housing, public health services, and community revenues.*
			Internal by your community: *Starting immediately, community presses country and state to institute policies and programs that reduce vulnerability country and state-wide with special efforts (as listed for other areas) to greatly reduce its vulnerability on job and income loss, affordable and healthy foods, affordable housing, public health services, and community revenues.*
		Internal: *Internally, community should reduce its vulnerabilities with special efforts (as listed for other areas) to greatly reduce its vulnerability on job and income loss, affordable and healthy foods, affordable housing, public health services, and community revenues.*	**Internal by your community**: *Within 2 years, community substantially reduces its vulnerabilities with special efforts (as listed for other areas) to greatly reduce its vulnerability on job and income loss, affordable and healthy foods, affordable housing, public health services, and community revenues.*

Producing personal/ public goods?	*Community should produce a wider range of products and services for city of its size, a substantially higher percentage of higher quality manufactured products, a high percentage of healthy and well educated children and a range of recreational activities in the top 10% of cities of its size.*	**External**: *Externally, employers should bring more and a wider range of jobs and higher quality manufacturing; country and state provide added education resources; country and state add recreational resources to community.*	**External by others**: *Employers bring more and a wider range of jobs and higher quality manufacturing within 12 months; country and state provide added education resources this fiscal year; country and state add recreational resources this fiscal year to community.*
			Internal by your community: *Community recruits employers to bring more and a wider range of jobs and higher quality manufacturing within 12 months; starting immediately, community presses country and state to provide added education resources; starting immediately, community presses country and state to add recreational resources to community.*

		Internal: *Internally, community should ensure a wider range of products and services than other cities of its size, a substantially higher percentage of higher quality manufactured products, a high percentage of healthy and well educated children and a range of recreational activities in the top 10% of cities of its size.*	Internal by your community: *Community and private sector ensure a wider range of products and services than other cities of its size and a substantially higher percentage of higher quality manufactured products within 12 months; community ensures supportive resources this fiscal year to help ensure a high percentage of healthy and well educated children; and community provides resources this fiscal year to ensure a range of recreational activities in the top 10% of cities of its size.*
Stable, positive climate?	*Climate should continue to be good to very good.*	External: *Externally, country and state work to ensure climate is good to very good.*	External by others: *Country and state work to ensure climate is good to very good through environmental policy within 18 months and international agreements within 2 years.*
			Internal by your community:
		Internal:	Internal by your community:
Sustainable?	*Sustainability should be ensured and no longer be in question in spite of changing national and international economics and potential job outsourcing.*	External: *Externally, country and state support policies that reduce outsourcing and protect jobs in community.*	External by others: *Country and state execute policies that reduce outsourcing and protect jobs in community within 12 months.*

			Internal by your community: *Starting immediately, community presses country and state to support policies that reduce outsourcing and protect jobs in community*
		Internal: *Internally, community ensures sustainability is no longer in question in spite of changing national and international economics and potential job outsourcing.*	**Internal by your community**: *Starting immediately, community presses country and state to ensure climate is good to very good. Within 2 years, community ensures sustainability is no longer in question in spite of changing national and international economics and potential job outsourcing.*

Table 5.4. ***Thrive!* Strategy and Action Plan.** How well (surviving/thriving) should your community be in near/long term future? What external/internal changes are needed to achieve your community's thriving future? To make this happen, what external/internal actions are needed?

Community Characteristics	What is your community today?
Geographic boundaries	
Gender make-up	
Age make-up	
Racial make-up	
Ethnic make-up	
Lifestyle	
Type of work	
Financial situation	
Food/drink	
Housing	
Protection	
Education	
Physical / mental health	
Personal growth / development	
Habitat	
Producing what	
Climate	
Sustainability	

Table 5.1. What is your community today?

Thriving and Surviving	How well (surviving/ thriving) is your community?	What positively/ negatively impacts its thriving/ surviving?	What is its near/ long term behavior as to thriving/ surviving?
Performing (live/work/play) well?			
Well-off?			
Well nourished?			
Well housed?			
Well protected?			
Well educated?			
Physically/ mentally well?			
Growing/ developing well?			
Living in good habitat?			
Not vulnerable?			
Producing personal/ public goods?			
Stable, positive climate?			
Sustainable?			

Table 5.2. How well (surviving/thriving) is your community? What positively/ negatively impacts it? If no change, what is its near/long term future behavior?

Community Characteristics	What is your desired and/or likely future community?
Type of work/how people live	
Financial situation	
Food/drink	
Housing	
Protection	
Education	
Physical / mental health	
Personal growth / development	
Habitat	
Producing what	
Climate	
Sustainability	

Table 5.3. What is your desired and/or likely future community?

Thriving and Surviving	How well (surviving/ thriving) should your community be in near/long term future?	External/internal changes needed to achieve surviving and thriving future	Actions by your community and others - Who will do what to/with whom, where, when, and with what result?
Performing (live/work/ play) well?		External:	External by others:
			Internal by your community:
		Internal:	Internal by your community:
Well-off?		External:	External by others:
			Internal by your community:
		Internal:	Internal by your community:
Well nourished?		External:	External by others:
			Internal by your community:
		Internal:	Internal by your community:
Well housed		External:	External by others:
			Internal by your community:
		Internal:	Internal by your community:
Well protected?		External:	External by others:
			Internal by your community:
		Internal:	Internal by your community:
Well educated?		External:	External by others:
			Internal by your community:
		Internal:	Internal by your community:
Physically/ mentally well?		External:	External by others:
			Internal by your community:
		Internal:	Internal by your community:

Growing/ developing well?		External:	**External by others:**
			Internal by your community:
		Internal:	**Internal by your community:**
Living in good habitat?		External:	**External by others:**
			Internal by your community:
		Internal:	**Internal by your community:**
Not vulnerable?		External:	**External by others:**
			Internal by your community:
		Internal:	**Internal by your community:**
Producing personal/ public goods?		External:	**External by others:**
			Internal by your community:
		Internal:	**Internal by your community:**
Stable, positive climate?		External:	**External by others:**
			Internal by your community:
		Internal:	**Internal by your community:**
Sustainable?		External:	**External by others:**
			Internal by your community:
		Internal:	**Internal by your community:**

Table 5.4. *Thrive!* **Strategy and Action Plan.** How well (surviving/thriving) should your community be in near/long term future? What external/internal changes are needed to achieve your community's thriving future? To make this happen, what external/internal actions are needed?

Example and Worksheets
for
You and Your Country

Thrive! **Strategy and Action Plan** (Example of surviving and somewhat thriving).

Thriving and Surviving	How well (surviving/thriving) should your country be in near/long term future?	External/internal changes needed to achieve surviving and thriving future	Actions by your country and others - Who will do what to/with whom, where, when, and with what result?
Performing (live/work/play) well?	*Country should perform better than countries on its continent with close to continent's average mix of lifestyles for country of its size.*	**External**: *Externally, more business, agriculture and light industry should move into country with more employment for blue collar and agriculture workers.*	**External by others**: *Twenty-five percent more business, agriculture and light industry move into country with more employment for blue collar and agriculture workers within 2 years.*
			Internal by your country:
	Unemployment should be lower than its continent; mix of work should be similar to that of its continent but with a larger percentage of blue collar and of agricultural workers and light industry.	**Internal**: *Internally, country should have a better, more collaborative government with a collaborative partnership with the private sector committed to perform better than countries on its continent. Internally, more business, agriculture and light industry should stay in country with more employment for blue collar and agriculture workers.*	**Internal by your country**: *Within 1 year, country builds and sustains a better, more collaborative government with a collaborative partnership with the private sector committed to perform better than countries on its continent. With small incentives added by government, 95% of business, agriculture and light industry stay in country with more employment for blue collar and agriculture workers. With small incentives added by government, 25 percent more business, agriculture and light industry move into country within 2 years with more employment for blue collar and agriculture workers.*
Well-off?	*Financial condition of country should*	**External**:	**External by others**:
			Internal by your country:

	blue collar workers who should not face potential moving of jobs out of country.	**Internal**: *Internally, government and private sector should collaborate and ensure financial condition is stable and sufficient to support needed public services; employers should be committed to blue collar workers and not moving their jobs out of country; country and employers should have expanded job training.*	**Internal by your country**: *Government and private sector collaborate and come to agreement this year and ensure financial condition is stable and sufficient to support needed public services for at least next 5 years; employers commit to blue collar workers and not moving their jobs out of country for at least next 5 years; country and employers expand job training by 50% within 1 year with 50/50 funding.*
Well nourished?	*Food and drink should be available and prices should be 10% below average for its continent; country should have sufficient sources of healthy food; low income people should have resources for healthy food and for food generally; country should have sufficient resources to feed very poor.*	**External**:	**External by others**:
			Internal by your country:
		Internal: *Internally, food and drink producers, wholesalers and retailers should ensure food and drink is available and 10% below average cost for its continent; country and food industry should ensure sufficient sources of healthy food; country should ensure low income people have resources for healthy food and for food generally; country should ensure sufficient resources to feed very poor.*	**Internal by your country**: *Food and drink producers, wholesalers and retailers ensure food and drink is available and 10% below average cost for its continent for at least next 3 years; country and food industry agree to and ensure sufficient sources of healthy food for at least next 3 years; country comes to agreement, provides funding and helps ensure low income people have resources for healthy food and for food generally for at least next 5 years; country comes to agreement, provides funding and ensures sufficient resources to feed very poor for at least next 5 years.*
Well housed	*Housing for upper and middle income*	**External**:	**External by others**:
			Internal by your country:

	and lower middle income people should be available, affordable and adequate.	**Internal**: *Internally, banks and housing industry should ensure housing for upper and middle income people is available and affordable; government, bankers and builders should ensure housing for low and lower middle income people is available, affordable and adequate.*	**Internal by your country**: *Banks and housing industry continue to ensure housing for upper and middle income people is available and affordable for at least next 5 years; government, bankers and builders come to agreement, government provides incentive funding and all ensure housing for low and lower middle income people is available, affordable and adequate within 5 years.*
Well protected?	*Country local police force, state police force and country military should be best for its continent.*	**External**:	**External by others**: **Internal by your country**:
		Internal: *Internally, country and its local police force, state police force and country military should ensure it is best of its continent, including adequate resourcing.*	**Internal by your country**: *Country and its local police force, state police force and country military ensure it is best of its continent, including strong management and adequate resourcing for at least next 5 years.*
Well educated?	*Education availability and quality should be best on its continent; country should have 10 percent more college educated than its continent.*	**External**:	**External by others**: **Internal by your country**:
		Internal: *Internally, country and its education people should ensure education availability and quality is best on its continent and should ensure country has 10 percent more college educated than its continent.*	**Internal by your country**: *Country and its education people come to agreement within 1 year; government provides funding; and all ensure education availability and quality is best on its continent and ensure country has 10 percent more college educated than its continent for at least next 5 years.*
Physically/ mentally well?	*Physical and mental health should be best*	**External**:	**External by others**: **Internal by your country**:

	substantially less occupationally related illness; private and public health services should be best on its continent.	**Internal**: *Internally, country and its private and public health services should ensure physical and mental health is best compared to other countries on its continent; country and employers should ensure workers have substantially less occupationally related illness; country and private and public health services should ensure services are best on its continent; country should ensure every person without private insurance has financial access to needed health services; country and its people should ensure each person is improving personal and family health.*	**Internal by your country**: *Country and its private and public health services agree and within 2 years ensure physical and mental health is best compared to other countries on its continent; country and employers agree within 1 year and ensure workers have substantially less occupationally related illness; country and private and public health services agree within 1 year and ensure services are best on its continent within 2 years; country agrees within 1 year, provides funding for at least 5 years, and ensures every person without private insurance has financial access to needed health services for at least the next 5 years; country and its people begin collaborative effort this year and ensure each person is improving personal and family health starting within 2 years.*
Growing/ developing well?	*Personal growth and development should be better than countries on its continent and have substantially more job training.*	**External**:	**External by others**:
			Internal by your country:
		Internal: *Internally, country and its people should ensure personal growth and development is better than countries on its continent; country and employers should ensure substantially more job training.*	**Internal by your country**: *Country and its people begin collaborative effort this year and ensure personal growth and development is better than countries on its continent within 2 years; country and employers agree within 1 year and agree to 50/50 funding ensure substantially more job training within 1 year.*

Living in good habitat?	*Habitat should have the best mix of pleasant and harsh and healthy and unhealthy on its continent.*	**External**: *Externally, country and its neighboring countries should jointly ensure habitat has the best mix of pleasant and harsh and healthy and unhealthy.*	**External by others**: *Neighboring countries agree within 1 year and jointly help ensure habitat has the best mix of pleasant and harsh and healthy and unhealthy with phased plan over next 5 years.*
			Internal by your country: *Starting immediately, country joins with neighboring countries, agree within 1 year, and jointly help ensure habitat has the best mix of pleasant and harsh and healthy and unhealthy with phased plan over next 5 years.*
		Internal: *Internally, country and its people should ensure habitat has the best mix of pleasant and harsh and healthy and unhealthy on its continent.*	**Internal by your country**: *Country and its people develop collaborative effort and strategy and, within 5 years, ensure habitat has the best mix of pleasant and harsh and healthy and unhealthy on its continent.*
Not vulnerable?	*While country has had much vulnerability, it should no longer be vulnerable on job loss, limited income, lack of affordable and healthy foods, lack of affordable and adequate housing for poorer people, inadequate private and public health services, and low country revenues.*	**External**:	**External by others**:
			Internal by your country:
		Internal: *Internally, while country has had much vulnerability, country and its people should ensure it is no longer vulnerable on job loss, limited income, lack of affordable and healthy foods, lack of affordable and adequate housing for poorer people, inadequate private and public health services, and low country revenues.*	**Internal by your country**: *While country has had much vulnerability, country and its people collaborate, develop strategy and, within 1 year start to ensure it is no longer vulnerable on job loss, limited income, lack of affordable and healthy foods, lack of affordable and adequate housing for poorer people, inadequate private and public health services, and low country revenues.*
Producing personal/ public	*Compared to its continent, country should*	**External**:	**External by others**:
			Internal by your country:

		Internal: *Internally and compared to its continent, country and its people should ensure it produces an optimal range of products and services for its continent, a substantially higher percentage of high quality manufactured products, the best percentage of healthy and well educated children and a wide range of recreational activities.*	Internal by your country: *Within 5 years and compared to its continent, country and its people work together to ensure it produces an optimal range of products and services for its continent, a substantially higher percentage of high quality manufactured products, the best percentage of healthy and well educated children on its continent and a wide range of recreational activities.*
Stable, positive climate?	*Climate should be very good and stay that way.*	External: *Externally, country should join with international community to ensure climate is very good and stays that way.*	External by others: *International community comes to agreement within 2 years and ensures climate is very good and stays that way for centuries to come.*
			Internal by your country: *Starting immediately, country joins with international community, comes to agreement within 2 years and ensures climate is very good and stays that way for centuries to come.*
		Internal:	Internal by your country:
Sustainable?	*Sustainability should be ensured and no longer be in question due to potential job losses, limited income and country revenues, lower education and health, under developed natural resources and changing national and international*	External: *Externally, country should join with neighboring countries and international community to ensure no negative impact from changing national and international economics.*	External by others: *Neighboring countries and international community come to agreement within 1 year and help ensure no negative impact from changing national and international economics for at least next 10 years.*
			Internal by your country: *Starting immediately, country joins with neighboring countries and international community, comes to agreement within 1 year and helps ensure no negative impact from changing national and international economics for at least the next 10 years.*

	economics.	**Internal**: *Internally, country and its people should ensure sustainability and that there is no longer job losses, limited income and country revenues, lower education and health, under developed natural resources and no negative impact from changing national and international economics.*	**Internal by your country**: *Country and its people collaborate, develop strategy and, within 1 year work to ensure sustainability and that there is no longer job losses, limited income and country revenues, lower education and health, under developed natural resources and negative impact from changing national and international economics for at least next 10 years.*

Table 6.4. *Thrive!* **Strategy and Action Plan.** How well (surviving/thriving) should your country be in near/long term future? What external/internal changes are needed to achieve your country's thriving future? To make this happen, what external/internal actions are needed?

Country Characteristics	What is your country today?
Geographic boundaries	
Gender make-up	
Age make-up	
Racial make-up	
Ethnic make-up	
Lifestyle	
Type of work	
Financial situation	
Food/drink	
Housing	
Protection	
Education	
Physical / mental health	
Personal growth / development	
Habitat	
Producing what	
Climate	
Sustainability	

Table 6.1. What is your country today?

Thriving and Surviving	How well (surviving/ thriving) is your country?	What positively/ negatively impacts its thriving/ surviving?	What is its near/ long term behavior as to thriving/ surviving?
Performing (live/work/play) well?			
Well-off?			
Well nourished?			
Well housed?			
Well protected?			
Well educated?			
Physically/ mentally well?			
Growing/ developing well?			
Living in good habitat?			
Not vulnerable?			
Producing personal/ public goods?			
Stable, positive climate?			
Sustainable?			

Table 6.2. How well (surviving/thriving) is your country? What positively/ negatively impacts it? What is its near/long term future behavior?

Country Characteristics	What is your desired and/or likely future country?
Type of work/how people live	
Financial situation	
Food/drink	
Housing	
Protection	
Education	
Physical / mental health	
Personal growth / development	
Habitat	
Producing what	
Climate	
Sustainability	

Table 6.3. What is your desired and/or likely future country?

Thriving and Surviving	How well (surviving/thriving) should your country be in near/long term future?	External/internal changes needed to achieve surviving and thriving future	Actions by your country and others - Who will do what to/with whom, where, when, and with what result?
Performing (live/work/play) well?		External:	External by others:
			Internal by your country:
		Internal:	Internal by your country:
Well-off?		External:	External by others:
			Internal by your country:
		Internal:	Internal by your country:
Well nourished?		External:	External by others:
			Internal by your country:
		Internal:	Internal by your country:
Well housed		External:	External by others:
			Internal by your country:
		Internal:	Internal by your country:
Well protected?		External:	External by others:
			Internal by your country:
		Internal:	Internal by your country:
Well educated?		External:	External by others:
			Internal by your country:
		Internal:	Internal by your country:
Physically/mentally well?		External:	External by others:
			Internal by your country:
		Internal:	Internal by your country:

Growing/ developing well?		External:	External by others:
			Internal by your country:
		Internal:	Internal by your country:
Living in good habitat?		External:	External by others:
			Internal by your country:
		Internal:	Internal by your country:
Not vulnerable?		External:	External by others:
			Internal by your country:
		Internal:	Internal by your country:
Producing personal/ public goods?		External:	External by others:
			Internal by your country:
		Internal:	Internal by your country:
Stable, positive climate?		External:	External by others:
			Internal by your country:
		Internal:	Internal by your country:
Sustainable?		External:	External by others:
			Internal by your country:
		Internal:	Internal by your country:

Table 6.4. ***Thrive!* Strategy and Action Plan.** How well (surviving/thriving) should your country be in near/long term future? What external/internal changes are needed to achieve your country's thriving future? To make this happen, what external/internal actions are needed?

Example and Worksheets
for
Our World

Thrive! **Strategy and Action Plan** (Example of surviving and thriving).

Thriving and Surviving	How well (surviving/ thriving) should our world be in near/long term future?	Changes needed to achieve surviving and thriving future	Actions - Who will do what to/with whom, where, when, and with what result?
			Starting immediately, we (people, business/industry, private organizations (local, country), governments (local, country) and international organizations) build, achieve, and sustain a surviving and thriving future for our world and for all forever, including:
Performing (live/work/ play) well?	Our world and our people should be performing (living, working, recreating, learning) well enough to survive and thrive. *For example. All live, work, recreate and learn well.*	*People, business/industry, private organizations (local, country), governments (local, country) and international organizations act to ensure a) all (who are able and not appropriately retired) can work and earn a living income sufficient to survive and thrive and b) all have sufficient resources for and are living, recreating, learning so that they are surviving and thriving to maximum extent feasible.*	*Starting immediately, people, business/industry, private organizations (local, country), governments (local, country) and international organizations act to ensure, within the next 20 years, a) all (who are able and not appropriately retired) can work and earn a living income sufficient to survive and thrive and b) all have sufficient resources for and are living, recreating, learning so that they are surviving and thriving to maximum extent feasible.*
Well-off?	Our world and our people should be well-off (financially) enough to survive and thrive. *For example. A living income for all, eliminate poverty.*	*People, business/industry, private organizations (local, country), governments (local, country) and international organizations act to ensure a) all have sufficient income/resources to survive and thrive and b) all governments have sufficient resources to*	*Starting immediately, people, business/industry, private organizations (local, country), governments (local, country) and international organizations act to ensure, within the next 20 years, a) all have sufficient income/resources to survive and thrive and b) all governments have*

		provide needed (supporting surviving) and desired (supporting thriving) public programs and policies.	*sufficient resources to provide needed (supporting surviving) and desired (supporting thriving) public programs and policies.*
Well nourished?	Our world and our people should be well nourished (food and drink) enough to survive and thrive. *For example, Affordable and healthy food for all.*	*People, business/industry, private organizations (local, country), governments (local, country) and international organizations act to ensure that all people have access to, be able to afford and consume healthy foods enough to survive and thrive.*	*Starting immediately, people, business/industry, private organizations (local, country), governments (local, country) and international organizations act to ensure, within the next 20 years, that all people have access to, be able to afford and consume healthy foods enough to survive and thrive.*
Well housed?	Our world and our people should be well housed enough to survive and thrive. *For example. Affordable and adequate housing for all.*	*People, business/industry, private organizations (local, country), governments (local, country) and international organizations act to ensure all have access to, be able to afford and live in adequate and preferably high performing housing that supports surviving and thriving.*	*Starting immediately, people, business/industry, private organizations (local, country), governments (local, country) and international organizations act to ensure, within the next 20 years, all have access to, be able to afford and live in adequate and preferably high performing housing that supports surviving and thriving.*
Well protected?	Our world and our people should be well protected (exposures, crime) enough to survive and thrive. *For example. All are protected from crime and environmental threats.*	*People, business/industry, private organizations (local, country), governments (local, country) and international organizations act to ensure a) environmental exposures in home, workplace and elsewhere are minimized so as to not prevent surviving and thriving and b) crimes are minimized in terms of frequency and impact so as to not prevent surviving and thriving.*	*Starting immediately, people, business/industry, private organizations (local, country), governments (local, country) and international organizations act to ensure, within the next 20 years, a) environmental exposures in home, workplace and elsewhere are minimized so as to not prevent surviving and thriving and b) crimes are minimized to the extent feasible in terms of frequency and impact so as to not prevent surviving*

			and thriving.
Well educated?	Our world and our people should be well educated enough to survive and thrive. *For example. All are well educated with all reaching optimum educational levels.*	*People, business/industry, private organizations (local, country), governments (local, country) and international organizations act to ensure all people are educated to the full extent of their abilities, needs and desires and to support their surviving and thriving.*	*Starting immediately, people, business/industry, private organizations (local, country), governments (local, country) and international organizations act to ensure, within the next 20 years, all people are educated to the full extent of their abilities, needs and desires and to support their surviving and thriving.*
Physically/ mentally well?	Our world and our people should be physically and mentally well enough to survive and thrive. *For example. All are physically and mentally healthy.*	*People, business/industry, private organizations (local, country), governments (local, country) and international organizations act to ensure a) all people receive the optimal health support to ensure surviving and thriving and b) all people's physical and mental health is optimized to best ensure surviving and thriving.*	*Starting immediately, people, business/industry, private organizations (local, country), governments (local, country) and international organizations act to ensure, within the next 20 years, a) all people receive the optimal health support to ensure, within the next 20 years, surviving and thriving and b) all people's physical and mental health is optimized to best ensure surviving and thriving.*
Growing/ developing well?	Our world and our people should be personally growing/develo ping well enough to survive and thrive. *For example. All are growing and developing to their full potential.*	*People, business/industry, private organizations (local, country), governments (local, country) and international organizations act to ensure all people are personally growing and developing to best ensure surviving and thriving.*	*Starting immediately, people, business/industry, private organizations (local, country), governments (local, country) and international organizations act to ensure, within the next 20 years, all people are personally growing and developing to best ensure surviving and thriving.*
Living in good habitat?	Our world should be good habitat enough	*People, business/industry, private organizations (local, country),*	*Starting immediately, people, business/industry, private organizations*

	to survive and thrive. *For example. All live in good, sustainable habitat including housing, community, and natural environment.*	*governments (local, country) and international organizations act to ensure a) all people have access to habitat that best supports their surviving and thriving and b) our world has the optimal mix, quantity and quality of habitat to best support our world and its inhabitants' surviving and thriving.*	*(local, country), governments (local, country) and international organizations act to ensure, within the next 20 years, a) all people have access to habitat that best supports their surviving and thriving and b) our world has the optimal mix, quantity and quality of habitat to best support our world and its inhabitants' surviving and thriving.*
Not vulnerable?	Our world and our people should not be vulnerable. *For example. Vulnerability is minimized in terms of frequency, level, duration and impact.*	*People, business/industry, private organizations (local, country), governments (local, country) and international organizations act to ensure our world and all of its people, if vulnerable, are vulnerable only to the minimum extent feasible.*	*Starting immediately, people, business/industry, private organizations (local, country), governments (local, country) and international organizations act to ensure, within the next 20 years, our world and all of its people, if vulnerable, are vulnerable only to the minimum extent feasible.*
Producing personal/ public goods?	Our world and our people should be producing personal and public goods enough to survive and thrive. *For example. Should produce optimal personal income/resources, housing, food and drink, energy, education, health, protection, personal growth and development, and habitat.*	*People, business/industry, private organizations (local, country), governments (local, country) and international organizations act to ensure our people produce personal and public goods (including personal income/resources, housing, food and drink, energy, education, health, protection, personal growth and development, and habitat) so as to support surviving and thriving for all persons and for our world overall.*	*Starting immediately, people, business/industry, private organizations (local, country), governments (local, country) and international organizations act to ensure, within the next 20 years, our people produce personal and public goods (including personal income/resources, housing, food and drink, energy, education, health, protection, personal growth and development, and habitat) so as to support surviving and thriving for all persons and for our world overall.*

Stable, positive climate?	Our world should have a stable, positive climate. *For example. Our climate should help support all human, animal and plant life forever.*	*People, business/industry, private organizations (local, country), governments (local, country) and international organizations act to ensure all people behave so as to avoid negative impacts and support positive impacts so as to help ensure a stable, positive climate.*	*Starting immediately, people, business/industry, private organizations (local, country), governments (local, country) and international organizations act to ensure, within the next 10 years, all people behave so as to avoid negative impacts and support positive impacts so as to help ensure a stable, positive climate.*
Sustainable?	Our world and our people should be sustained. *For example. Our people and our earth are sustained for all forever.*	*People, business/industry, private organizations (local, country), governments (local, country) and international organizations act to ensure all people behave so as to ensure the sustainability of our world <u>and</u> its people.*	*Starting immediately, people, business/industry, private organizations (local, country), governments (local, country) and international organizations act to ensure, within the next 5 years, all people behave so as to ensure the sustainability of our world <u>and</u> its people.*

Table 7.4. ***Thrive!* Strategy and Action Plan.** How well (surviving/thriving) should our world be in near/long term future? What changes are needed to achieve our world's thriving future? To make this happen, what actions are needed?

World Characteristics	What is our world today?
Geographic boundaries	
Gender make-up	
Age make-up	
Racial make-up	
Ethnic make-up	
Lifestyle	
Type of work	
Financial situation	
Food/drink	
Housing	
Protection	
Education	
Physical / mental health	
Personal growth / development	
Habitat	
Producing what	
Climate	
Sustainability	

Table 7.1. What is our world today?

Thriving and Surviving	How well (surviving/ thriving) is our world?	What positively/ negatively impacts its thriving/ surviving?	What is its near/ long term behavior as to thriving/ surviving?
Performing (live/work/play) well?			
Well-off?			
Well nourished?			
Well housed?			
Well protected?			
Well educated?			
Physically/ mentally well?			
Growing/ developing well?			
Living in good habitat?			
Not vulnerable?			
Producing personal/ public goods?			
Stable, positive climate?			
Sustainable?			

Table 7.2. How well (surviving/thriving) is our world? What positively/ negatively impacts it? What is its near/long term future behavior?

World Characteristics	What is our desired and/or likely future world?
Type of work/how people live	
Financial situation	
Food/drink	
Housing	
Protection	
Education	
Physical / mental health	
Personal growth / development	
Habitat	
Producing what	
Climate	
Sustainability	

Table 7.3. What is our desired and/or likely future world?

Thriving and Surviving	How well (surviving/ thriving) should our world be in near/long term future?	Changes needed to achieve surviving and thriving future	**Actions** - Who will do what to/with whom, where, when, and with what result?
Performing (live/work/play) well?			
Well-off?			
Well nourished?			
Well housed?			
Well protected?			
Well educated?			
Physically/ mentally well?			
Growing/ developing well?			
Living in good habitat?			
Not vulnerable?			
Producing personal/ public goods?			
Stable, positive climate?			
Sustainable?			

Table 7.4. *Thrive!* **Strategy and Action Plan.** How well (surviving/thriving) should our world be in near/long term future? What changes are needed to achieve our world's thriving future? To make this happen, what actions are needed?

Thrive!

Thrive!® - **People's Guide**

To A Thriving Future

[For All Forever]

<u>Complete Guide</u> To A Thriving Future

Chapter 1: How to use this <u>People's Guide</u>.

How to use this **<u>People's Guide</u>** to help you and your family and friends, community, country and world survive and thrive forever.

This **<u>People's Guide To A Thriving Future [For All Forever]</u>** is provided to help you and your family and friends, community, country and world survive and thrive forever. [50] For our selves, our future generations and the Earth on which we depend, you and we must, can and will achieve a surviving and thriving future for all forever. [51] This future is *Thrive!*, a bold vision and mission.

In this Guide, the term *Thrive!* has several meanings: [52]
- *Thrive!* is the <u>vision</u> of a thriving and surviving future forever for all (our selves, family and friends, communities, countries and world).
- *Thrive!* is the <u>human aspiration</u> to build, achieve and sustain a surviving and thriving future for all forever.
- *Thrive!* is the <u>mission</u> to create and sustain large, positive and timely change that builds and achieves a surviving and thriving future for all forever.

---

[50] This **<u>People's Guide</u>**, including fillable worksheets, can be downloaded free from <u>www.ThrivingFuture.org</u>

[51] Whenever the term "thriving future" is used, it means "a thriving future for all forever", to the maximum extent possible. For example, while an individual person may not survive (live) and thrive forever, people (human race) may survive and thrive forever, whether on Earth or another inhabitable planet.

[52] The *Thrive!* trademark is registered to Gary Christopherson.

Thrive!

- ***Thrive!*** is the <u>call to action and rallying cry</u> to build, achieve and sustain a surviving and thriving future for all forever.
- ***Thrive!*** is the vast <u>***Thrive!* Endeavor**</u> by all of us to build, achieve and sustain a surviving and thriving future for all forever.

This Guide describes what your life and your world will be in a thriving future where all survive and thrive forever, to the maximum extent possible. It lays out why you and we must care about a surviving and thriving future for you, your friends and family, your community, your country and our world. You and all of us want and need that future because of our endangered future and our human need to survive and desire to thrive. This Guide shows you how to build, achieve and sustain a surviving and thriving future for you, your friends and family, your community, your country and our world. And yes, we can as we are now the most able in human history. To help, ***Thrive!*** provides next generation strategy and tools. Finally, this guide shows how the ***Thrive!* Endeavor**, you and all of us together, builds, achieves and sustains <u>a surviving and thriving future</u> <u>for all</u> <u>forever</u>.

More specifically, this Guide describes what your life and your world will be in a thriving future where all survive and thrive forever, to the maximum extent possible. ***Thrive!*** is different and arguably better than anything tried or achieved in human history. It is a <u>thriving</u> future. Not just getting by or achieving a surviving future. A surviving future is necessary but not sufficient. It is a thriving future for <u>all people and all future generations</u>, a "50+ generation" strategy. Not just for some people or just for the current and next generation. It is a thriving future <u>forever</u>, a 1000+ year strategy. Not just for today or just 100 years. It is also for <u>Earth on which we live and depend</u>, not just for people.

So, the first question to ask yourself is whether or not this surviving and thriving future is the future you want? Regardless of how you answer for yourself, then follow other questions. Is this the future your family and friends want? Your community wants? Your

-4-

country wants? Our world wants?   The answer for each of these may be yes, no or not sure.

If you are not sure or do not want this surviving and thriving future, you should read just a bit further. To convince you, this Guide lays out why you and all of us must care about a surviving and thriving future for you, your friends and family, your community, your country and our world. First, you and all of us want and need that future because our future is endangered if we continue our current path. Second, you and all of us want and need that future because we as humans need to survive and strongly desire to thrive in the current world and a sustainable future world. Third, we have an obligation. Because it is people who broke much of the world and endangered its future, it is people who must fix what is broken and build a survivable and thriving future.

But, if you do not want a surviving and thriving future, this Guide has failed in its mission and is probably not for you. Hopefully, you might change your mind in the future.

If you want this future or if you are not sure, you are going to ask if you and we <u>can</u> build, achieve and sustain a surviving and thriving future. You are going to ask <u>how</u>. Chapters 4 through 7 lay out why you and all of us can and how to do it.

You and all of us <u>can</u> because we are more capable than any time in human history. We can build a thriving future by effectively and collaboratively using all available knowledge and tools, including next generation *Thrive!* strategy and tools. Next generation *Thrive!* is different and better than anything in human history. It is <u>achieving</u> a thriving future at each level. It understands that <u>people's behavior</u>, including yours, makes (or breaks) a thriving future. Its knowledge and tools help people, including you, achieve the behavior that in turn achieves a thriving future at each level (family and friends, community, country, world).

<u>How</u> to build and achieve a thriving future for any or all of those you and we care about is laid out as follows.[53]

- Chapter 4 shows you how to build, achieve and sustain that future for <u>you and your friends and family</u>.
- Chapter 5 shows you how to build, achieve and sustain that future for <u>you and your community</u>.
- Chapter 6 shows you how to build, achieve and sustain that future for <u>you and your country</u>.
- Most ambitiously, Chapter 7 shows you how to build, achieve and sustain that future for <u>our world</u>.

This Guide argues <u>why you and all of us should</u> build, achieve and sustain a surviving and thriving future. It argues <u>why we can</u> do it. It walks through <u>how to</u> do it for you and those you and all of us care about. But it will take more than just knowledge and tools and more than just each of us individually. It will take <u>all of us together, including you</u>.

Together, you and all of us must and can build, to the maximum extent possible, a thriving future for all forever via the *Thrive!* **Endeavor**. It is only people that can and must fix what is broken and build a survivable and thriving future. This mission to achieve a thriving future is greater than any in human history and must be sustained for as long as humans exist. To succeed in this mission, it will take all of us working together. For these reasons, *Thrive!* is and requires a vast, sustained endeavor building, achieving and sustaining a surviving and thriving future for all forever. Creating and sustaining the *Thrive!* **Endeavor** is the driving purpose of this **People's Guide**.[54]

---

[53] In order to make each "how-to" chapter self-sufficient, there is some necessary repetition. The intent is that each chapter stands on its own depending on who and what are your priorities (family and friends, community, country, world).

[54] You might also want to use *__Thrive! - Building a Thriving Future__* - a manual providing greater depth on strategy and tools and which is available via <u>www.Amazon.com</u> or as free download from <u>www.ThrivingFuture.org</u>.

Chapter 2: What a thriving future will be.

What your life and your world will be in a thriving future where all survive and thrive forever, to the maximum extent possible.

This Guide describes what your life and your world will be in a thriving future where all survive and thrive forever, to the maximum extent possible. This future is *Thrive!* and is a bold vision and mission.

For you and your family and friends, a thriving future is a better life now and for the near and long term future for all of you and for future generations.

For you and your community, a thriving future is a better life now and for the near and long term future for the whole community and for all of the community's people.

For you and your country, a thriving future is a better life now and for the near and long term future for the whole country and for all of the country's people.

For our world, a thriving future is a better life now and for the near and long term future for the whole world (people and Earth) and for all of the world's people and the Earth itself.

For you and all that you and we care about, it is a much better life and future with less vulnerability, with surviving and with sustained thriving.

When a surviving and thriving future is achieved, you, families and friends, communities, states, countries and the world will be:
- Performing well,
- Well-off (financially),
- Well nourished,
- Well housed,
- Well protected (exposures, crime),
- Well educated,
- Physically and mentally well (people),
- Growing/developing well,
- Living within good habitat,
- Physically well (Earth, plants, animals, environment),
- Not vulnerable,
- Producing personal and public goods,
- Living within a stable, positive climate, and
- Sustained.

When achieved, we will have helped you, families and friends, communities, states, countries and the world move up from:
- Performing poorly or badly,
- Being poor (financially),
- Being poorly nourished,
- Being poorly housed,
- Being poorly protected (exposures, crime),
- Being poorly educated,
- Being physically or mentally ill (people),
- Growing and developing poorly or badly,
- Not doing well "physically" (Earth, plants, animals, environment),
- Living within poor or bad habitat,
- Being excessively vulnerable,
- Living in an unstable, destructive climate, and
- Not being sustained.

Thrive!

When achieved, we will have fulfilled the hope of all, and especially:
- Vulnerable individual people (persons),
- Vulnerable families and friends,
- Vulnerable communities (including neighborhoods, villages, towns, cities, counties, regions),
- Vulnerable states,
- Vulnerable countries, and
- A vulnerable world.

When achieved, we will have:
- Thriving individual people (persons),
- Thriving families and friends,
- Thriving communities (including neighborhoods, villages, towns, cities, counties, states, regions),
- Thriving countries, and
- A thriving world.

Thrive!, a thriving future, is different and arguably better than anything tried or achieved in human history. Not just getting by or achieving a surviving future. A surviving future is necessary but not sufficient. It is a thriving future for <u>all people and all future generations</u>, a "50+ generation" strategy. Not just for some people or just for the current and next generation. It is a thriving future <u>forever</u>, a 1000+ year strategy. Not just for today or just 100 years. It is also for <u>Earth on which we live and depend</u>, not just for people.

Helping achieve this surviving and thriving future is ***Thrive!*** - a vast human endeavor of you and all of us together striving for a surviving and thriving future. ***Thrive!*** strives for and envisions a surviving and thriving future, to the maximum extent possible, forever for all (you, family and friends, communities, countries and the world (including the Earth on which it depends).

Chapter 3: Why care about a thriving future.

Why you and we must care about a surviving and thriving future for you. Your friends and family. Your community. Your country. Our world.

This Guides lays out why you and we must care about a surviving and thriving future for you and your friends and family, your community, your country and our world. You and all of us want and need that future because of our endangered future and our human need to survive and desire to thrive. What drives us is that a person and a people <u>need to survive</u> and <u>desire to thrive</u> in the current world and a sustainable future world.

Our needing and desiring a surviving and thriving future is driven by a natural human force - "a person needs to survive and desires to thrive." To truly satisfy this need and desire, we need the following:

6) we, as a person <u>and</u> a people, need to survive and desire to thrive,
7) we depend on <u>other persons</u> (a people) for survival and thriving, especially in the long term,
8) our need and desire applies to both the current <u>and</u> future world,
9) our <u>future</u> survival and thriving depends on there being a <u>future world</u>, and
10) our future world must be <u>sustainable</u> and <u>sustained</u> to fully meet our need and desire.

For these reasons, building, achieving and sustaining a thriving future forever (to the maximum extent possible) for you, your family and friends, your community, your country and our world is <u>the</u> human endeavor and <u>the</u> ideal.

This is why you and we care about a thriving future. But let's be a bit more specific.

What future must you and we build, achieve and sustain? You, your family and friends, your community, your country and our world want to and must <u>build, achieve and sustain a surviving and thriving future</u>.

All of us, almost without exception, want to <u>thrive</u>. Thriving means:
- Performing well,
- Being well-off (financially),
- Being well nourished,
- Being well housed,
- Being well protected (exposures, crime),
- Being well educated,
- Being physically and mentally well (people),
- Growing/developing well,
- Living within good habitat,
- Being physically well (Earth, plants, animals, environment),
- Not being vulnerable,
- Producing personal and public goods,
- Living within a stable, positive climate, and
- Being sustained.

This is the best future for you, your family and friends, your community, your country and our world (including the Earth on which we depend).

All of us, almost without exception, want to and must <u>survive</u>. Surviving means at least:
- Performing at a minimal level,
- Having the minimum levels of resources, food, housing, protection, education, physical and mental health (people), personal growth and development, and habitat,
- Surviving "physically" (Earth, plants, animals, environment),
- Not being excessively vulnerable,

- Producing minimum levels of personal and public goods, e) being in an humanly survivable climate, and
- Being sustained at a minimal survival level.

This is not the best future but it is far better than not surviving.

What future must we avoid? You, your family and friends, your community, your country and our world want to and must <u>avoid a bad or endangered future</u>. A bad future means:
- Performing poorly or badly,
- Being poor (financially),
- Being poorly nourished,
- Being poorly housed,
- Being poorly protected (exposures, crime),
- Being poorly educated,
- Not being physically or mentally well (people),
- Not growing and developing well,
- Not doing well "physically" (Earth, plants, animals, environment),
- Living within poor or bad habitat,
- Being excessively vulnerable,
- Living in an unstable, destructive climate, and/or
- Not being sustained.

In an endangered future, there is the risk of any or all of these. No one wants to risk this bad future let alone live this bad future.

A bad future also means not fixing what we already know is broken and likely to stay broken.

As we look around us at the people and the world which we care about, much of what is important to us is already broken or is endangered, much of it unnecessarily so. This is probably true for you and your family. This is true for your community, your country and our world.

For example, in the United States, our financial systems' failure did and still could bring down countries' and the world's financial system. Housing bubbles have burst and lifetime savings lost.

While some of our housing markets improve, many people cannot buy homes (lack resources, can't get loans, job insecurity) or they own homes they cannot afford or sell. Even with the Affordable Care Act, our health care remains inaccessible, unaffordable and of poor quality for many people. Our education systems leave children behind and fail to educate children to their full potential. Our economic system rewards many people far beyond their contribution, holds many far below their potential contribution, and keeps many in or near poverty. Our environment is under more stress than it can handle in the decades and centuries to come. On energy, our future was bet on non-renewable energy sources and we have yet to turn to conservation and renewable energy at a level commensurate with long term energy needs and supply.

For some countries, the situation is better. For some, it is worse. All countries and the world as a whole are and will continue to be broken to some greater or lesser extent.

But these are only individual broken pieces for us to fix. In the real world, fixing the future means fixing these broken pieces together with fixing related broken pieces, e.g. health with the economy, education with food, energy with the environment, and housing with protection. Fixing these together is more likely to achieve a surviving and thriving future. Fixing all of these together is the most likely to achieve a thriving future.

Because it is people who have broken much of the world and endangered its future, it is people who must care about and must fix what is broken and build a survivable and thriving future. Because it is only people who can change our future, it is people who must build, achieve and sustain a surviving and thriving future.

All of this is why you and we care about a surviving and thriving future.

Chapter 4: How <u>you and your family and friends</u> can thrive.

How to build, achieve and sustain a surviving and thriving future for you and your family and friends.

Why you and your family and friends <u>can.</u>

You and your family and friends <u>can</u> have a surviving and thriving future. To get to that future, keep in mind that each of them is different with a different future already beginning. Each and all of them <u>can</u> do better whether that future appears bad or good. To build a better future, *Thrive!* strategy and tools have been used successfully at the personal level and on larger scales (community, country). They can work for you and the people closest to you. As they have for others, *Thrive!* can help you and your peoples build, achieve and sustain a surviving and thriving future.

Thrive!
Keep in mind that we are more capable than any time in human history. We can build a thriving future by effectively and collaboratively using all available knowledge and tools, including next generation *Thrive!* strategy and tools. Next generation *Thrive!* is different and better than anything in human history. It is <u>achieving</u> a thriving future at each level. It understands that <u>people's behavior</u>, including yours, makes (or breaks) a thriving future. It helps people, including you, achieve the behavior that in turn achieves a thriving future at each level and for all forever.

Why you and your family and friends <u>must</u>.

You and your family and friends <u>must</u> have a surviving and thriving future. Each and all of your people <u>must</u> do better whether that future appears bad or good. Why? Even those that have a good future are not fully thriving, are not likely to be fully thriving in the future, and are still facing uncertainties about the long term future. You and your people all want and need that future because your and their future is endangered and because of your and their need to survive and desire to thrive. What drives each of them is their need to survive and desire to thrive in the current world and a sustainable future world. Further, because some or all of them have broken some part of their world and endangered its future, you and your people must help fix what is broken and help build a survivable and thriving future.

How to build, achieve, and sustain a surviving and thriving future for you and your family and friends.[55]

To build a surviving and thriving future for you and your family and friends, they should be partners in this endeavor from the beginning and through each step. A collaborative approach where they jointly provide leadership, vision, motivation, strategy and successful execution probably has the greater potential to create <u>and</u> sustain large, positive change and a surviving and thriving future. Key to success is the strong desire to move current vulnerabilities through and beyond surviving to a sustained thriving future. *Thrive!* can be helpful to you and is laid out in the following steps.

---

[55] The following strategy is adapted from the *Thrive!* **Next Generation Toolkit** contained in the Appendix. It is customized to help you and your people build, achieve and sustain a surviving and thriving future. More is available in ***Thrive! - Building a Thriving Future*** - a manual providing greater depth on strategy and tools and is available via www.Amazon.com or free download from www.ThrivingFuture.org.

Step 1.

Step 1. Current state of you and your family and friends. The first major step is to understand the current state of you and your family and friends. This "how-to" works whether it is you alone, you and your immediate family, you and a more extended family, and/or you and your friends. In this chapter, the short-hand term "your people" is used and lets you decide on whom (you alone, you and your immediate family, you and a more extended family, and/or you and your friends) you want to focus your efforts. *[Note: For each step, an example is provided to give a sense of how to do that step. The example of a family provides highlights but not the full working of a step.]*

a. Who are your people? Let's first go through who are you and your people currently.[56] Who are your people? Use Table 4.1 (end of chapter) to describe each of your people.[57] For each person, have the person independently do a one-paragraph description in her/his own words. If the person can't, do one for the person as best you can. Who is the person with respect to working and living? Financial situation? Eating and drinking? Housing? Protection? Education? Physical and mental health? Personal growth and development? Habitat (living environment)? Producing what? Climate? With this information on individual persons and as best you can, do a summary of your people as a whole.

Example of a family. Jane is 38, female living in small rural community in upper Midwest and working includes drilling and sanding steel. John is 39, male working as independent electrician. They are married. Children Jim is 8 years old and Joan is 15 years old. Jane works in small factory. Jane makes $25,000/year; John makes $18,000/year; both have house mortgage of $150,000. Purchase weekly food from local grocery; mainly cook evenings and weekends. Housing is 70s ranch style home. Protection by county police and by taser and pepper spray in house. Both have high school education. Jane and John have physical health problems. Jane and John have physical exercise at work; all hike most

---

[56] Uses the Toolkit's "Systems Model (including Ideal Systems)".

[57] Free download of larger, fillable worksheets at www.ThrivingFuture.org

weekends. Habitat is relatively clean environment and is large river, hills, valleys. Both produce family life; Jane produces factory products; and John produces services. Climate is upper Midwest, United States.

b. How well are they? How well (surviving and thriving) are your people?[58] Use Table 4.2a (end of chapter) to describe how well is each person.[59] How well is each person in terms of performing well? Being well-off (financially)? Being well nourished (food and drink)? Being well housed? Being well protected (exposures, crime)? Being well educated? Being physically and mentally well? Personally growing/developing well? Living within good habitat? Not being vulnerable? Producing personal and public goods? Living within a stable, positive climate? Being sustained? With this information and as best you can, create a summary for your people as a whole. Use Table 4.2b (end of chapter) to describe how well are your people as a whole.[60]

Answering "yes" to all indicates current surviving and thriving. Though the "yes" answers are good, there is still future work to make sure this continues. "No" answers are bad and mean there is current <u>and</u> future work to be done.

> ***Example of a family.*** *Jane's small factory has uncertain future. John's work is intermittent and about ¾ time. Both are low-middle income with Social Security as only retirement. They have enough food but diet has too much salt and saturated fat. Home is in decent shape but not energy efficient. Jane has some job exposure to metal dust; John may or may not have job exposure. There is only low crime in work and home area. Both graduated high school in middle of class. The family's mental health is okay but not great. Physical health issues include Jane's cardiovascular risks and John's knee problems. Jane and John's personal growth and development have essentially stopped. Habitat is beautiful and good. Family is vulnerable to job loss, health problems, children's school problem, low retirement resources. Family is producing decent family life and good factory*

---

[58] Uses the Toolkit's "Status Model".
[59] Free download of larger, fillable worksheets at www.ThrivingFuture.org
[60] Free download of larger, fillable worksheets at www.ThrivingFuture.org

products and services. Climate has harsh, cold winters. Sustainability is uncertain to unlikely due to family stressors, poor retirement and savings, and growing health problems.

c. What positively or negatively impacts them? What positively or negatively impacts or is likely to impact you and your people's surviving and thriving? Use Table 4.2a (individuals) and 4.2b (summary of your people) to describe all of the following impacts (positive and negative; current and future). What impacts your people's performing well? Being well-off (financially)? Being well nourished (food and drink)? Being well housed? Being well protected (exposures, crime)? Being well educated? Being physically and mentally well? Personally growing/developing well? Living within good habitat? Not being vulnerable? Producing personal and public goods? Living within a stable, positive climate? Being sustained?

Good impacts improve and/or sustain surviving and thriving. If they will continue, you probably can focus on other things. If they may or may not continue, your action is needed to make them continue and/or to develop other things to compensate. Bad impacts prevent or limit surviving and thriving. If they will not continue, you probably can focus on other things. If they may or may not continue, your action is needed to stop them or to avoid or minimize their impact.

> ***Example of a family.*** *Jane's small factory may be moved far away and her job may end. John's work is not improving as there is not much local construction. Local grocery sells very little healthy food. Heating costs are rising and few incentives are available for making home energy improvements. OSHA and factory doing little to reduce job exposure to metal dust. Police force and protection may be reduced due to lower tax revenues. Re-training is expensive and not local. No real insurance coverage for mental health. Limited health insurance and limited local health care are available. No local support for personal growth and development. Community water supply is under stress. Local school has few resources for children with problems. Combination of these pressures increase risk to sustainability.*

Optional.

Want more on your people's future behavior? At this point, you should have enough good information to move to Step 2 and to develop strategy for you and your people. If you want to develop your strategy and actions further, you may want to use more of the tools and models already mentioned. See the *Thrive!* **Next Generation Toolkit** (Appendix) and optional Sections d-e below.[61] The following **Sections d-e** on your people's future behavior are optional but can be helpful. Section d focuses on each of your people. Section e focuses on your people as a whole.

d. What is near and long term future behavior of each of your people? How are individual persons likely to behave in the near and long term future.[62] Use Table 4.2a to describe all of the following behaviors. If no change, how will your people individually behave with respect to performing well? Being well-off (financially)? Being well nourished (food and drink)? Being well housed? Being well protected (exposures, crime)? Being well educated? Being physically and mentally well? Personally growing/developing well? Living within good habitat? Not being vulnerable? Producing personal and public goods? Living within a stable, positive climate? Being sustained?

---

[61] Using the full *Thrive!* **Next Generation Toolkit** (Appendix) may be useful because it includes more strategy, policy and tools for creating and sustaining large, positive change and building a surviving and thriving future. You might also want to use *Thrive! - **Building a Thriving Future*** - a manual providing greater depth on strategy and tools and available via www.Amazon.com or as free download from www.ThrivingFuture.org.

   If you want to dig deeper, you may want to use the Behavioral Effectiveness Model (BEM) to more deeply assess what your people will do (behavior) in the future.   What this does is assess how your people's motivation and ability will impact future behavior and how actions by people outside your people will impact your people's motivation, ability and behavior. A full description of BEM and how to use it is included in the Appendix.

[62] Uses the Toolkit's "Person Model".

> *Example of a family. Jane may look for another job within 35 miles. John is resisting changing professions. While income is okay now, both may lose job income and children may produce future college costs. They are unlikely to improve diet on own. They are unlikely to improve home's energy efficiency. Jane may look for job with less occupational exposure. Jane is looking into re-training options. Family is unlikely to work on health problems. Jane and John may seek help with marriage and children stresses. Jane and John are only looking into job-related personal growth and development options. Family will continue to enjoy habitat. Family may remain vulnerable to income loss or reduction. Jane and John will talk to school about helping children. Jane and John are unlikely to act to further improve sustainability.*

e. For your people as a whole, what is near/ long term future behavior with respect to thriving/surviving? With individual person information and as best you can, do the same for your people as a whole.[63] Use Table 4.2b to describe all of the following behaviors. If no change, how will your people as a whole behave with respect to performing well? Being well-off (financially)? Being well nourished (food and drink)? Being well housed? Being well protected (exposures, crime)? Being well educated? Being physically and mentally well? Personally growing/developing well? Living within good habitat? Not being vulnerable? Producing personal and public goods? Living within a stable, positive climate? Being sustained?

> *Example of a family. Family may try to improve job and income situation but uncertain; family may look for help with college financing. Family is unlikely to improve diet on own. Family is unlikely to improve home's energy efficiency. Family may try to reduce occupational exposure. Family is looking into re-training options for both. Family is unlikely to work on health problems. Family may seek help with marriage and children stresses. Family is only looking into job-related personal growth and development options. Family will continue to enjoy habitat. Family may remain vulnerable to income loss or reduction. Family will talk to school*

---

[63] Uses the Toolkit's "Population Model".

about helping children. Family is unlikely to act to further improve sustainability.

Step 2.

Step 2. Strategy to achieve you and your family and friends' surviving and thriving future. The next major step is to develop the strategy that will help your people build and achieve a surviving and thriving future.

a. Who will your people be in the future? Who will be your future people?[64] If there are any changes to your people that are desired or likely, take them into account. You may want to leave out persons that should not or will not be one of your people. You may want to include future persons that should or will become one of your people (for example, new children, spouse, friend).

For each new person and as you did in Step 1, briefly describe the person to the extent possible. Use Table 4.1 to describe your future people individually and as a whole. What will this person do working and living? Financial situation? Eating and drinking? Housing? Protection? Education? Physical and mental health? Personal growth and development? Quality of habitat (living environment)? Producing what? Climate? If there are likely to be changes on these characteristics with existing members of your people in the future, make these changes as best you can. Also in Table 4.1, do a summary of your people as a whole. This should provide a full picture of your future people (individually and as a whole) as it will be and as desired.

> ***Example of a family.*** *Jane and John may be able to stay married. Try to stay in their community and home. No new children. Children likely to leave after high school and one may go to public college. Jane's grandfather experiencing dementia and may need to live with them or assisted living. Boating and hiking. Jane wants to work at better job and make much more than $25,000/year with*

---

[64] Uses the Toolkit's "Systems Model (including Ideal Systems)".

cost-of-living increases. John hopes construction will increase. Weekly food from local grocery supplemented by healthier food from internet and regional health coop; cooks evenings and weekends. 70s ranch style home. Jane's work still includes drilling and sanding steel. John's work still puts pressure on knees. County police protection; taser and pepper spray in house. High school education. Physical exercise at work (Jane and John) and hiking on weekends (all). Habitat is river, hills, valleys. Producing family life and products/services. Climate is upper Midwest US.

b. How well should your people be in the near and long term future? How well should your people as a whole be in the future?[65] Overall, they should be <u>surviving and thriving</u>. With this as a guide, you and your people choose the surviving and thriving future your people want to build and achieve. The *"**Thrive!** strategy"* will help you accomplish that.

Use Table 4.3a/b (end of chapter) to describe how well your people should be.[66] Table 4.3a is the simpler version. Table 4.3b is the more detailed and powerful version.

From you and your people's view and to be surviving and thriving, indicate to what extent your people should be performing well. Be well-off (financially). Be well nourished (food and drink). Be well housed. Be well protected (exposures, crime). Be well educated. Be physically and mentally well. Be personally growing/developing well. Be living within good habitat. Not be vulnerable. Be producing personal and public goods. Be living within a stable, positive climate. Be sustained. Again, your people should be surviving and thriving.

> ***Example of a family.*** *Jane has better job with better income, more certainty, pension, health benefits and no occupational exposure. John likes being electrician and continues but with more construction work. Jane and John's employers provide better income security. Family has enough food but needs healthier diet, including reduced salt and saturated fat. Family improves home*

---

[65] Uses the Toolkit's "Status Model".
[66] Free download of larger, fillable worksheets at <u>www.ThrivingFuture.org</u>

energy efficiency. Low crime is in work and home area. Jane and John have improved job skills for new and future jobs. Family improves mental health; Jane and John's job improvement helps. Family has improved physical and mental health by eating better, lowering stress, changing jobs, getting health benefits, and seeking better health care for more complex health problems. Family has improved personal growth and development at least in job/career. Habitat is beautiful and good. Family minimizes vulnerability to job loss, health problems, low retirement resources. Children's school situation is good. Family produces thriving family life and high quality work products. Family is more energy efficient, especially for heating, to help with harsh, cold winters. Family takes positive advantage of climate. Family may move to more positive climate. Family ensures sustainability by working though marital issues, working through children's school issues, minimizing family stressors, improve retirement and savings, and improve health.

c. What has to change externally and internally to achieve your people's thriving future? What has to change externally (outside your people) and internally (within your people) to progress from your people's current status to achieve your desired surviving and thriving status?[67] In Step 1, you identified what positively and negatively impacts or is likely to impact your people. Update those, taking into account any changes to who are your people in the future.

Given those, what has to change externally and internally to achieve a surviving and thriving future? Use Table 4.3a/b to describe all that has to change for the following. To achieve performing well? Being well-off (financially)? Being well nourished (food and drink)? Being well housed? Being well protected (exposures, crime)? Being well educated? Being physically and mentally well? Personally growing/developing well? Living within good habitat? Not being vulnerable? Producing personal and public goods? Living within a stable, positive climate? Being sustained?

---

[67] Uses the Toolkit's "Performance Improvement Model" and "via Model".

Good changes improve and/or sustain surviving and thriving. Bad changes prevent and/or limit surviving and thriving.

> ***Example of a family.*** *Jane needs employer (current or a new one) to give her job with better income, more certainty, pension, health benefits and no occupational exposure. John needs home and business owners to do more construction and repair. Need no-cost nutritionist/dietician to help buying/preparing healthier diet, including reduced salt and saturated fat. Need financial incentives to improve home energy efficiency, especially for heating during cold, harsh winters. Need police to continue to keep crime low in work and home area. Need physically and financially accessible training program to improve job skills for new and future jobs. Need physically and financially accessible mental health and physical health services that can successfully treat fairly complex problems. Need accessible and affordable healthy food source. Need local heating fuel supplier to provide lower price heating fuel. Need community, state and Federal social safety programs to receive stronger support and provide more assurance to family within 6 months. Need school and counselors to work successfully with Jane, John, Jim and Joan on improving children's school situation.*

d. What actions by your people are needed to achieve their thriving future? What internal actions (by you and your people) and external actions (by others) are needed to bring about the needed external and internal changes (identified in "c") that improve your people's current status enough to achieve the desired surviving and thriving status?[68] [See Figure 4.1] [69]

External actions by others. There are very important <u>external</u> actions that are needed to support the ***Thrive!*** strategy. You already identified what has to change externally to achieve your people's surviving and thriving future. What external actions by others will bring about the needed changes?

---

[68] Uses the Toolkit's "Strategy Model".
[69] An action is defined as "who will do what to/with whom, where, when, and with what result."

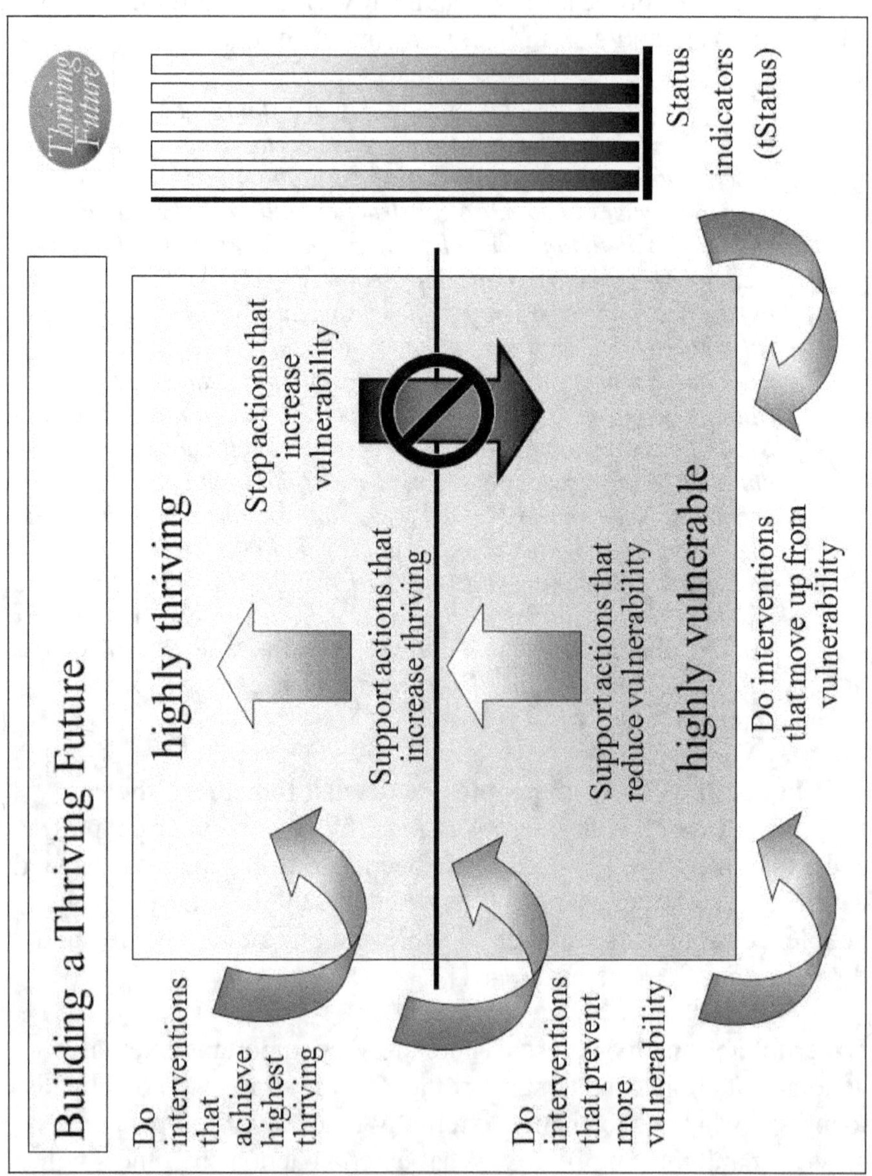

Figure 4.1. Building a Thriving Future.

Use Table 4.3a/b to describe all the external actions to be taken.

Identify external actions by others that support <u>good</u> changes that
will help improve and/or sustain surviving and thriving. If good

changes are likely to occur, together with others support them. If good changes are not likely to occur, together with others support them and develop other good changes to compensate.

Identify external actions by others that stop <u>bad</u> changes that prevent or limit surviving and thriving. If bad changes are not likely to occur, together with others ensure that they do not. If bad changes are likely to occur, together with others change them, stop them or avoid/reduce their impact.

> ***Example.*** *Jane's employer may leave area and take her job with it but other employers may be open to hiring her. Home owners and businesses may reduce or increase their business with John. The local grocery store may carry less or more healthy food at affordable prices. Federal, state, local or private utilities may provide lesser or greater financial incentives for energy efficiency; local heating fuel supplier may raise or lower prices. Local government could reduce or increase support for police; police may be less or more effective at protecting. Accessible re-training programs may become less or more available (distance, hours, cost). Nearby physical and mental health providers may reduce/increase services and/or may raise/lower costs. In addition to local grocery, internet grocery may reduce/increase availability of affordable healthy foods. School and its staff provide less/greater support to family. Social safety net becomes less/ more helpful and provides less/more assurance to families like theirs.*

Internal actions by your people. There are very important <u>internal</u> actions by you and your people that support the *Thrive!* strategy. Individual members and your people as a whole should support your strategy to ensure your people (individually and as a whole) are performing well. Being well-off (financially). Being well nourished (food and drink). Being well housed. Being well protected (exposures, crime). Being well educated. Being physically and mentally well. Personally growing/developing well. Living within good habitat. Not being vulnerable. Producing personal and public goods. Living within a stable, positive climate. Being sustained.

Use Table 4.3a/b to describe all the internal actions to be taken.

Identify internal actions by your people that support <u>good</u> changes that will help improve and/or sustain surviving and thriving. If good changes are likely to occur, support them. If good changes are not likely to occur, support them and develop other good changes to compensate. [Use Table 4.3a/b]

Identify internal actions by your people that stop <u>bad</u> changes that prevent or limit surviving and thriving. If bad changes are not likely to occur, ensure that they do not. If bad changes are likely to occur, change them, stop them or avoid/reduce their impact.

> ***Example.*** *Jane will more actively seek and change jobs. John will market himself more and travel more. Family will shop for and help prepare healthier diet. Both avoid eating out in less healthy restaurants. Family will work to improve home energy efficiency. Family will avoid situations where crime is more likely. Jane and John will go through re-training. Family will assist and support each other to improve mental health. Family will work together to improve physical and mental health. Family will improve personal growth and development. Family will enjoy the beautiful and good habitat. Family will work with school and counselors and with children to improve children's school situation. Family will join together to produce thriving family life. Jane and John will produce high quality work products/services. Family will increase heating efficiency to help with harsh, cold winters. Family will take better advantage of climate and may consider moving to more positive climate. Family will ensure sustainability to extent it can internally.*

e. Overall *Thrive!* strategy and actions. Your overall ***Thrive!*** strategy and actions need to be documented and agreed to by your people. Different members of your people will take on different responsibilities. For each action, designate who of your people will do what to/with whom, where, when, and with what result. [See example below.] Use Table 4.3a/b to document these actions and responsibilities. [See example table at end of Chapter.]

Thrive!

Example of a family surviving and somewhat thriving. *[Who will do what to/with whom, where, when, and with what result?] See Example **Thrive! Strategy and Action Plan** in list and table at end of Chapter. With these actions, family would be surviving and doing better but would not yet have achieved full thriving.*

- *Jane will more actively seek new job starting next Monday and, if feasible, change jobs to one with better income, more certainty, pension, health benefits and no occupational exposure within 3 months. John likes being electrician and continues but will market himself more and travel more within next two weeks. Community has begun seeking new employers with the intent of having 1000 new jobs within 12 months.*

- *Family will shop for and help prepare healthier diet, including reduced salt and saturated fat, starting next Saturday. Family will avoid eating out in less healthy restaurants from today forward. Local grocery agrees to add more healthy food, on trial basis, within 30 days.*

- *Family will work to improve home energy efficiency doing as much as they can themselves and starting immediately. State may provide new energy efficiency incentives within 12 months but needs substantial public pressure within next 2 months.*

- *Family will avoid situations where crime is more likely starting next weekend. Low crime in work and home area may be enough. Community commits to sufficient funding to sustain effective police protection from this time forward.*

- *Jane and John will go through re-training to improve job skills for new and future jobs within next 6 months. Nearby community college will add re-training programs starting this fall session.*

- *Family will assist and support each other to improve mental health starting immediately. Job change and improvement will help (see above). Family will work together to improve physical and mental health by eating better, lowering stress, changing or improving jobs, getting health benefits, and seeking better health care from better providers for more complex health problems starting immediately. Local health provider will add more mental health services within 12 months. More public health insurance programs are available that include physical and mental health services within 6 months.*

- *Family will improve personal growth and development, at least in job/career and re-training (see above).*

- *Family will enjoy the beautiful and good habitat starting next weekend. Family will do volunteer work on protecting environment.*
- *Jane and John will improve income security (see above). Family will work with school and counselors and with children to improve children's school situation starting with new school year.*
- *Family will join together to produce thriving family life (see above). Jane and John will produce high quality work products/services (see above). School agrees to provide more support to children to produce better learning starting with new school year.*
- *Family will be more energy efficient, especially for heating, which will help with harsh, cold winters starting this winter. Local heating fuel supplier provides lower price heating fuel to avoid more competition effective immediately. Family will take better advantage of climate starting immediately. If they don't, they will explore moving to more positive climate within 2 years.*
- *Family will ensure sustainability by getting better job situation, working though marital issues, working through children's school issues, minimizing family stressors, improve retirement and savings, and improve health within 12 months. Community, state and Federal social safety programs receive stronger support and can provide more assurance to family within 6 months.*

This is your *Thrive!* **Strategy and Action Plan**. As the strategy is executed, you strategy, actions and results should be updated.

Periodically, you and your people should assess your strategies/actions near and long term impact on near and long term surviving and thriving.

When a) your strategies and actions are not building and sustaining a thriving future and/or b) there are changes in the external world and in your people, you and your people should adjust your overall *Thrive!* **Strategy and Action Plan**.

Thrive!

The key is to successfully execute your strategy and actions and to build a near and long term surviving and thriving future.[70] Each and all must successfully carry out the assigned action. That is, each/all must successfully do what is required to/with whoever is required, where required, when required, and with what needed/desired result.

A ***Thrive!* Strategy and Action Plan** is only as good as its successful execution and successful achievement of the desired outcome - a surviving and thriving future.

But, we want a <u>thriving</u> future for you and your family and friends. To build, achieve and sustain a surviving <u>and</u> thriving future, the ***Thrive!* Strategy and Action Plan** should be more like the following example:

> ***Example of you and your family surviving <u>and</u> thriving.*** *[Who will do what to/with whom, where, when, and with what result?] Starting immediately, you and your family and friends build, achieve, and sustain a surviving and thriving future, including:*
> - Performing well. *Starting immediately, you and your family and friends act to ensure, within the next 10 years, a) all (who are able and not appropriately retired) can work and earn a living income sufficient to survive and thrive and b) all have sufficient resources for and are living, recreating, learning so that they are surviving and thriving to maximum extent feasible.*

---

[70] At this point, you should have enough good information to execute you and your people's ***Thrive!*** Strategy and Action Plan. If you want to develop your strategy and actions further, you may want to use more of the tools and models already mentioned and the ***Thrive!* Next Generation Toolkit** (Appendix).

The full ***Thrive!* Next Generation Toolkit** includes strategy, policy and tools for creating and sustaining large, positive change and building a thriving future. You might also want to use ***Thrive! - Building a Thriving Future*** - a manual providing greater depth on strategy and tools and available via www.Amazon.com or as a free download from www.ThrivingFuture.org.

If you want to dig deeper, you may want to use the Behavioral Effectiveness Model (BEM) to more deeply assess what your people will do (behavior) in the future.   What this does is assess how your people's motivation and ability will impact future behavior and how actions by people outside your people will impact your people's motivation, ability and behavior. A full description of BEM and how to use it is included in the Appendix.

- Being well-off (financially). *Starting immediately, you and your family and friends act to ensure, within the next 10 years, a) all have sufficient income/resources to survive and thrive.*
- Being well nourished (food and drink). *Starting immediately, you and your family and friends act to ensure, within the next 5 years, that all have access to, be able to afford and consume healthy foods enough to survive and thrive.*
- Being well housed. *Starting immediately, you and your family and friends act to ensure, within the next 10 years, all have access to, be able to afford and live in adequate and preferably high performing housing that supports surviving and thriving.*
- Being well protected (exposures, crime). *Starting immediately, you and your family and friends act to ensure, within the next 5 years, environmental exposures in home, workplace and elsewhere are minimized so as to not prevent surviving and thriving.*
- Being well educated. *Starting immediately, you and your family and friends act to ensure, within the next 10 years, all are educated to the full extent of their abilities, needs and desires and to support their surviving and thriving.*
- Being physically and mentally well. *Starting immediately, you and your family and friends act to ensure, within the next 5 years, a) all receive the optimal health support to ensure, within the next 20 years, surviving and thriving and b) physical and mental health is optimized to best ensure surviving and thriving.*
- Personally growing/developing well. *Starting immediately, you and your family and friends act to ensure, within the next 10 years, all people are personally growing and developing to best ensure surviving and thriving.*
- Living within good habitat. *Starting immediately, you and your family and friends act to ensure, within the next 20 years, a) all have access to habitat that best supports their surviving and thriving.*
- Not being vulnerable. *Starting immediately, you and your family and friends act to ensure, within the next 20 years, all, if vulnerable, are vulnerable only to the minimum extent feasible.*
- Producing personal and public goods. *Starting immediately, you and your family and friends act to ensure, within the next 10 years, all produce personal and public goods (including personal income/resources, housing, food and drink, energy, education, health, protection, personal growth and development, and habitat) so as to support surviving and thriving for all.*

Thrive!

- Living within a stable, positive climate. *Starting immediately, you and your family and friends act to ensure, within the next 2years, all behave so as to avoid negative impacts and support positive impacts so as to help ensure a stable, positive climate.*
- Being sustained. *Starting immediately, you and your family and friends act to ensure, within the next 5 years, all behave so as to ensure the sustainability of you and your family and friends.*

Thrive!

***Thrive!* Strategy and Action Plan** (Example of surviving and somewhat thriving).

Thriving and Surviving	How well (surviving/ thriving) should your people as a whole be in near/long term future?	External/internal changes needed to achieve surviving and thriving future	Actions by your people and others Who will do what to/with whom, where, when, and with what result?
Performing (live/work/ play) well?	*Jane has better job with better income, more certainty, pension, health benefits and no occupational exposure. John likes being electrician and continues but with more construction work.*	**External**: *Jane needs employer (current or a new one) to give her job with better income, more certainty, pension, health benefits and no occupational exposure. John needs home and business owners to do more construction and repair.*	**External by others**: *Community has begun seeking new employers with the intent of having 1000 new jobs within 12 months.* **Internal by your people**: *Jane will talk to current employer about higher pay and change in job to avoid exposure. John will approach home and business owners to get more jobs.*
		Internal:	**Internal by your people**: *Jane will more actively seek new job starting next Monday and, if feasible, change jobs to one with better income, more certainty, pension, health benefits and no occupational exposure within 3 months. John likes being electrician and continues but will market himself more and travel more within next two weeks.*
Well-off?	*Jane and John's employers provide better income security.*	**External**: *Need employers to provide better income security.*	**External by others**: *See above* **Internal by your people**: *See above*
		Internal:	**Internal by your people**: *See above*
Well nourished?	*Family has enough food but needs healthier diet, including reduced salt and saturated fat.*	**External**: *Need no-cost nutritionist/ dietician to help buying/preparing healthier diet, including reduced*	**External by others**: *Local grocery agrees to add more healthy food, on trial basis, within 30 days.*

		salt and saturated fat. situation. Need accessible and affordable healthy food source.	**Internal by your people:**
		Internal:	**Internal by your people:** *Family will shop for and help prepare healthier diet, including reduced salt and saturated fat, starting next Saturday. Family will avoid eating out in less healthy restaurants from today forward.*
Well housed	*Family improves home energy efficiency.*	**External:** *Need financial incentives to improve home energy efficiency, especially for heating during cold, harsh winters.*	**External by others:** *State may provide new energy efficiency incentives within 12 months but needs substantial public pressure within next 2 months.*
			Internal by your people:
		Internal:	**Internal by your people:** *Family will work to improve home energy efficiency doing as much as they can themselves and starting immediately.*
Well protected?	*Low crime is in work and home area.*	**External:** *Need police to continue to keep crime low in work and home area.*	**External by others:** *Low crime in work and home area may be enough. Community commits to sufficient funding to sustain effective police protection from this time forward.*
			Internal by your people:
		Internal!	**Internal by your people:** *Family will avoid situations where crime is more likely starting next weekend.*

Well educated?	*Jane and John have improved job skills for new and future jobs.*	**External**: *Need physically and financially accessible training program to improve job skills for new and future jobs.*	**External by others**: *Nearby community college will add re-training programs starting this fall session.* **Internal by your people**:
		Internal:	**Internal by your people**: *Jane and John will go through re-training to improve job skills for new and future jobs within next 6 months.*
Physically/ mentally well?	*Family improves mental health; Jane and John's job improvement helps. Family has improved physical and mental health by eating better, lowering stress, changing jobs, getting health benefits, and seeking better health care for more complex health problems.*	**External**: *Need physically and financially accessible mental health and physical health services that can successfully treat fairly complex problems.*	**External by others**: *Local health provider will add more mental health services within 12 months. More public health insurance programs are available that include physical and mental health services within 6 months.* **Internal by your people**:
		Internal:	**Internal by your people**: *Family will assist and support each other to improve mental health starting immediately. Job change and improvement will help (see above). Family will work together to improve physical and mental health by eating better, lowering stress, changing or improving jobs, getting health benefits, and seeking better health care from better providers for more complex health problems starting immediately.*
Growing/ developing	*Family has improved personal growth and*	**External**: *Need physically and*	**External by others**:

well?	*development at least in job/career.*	*financially accessible re-training programs.*	**Internal by your people:**
		Internal:	**Internal by your people:** *Family will improve personal growth and development, at least in job/career and re-training (see above)*
Living in good habitat?	*Habitat is beautiful and good.*	**External:** *No change needed, except to sustain habitat.*	**External by others:**
			Internal by your people: *Family will do volunteer work on protecting environment.*
		Internal:	**Internal by your people:** *Family will enjoy the beautiful and good habitat starting next weekend.*
Not vulnerable?	*Family minimizes vulnerability to job loss, health problems, low retirement resources. Children's school situation is good.*	**External:** *Need school and counselors to work successfully with Jane, John, Jim and Joan on improving children's school*	**External by others:**
			Internal by your people:
		Internal:	**Internal by your people:** *Jane and John will improve income security (see above). Family will work with school and counselors and with children to improve children's school situation starting with new school year.*
Producing personal/ public goods?	*Family produces thriving family life and high quality work products.*	**External:** *See above*	**External by others:** *School agrees to provide more support to children to produce better learning starting with new school year.*
			Internal by your people:

		Internal:	**Internal by your people**: *Family will join together to produce thriving family life (see above). Jane and John will produce high quality work products/services (see above).*
Stable, positive climate?	*Family is more energy efficient, especially for heating, to help with harsh, cold winters. Family takes positive advantage of climate. Family may move to more positive climate.*	**External**: *Need local heating fuel supplier to provide lower price heating fuel.*	**External by others**: *Local heating fuel supplier provides lower price heating fuel to avoid more competition effective immediately.*
			Internal by your people:
		Internal:	**Internal by your people**: *Family will be more energy efficient, especially for heating, which will help with harsh, cold winters starting this winter. Family will take better advantage of climate starting immediately. If they don't, they will explore moving to more positive climate within 2 years.*
Sustainable?	*Family ensures sustainability by working though marital issues, working through children's school issues, minimizing family stressors, improve retirement and savings, and improve health.*	**External**: *Need community, state and Federal social safety programs to receive stronger support and provide more assurance to family within 6 months. Need school and counselors to work successfully with Jane, John, Jim and Joan on improving children's school situation.*	**External by others**: *Community, state and Federal social safety programs receive stronger support and can provide more assurance to family within 6 months.*
			Internal by your people:

		Internal:	**Internal by your people**: *Family will ensure sustainability by getting better job situation, working though marital issues, working through children's school issues, minimizing family stressors, improve retirement and savings, and improve health within 12 months.*

Table 4.3b. How well should your future people as a whole be in near/long term future? What external/internal changes are needed to achieve your people's thriving future? To make this happen, what external/internal actions are needed?

Current and Future Persons (name)	For each person, have the person independently do a one-paragraph description in her/his own words. If the person can't, do one for the person. Cover things like work/living/playing, financial situation, eating/drinking, housing, protection, education, physical/mental health, growth/development, habitat, producing what, and climate. Enter the descriptions into this worksheet/table. Do a summary of your people as a whole.
Your current and future people as a whole. [Summary]	

Table 4.1. Who are your current and future people?

Thrive!

Current/Future Person: _______________________ (Do for each person)

Thriving and Surviving	How well (surviving/ thriving) is the person?	What positively/ negatively impacts her/his thriving/ surviving?	[Optional] If no change, what is her/his near/ long term future behavior as to thriving/ surviving?
Performing (live/work/play) well?			
Well-off?			
Well nourished?			
Well housed?			
Well protected?			
Well educated?			
Physically/ mentally well?			
Growing/ developing well?			
Living in good habitat?			
Not vulnerable?			
Producing personal/ public goods?			
Stable, positive climate?			
Sustainable?			

Table 4.2a. How well (surviving/thriving) is the person? What positively/negatively impacts the person? What is her/his near/long term future behavior?

Thriving and Surviving	How well (surviving/ thriving) are your people as a whole?	What positively/ negatively impacts their thriving/ surviving?	[Optional] What is their near/ long term future behavior as to thriving/ surviving?
Performing (live/work/play) well?			
Well-off?			
Well nourished?			
Well housed?			
Well protected?			
Well educated?			
Physically/ mentally well?			
Growing/ developing well?			
Living in good habitat?			
Not vulnerable?			
Producing personal/ public goods?			
Stable, positive climate?			
Sustainable?			

Table 4.2b. How well (surviving/thriving) are your people as a whole? What positively/negatively impacts them? If no change, what is their near/long term future behavior?

Thriving and Surviving	How well (surviving/thriving) should your people as a whole be in near/long term future?	External/internal changes needed to achieve thriving/surviving future	External actions by others - Who externally will do what to/with whom, where, when, and with what result? How to make that happen?	Internal actions by your people - Who of your people will do what to/with whom, where, when, and with what result
Performing (live/work/play) well?				
Well-off?				
Well nourished?				
Well housed?				
Well protected?				
Well educated?				
Physically/mentally well?				
Growing/developing well?				
Living in good habitat?				
Not vulnerable?				
Producing personal/public goods?				
Stable, positive climate?				
Sustainable?				

Table 4.3a. *Thrive!* **Strategy and Action Plan.** How well (surviving/thriving) should your people as a whole be in near/long term future? What external/internal changes are needed to achieve your people's thriving future? To make this happen, what external/internal actions are needed?

Thriving and Surviving	How well (surviving/ thriving) should your people as a whole be in near/long term future?	External/internal changes needed to achieve surviving and thriving future	Actions by your people and others Who will do what to/with whom, where, when, and with what result?
Performing (live/work/ play) well?		External:	External by others:
			Internal by your people:
		Internal:	Internal by your people:
Well-off?		External:	External by others:
			Internal by your people:
		Internal:	Internal by your people:
Well nourished?		External:	External by others:
			Internal by your people:
		Internal:	Internal by your people:
Well housed		External:	External by others:
			Internal by your people:
		Internal:	Internal by your people:
Well protected?		External:	External by others:
			Internal by your people:
		Internal:	Internal by your people:
Well educated?		External:	External by others:
			Internal by your people:
		Internal:	Internal by your people:

Physically/ mentally well?		External:	External by others:
			Internal by your people:
		Internal:	Internal by your people:
Growing/ developing well?		External:	External by others:
			Internal by your people:
		Internal:	Internal by your people:
Living in good habitat?		External:	External by others:
			Internal by your people:
		Internal:	Internal by your people:
Not vulnerable?		External:	External by others:
			Internal by your people:
		Internal:	Internal by your people:
Producing personal/ public goods?		External:	External by others:
			Internal by your people:
		Internal:	Internal by your people:
Stable, positive climate?		External:	External by others:
			Internal by your people:
		Internal:	Internal by your people:
Sustainable?		External:	External by others:
			Internal by your people:
		Internal:	Internal by your people:

Table 4.3b. ***Thrive!* Strategy and Action Plan.** How well should your future people as a whole be in near/long term future? What external/internal changes are needed to achieve your people's thriving future? To make this happen, what external/internal actions are needed?

Chapter 5: How <u>you and your community</u> can thrive.

How to build, achieve and sustain a surviving and thriving future for you and your community.

Why you and your community <u>can</u>.

You and your community <u>can</u> have a surviving and thriving future. To get to that future, keep in mind that each community is different with a different future already beginning. [71] Whether that future appears bad or good, each community can do better. To build a better future, the *Thrive!* strategy and tools has been used successfully at the personal level and on larger scales (community, country). They can work for you and the community you care about. As they have for others, this strategy and these tools can help you and your community build, achieve and sustain a surviving and thriving future.

Thrive!
Keep in mind that we are more capable than any time in human history. We can build a thriving future by effectively and collaboratively using all available knowledge and tools, including "next generation" *Thrive!* strategy and tools. Next generation *Thrive!* is different and better than anything in human history. It is <u>achieving</u> a thriving future at each level. It understands that <u>people's behavior</u>, including yours, makes (or breaks) a thriving future. It helps people, including you, achieve the behavior that in turn achieves a thriving future at each level and for all forever.

---

[71] A community can be defined by geography (for example, a neighborhood, a region), by political boundaries (for example, a village, town, city, county, state), or by common population characteristics (e.g. racial/ethnic, gender, economics, political view, similar mission, religion, labor, profession, business).

Why you and your community <u>must</u>.

You and your community <u>must</u> have a surviving and thriving future. Each community <u>must</u> do better whether that future appears bad or good. Why? Even those communities that have a good future are not fully thriving, are not likely to be fully thriving in the future, and are still facing uncertainties about the long term future. You and your community want and need a surviving and thriving future because your community's future is endangered and because of our human need to survive and desire to thrive. What drives a community and its people is our human need to survive and desire to thrive now and in a sustainable future. Further, because your community's people (past and present) have broken some part of your community and endangered its future, you and your community's people (present and future) must help fix what is broken and build a survivable and thriving future for your community.

Why we all must and can do it together.

To build this better future, your community's people and leaders should be partners in this endeavor from the beginning and through each step. Success is dependent on positive and effective leadership from your community's leaders and people. How that leadership comes about is the subject of some debate. Some people argue for a leader driven approach where the leader creates the vision and motivation and the people join and/or follow. Some argue for bottom-up or self-organizing approaches where the people lead and the traditional leaders may or may not join and/or follow. Some argue for a collaborative approach where the traditional leaders and the people (also serving as leaders) jointly provide leadership, vision, motivation, strategy and successful execution. In general, the latter approach probably has the greater potential to create <u>and</u> sustain large, positive change and a surviving and thriving community.

Some communities will be geographic communities (including villages, towns, cities, counties and states). When feasible and when your community's governments are a positive force, governments should be part of the leadership and be partners in building a surviving and thriving community. However, it is not sufficient for governments to be the only leaders in this endeavor. Non-governmental organizations need to be leaders. Private businesses need to be leaders. Individual people need to be leaders. To be successful, this needs to be a whole community (people and leaders) endeavor.

Key to success is the strong desire by you and your community to move your community from its current vulnerabilities through and beyond surviving to a sustained thriving future.

How to build, achieve, and sustain a surviving and thriving future for you and your community.

To build a surviving and thriving future for you and your community, *Thrive!* can be helpful to you and is laid out in the following "how-to".[72,73] The following "how-to" is a relatively basic "how-to". The underlying principles and the strategy, models and tools apply to communities from small size and low complexity to very large size and very high complexity.

It is adapted from the *Thrive!* **Next Generation Toolkit** contained in the Appendix. It is customized to help you and your people build, achieve and sustain a surviving and thriving future. More is available in ***Thrive!* - Building a Thriving Future** - a manual

---

[72] Note that for each step, an example is provided to give a sense of how to do that step. The example provides highlights but not the full working of a step.
[73] Note that Using *Thrive!* for a community is very similar to using it for a country. If your primary interest is in a whole country, you may want to skip to the next chapter. A country is handled separately because of likely increased size and likely increased complexity and diversity of its people, its politics, its geography, its resources and its habitat.

providing greater depth on strategy and tools and available via www.Amazon.com or free download from www.ThrivingFuture.org.

Step 1.

Step 1. Current state of you and your community. The first major step is to understand the current state of your community.

a. What is your community? Let's first go through what is your community today.[74] A community can be defined by geography (for example, a neighborhood, a region), by political boundaries (for example, a village, town, city, county, state), or by common population characteristics (e.g. racial/ethnic, gender, economics, political view, similar mission, religion, labor, profession, business). It can be a combination of these.

For your community, what are its geographic boundaries and characteristics? Use Table 5.1 (end of chapter) to describe all of the following for your community.[75] Its gender, age, racial, ethnic make-up. Lifestyle. Type of work. Financial situation. Food and drink. Housing. Protection (crime, environmental hazards). Education. Physical and mental health. Personal growth and development. Habitat (living environment, neighboring communities, part of what state, country, continent). Producing what. Climate. Sustainability.

> ***Example.*** *Community is an incorporated city of 400,000 people occupying 40 square miles in the middle of the country. Gender mix is 51/49 female/male; age mix approximates that of the country as a whole but with slightly higher percentage under age 25; racial mix approximates that of the country as a whole but with a slightly higher percentage of all minorities. Lifestyle mix is similar to most cities of its size. Mix of work is similar to that of country as a whole but with a slightly larger percentage of blue collar workers and light industry. Financial basis is similar to*

---

[74] Uses the Toolkit's "Systems Model (including Ideal Systems)".
[75] Free download of larger, fillable worksheets at www.ThrivingFuture.org

most cities of its size but with slightly higher resources coming from light industry. Food and drink is similar to most cities of its size. A wide range of housing is available for those with the means to purchase or rent; community has adequate housing supply. Protection comes primarily from city police force with some neighborhood watch groups. Education is similar to most cities of its size but with slightly lower college education level. Physical and mental health is similar to most cities but with slightly less occupationally related illness. Personal growth and development is similar to most cities but with slightly more job re-training. Habitat consists of a small river and lake, mildly varying terrain, and moderate deciduous tree cover; located in medium-sized state in country. City produces usual range of products and services for city of its size, slightly higher percentage of manufactured products, relatively healthy and well educated children and range of recreational activities. Climate is moderate with slightly higher percentage of rainfall, slightly lower percentage of sunlight, slightly lower temperatures than other cities in country. Sustainability is in question due to changing national and international economics.

b. How well is your community? How well (surviving and thriving) is your community?[76] Use Table 5.2 (end of chapter) to describe how well is your community.[77] How well is your community in terms of performing well? Being well-off (financially)? Being well nourished (food and drink)? Being well housed? Being well protected (exposures, crime)? Being well educated? Being physically and mentally well? Personally growing/developing well? Living within good habitat? Not being vulnerable? Producing personal and public goods? Living within a stable, positive climate? Being sustained?

Answering "yes" to all indicates current surviving and thriving. Though the "yes" answers are good, there is still future work to make sure this continues. "No" answers are bad and mean there is current <u>and</u> future work to be done.

---

[76] Uses the Toolkit's "Status Model".

[77] Free download of larger, fillable worksheets at www.ThrivingFuture.org

Example. Community is performing okay with close to country's average mix lifestyles for city of its size. Unemployment is a 1 percentage point lower than country; mix of work is similar to that of country as a whole but with a slightly larger percentage of blue collar workers and light industry. Financial condition of community is generally stable and sufficient to support public services; community has slightly higher percentage of blue collar workers who are facing potential outsourcing of jobs and declining union effectiveness. Food and drink is available but prices are 5% above average for country; community lacks sufficient sources of healthy food; low income people lack resources for healthy food and for food generally; community lacks sufficient resources to feed very poor. Housing for upper and middle income people is available and affordable; housing for low and lower middle income people is unavailable, unaffordable and inadequate. Community police force is above average for country; some neighborhood watch groups exist and help but not without some problems. Education availability and quality is similar to most cities of its size; community has slightly lower percentage of college educated. Physical and mental health is about average compared to most cities of its size; community has slightly less occupationally related illness; private health services are average but public health services are only 75% of other cities of its size. Personal growth and development is about the same as most cities but it has slightly more job re-training. Habitat is pleasant and fairly healthy. While community has much vulnerability, it is most vulnerable on job and income loss, affordable and healthy foods, affordable housing, public health services, and community revenues. Community produces usual range of products and services for city of its size, slightly higher percentage of higher quality manufactured products, above average percentage of healthy and well educated children and an above average range of recreational activities. Climate is good. Sustainability is in question due to changing national and international economics and potential job outsourcing.

c. What positively or negatively impacts your community? What positively or negatively impacts or is likely to impact you and your community's surviving and thriving? Use Table 5.2 to describe all of the following impacts (positive and negative; current and future). What impacts your community's performing well? Being well-off (financially)? Being well nourished (food and drink)? Being well housed? Being well protected (exposures, crime)? Being well educated? Being physically and mentally well? Personally growing/developing well? Living within good habitat? Not being vulnerable? Producing personal and public goods? Living within a stable, positive climate? Being sustained?

Positive impacts improve and/or sustain surviving and thriving. If they will continue, you probably can focus on other things. If they may or may not continue, your action is needed to make them continue and/or to develop other things to compensate. Bad impacts prevent or limit surviving and thriving. If they will not continue, you probably can focus on other things. If they may or may not continue, your action is needed to stop them or to avoid or minimize their impact.

> ***Example.*** *Community is impacted by external lifestyle exposures. Employment is impacted by changing national and international economics and push for job outsourcing to places with lower cost labor; union effectiveness is impacted by country-wide changes in unions; businesses are impacted by overall economic climate. Financial condition of community is dependent on continuing support from state and national revenues. Food and drink is available but prices are 5% above average for country due to lack of competition; country as a whole lacks sufficient sources of healthy food; higher prices mean low income people lack resources for healthy food and for food generally; community lacks sufficient resources to feed very poor due to cutbacks in state and country food support. Housing for upper and middle income people is available and affordable and is positive; housing for low and lower middle income people is unavailable, unaffordable and inadequate and is negative. Community police force is losing good officers to communities with more resources. Education availability and quality is under pressure due to cutbacks in state and country aid; community's college educated are being drawn away by other communities and their higher pay. Physical and mental health services are impacted by high quality staff being recruited by other communities with higher pay; physical health is impacted by occupational health exposure; mental health is impacted by potential job losses due to outsourcing; public health*

services impacted by lower state and country funding. Personal growth and development is impacted by same forces as most cities of its size; pressure on jobs means more need for job re-training. Community has much vulnerability and is most vulnerable on job and income loss, affordable and healthy foods, affordable housing, public health services, and community revenues. Habitat is pleasant and fairly healthy and is only impacted by broader national environmental exposures. Community producing of products impacted by high competition from other communities and countries; producing healthy and well educated children is impacted by state and country program and funding; recreational activities are impacted by availability of community and personal resources which are impacted by jobs and external funding. Climate is good but is impacted by country and global changes. Sustainability is in question due to changing state and country funding, national and international economics, and potential job outsourcing.

d. What is near and long term future behavior of your community? How is your community likely to behave in the near and long term future.[78] For example, will it behave (individual behavior; group behavior, overall community behavior) so as to protect/improve public services, help each other survive/thrive, protect/increase jobs, maintain/improve community environment, and/or sustain the community near and long term.

Use Table 5.2 to describe all of the following behaviors. How will your community behave with respect to performing well? Being well-off (financially). Being well nourished (food and drink)? Being well housed? Being well protected (exposures, crime)? Being well educated? Being physically and mentally well? Personally growing/developing well? Living within good habitat? Not being vulnerable? Producing personal and public goods? Living within a stable, positive climate? Being sustained?

> **Example.** *Community will perform okay with close to country's average mix lifestyles for city of its size. Working will be similar to that of country as a whole but with a slightly larger percentage*

---

[78] Uses the Toolkit's "Population Model".

of blue collar workers and light industry. Community will continue to protect financial condition of community and supports public services; community will try to reduce outsourcing of jobs; union will try to increase effectiveness. Community will try to find sufficient sources of healthy food; low income people will continue to try to make do with a lack of resources for healthy food and for food generally; community will try to find sufficient resources to feed very poor. Upper and middle income people will live in housing that is available and affordable; low and lower middle income people will struggle to find and keep affordable and adequate housing. Community police force will continue protection above average for country; some neighborhood watch groups will continue but with some problems. Community will continue education availability and quality similar to or better than most cities of its size; community will try to hold on to and increase the percentage of college educated. Community will try to improve physical and mental health which is about average compared to most cities of its size; community will try to keep lowering occupationally related illness; community will try to improve private health services and public health services (beyond 75% compared to other cities of its size). Community will explore how to increase personal growth and development but especially job re-training. Community will try to address at least its major vulnerabilities. Habitat will likely be pleasant and fairly healthy. Community will try to protect its production of products and services, increase its percentage of higher quality manufactured products, increase its above average percentage of healthy and well educated children and increase its above average range of recreational activities. Community will explore what it can do collaboratively with other communities and countries to ensure climate is good. Community will explore how to ensure sustainability given changing national and international economics and potential job outsourcing.

e. Want more on your community's future and behavior? At this point, you have a baseline with which to measure progress for your community. You have enough information to move to Step 2 and to develop strategy for you and your community. If you want more information before moving to strategy, you may want to use more of the tools and models already mentioned and the *Thrive!* **Next Generation Toolkit** (Appendix).[79]

Step 2.

Step 2. Strategy to achieve you and your community's surviving and thriving future. The next major step is to develop the strategy that will help you and your community build and achieve a surviving and thriving future.

a. What will your community be in the future? What will be your desired and/or likely future community?[80] Use Table 5.3 (end of chapter) to describe the likely future.[81] If there are any changes to your community that are desired or likely, take them into account. You may want to leave out parts of the community that should not or will not be part of your community. You may want to include future additions that should or will be part of the community (for example, the next neighborhood, the next village/town/city, the surrounding area, another interest group, another population).

With this updated information, what will be your community's geographic boundaries and characteristics? Type of work/how people live. Financial situation. Food and drink. Housing. Protection (crime, environmental hazards). Education. Physical and mental health. Personal growth and development. Habitat (living

---

[79] Using the full *Thrive!* **Next Generation Toolkit** (Appendix) is recommended because it includes more strategy, policy and tools for creating and sustaining large, positive change and building a surviving and thriving future.[79] You might also want to use *Thrive!* **- Building a Thriving Future** - a manual providing greater depth on strategy and tools and available via www.Amazon.com or as free download from www.ThrivingFuture.org.

For example, if you want to develop and assess more in-depth strategies and actions, you may want to use the Behavioral Effectiveness Model (BEM). BEM helps assess a) how your community's and individual community member's motivation and ability will impact future behavior and b) how actions by people outside your community will impact your community's and individual community member's future motivation, ability and behavior. A description of BEM and how to use it is included in the Appendix.

[80] Uses the Toolkit's "Systems Model (including Ideal Systems)".

[81] Free download of larger, fillable worksheets at www.ThrivingFuture.org

environment, neighboring communities, part of what state, country, continent). Producing what. Climate. Sustainability. Update Table 5.3 with this information.

> ***Example.*** *Community will be an incorporated city with population increasing 2%/year from current 400,000 people still occupying 40 square miles in the middle of the country. Gender mix will still be about 51/49 female/male; age mix will continue to approximate that of the country as a whole but with slightly higher percentage under age 30; racial mix will have a 10% higher percentage of minorities than the country as a whole. Lifestyle mix will be similar to most cities of its size but with additional influence of under 30 population. Mix of work may be similar to that of country as a whole and with a similar percentage of blue collar workers and light industry due to recent losses due to outsourcing. Financial basis will be a bit lower than most cities of its size but with slightly lower coming from light industry. Food and drink will be similar to most cities of its size. A wide range of housing will be available for those with the means to purchase or rent; community will have an adequate housing supply. Protection will continue to come primarily from city police force with some decline in neighborhood watch groups. Education will be similar to most cities of its size but with a lower level of college educated. Physical and mental health will be similar to most cities but with less occupationally related illness and more job related stress. Personal growth and development will be similar to most cities but with substantially more job re-training. Habitat will continue to consist of a small river and lake, mildly varying terrain, and moderate deciduous tree cover; community will continue to be located in medium-sized state in country. City will produce usual range of products and services for city of its size, average percentage of manufactured products, relatively healthy and well educated children and slightly reduced range of recreational activities. Climate will likely continue to be moderate with slightly higher percentage of rainfall, slightly lower percentage of sunlight, slightly lower temperatures than other cities in country; community will be increasingly concerned about negative climate change. Sustainability will remain in question due to predicted changes in national and international economics.*

b. How well should your community be in the near and long term future? How well should your community as a whole be in the future?[82] Overall, it should be <u>surviving and thriving</u>. With this as a guide, you and your community choose the surviving and thriving future your community wants to build and achieve. The "*Thrive!* strategy" will help you accomplish that.

Use Table 5.4 (end of chapter) to describe how well your community should be.[83] From you and your community's view and to be surviving and thriving, indicate to what extent your community should be performing well. Be well-off (financially). Be well nourished (food and drink). Be well housed. Be well protected (exposures, crime). Be well educated. Be physically and mentally well. Be personally growing/developing well. Be living within good habitat. Not be vulnerable. Be producing personal and public goods. Be living within a stable, positive climate. Be sustained. Again, your community should be surviving and thriving.

> ***Example.*** *Community should perform well with close to country's average mix lifestyles for city of its size. Unemployment should be 2 percentage points lower than country; mix of work should be similar to that of country as a whole and continue with a slightly larger percentage of blue collar workers and light industry. Financial condition of community should be generally stable and sufficient to support public services; community should have slightly higher percentage of blue collar workers but who are no longer facing potential outsourcing of jobs and declining union effectiveness. Food and drink should be available and affordable with prices 5% below average for country; community should have sufficient sources of healthy food; low income people should have adequate resources for healthy food and for food generally; community should have sufficient resources to feed very poor. Housing for upper and middle income people should be available and affordable; housing for low and lower middle income people should be affordable, available and adequate. Community police force should be in top 10% for country; some neighborhood watch groups should exist but without any significant problems.*

---

[82] Uses the Toolkit's "Status Model".
[83] Free download of larger, fillable worksheets at <u>www.ThrivingFuture.org</u>

Education availability and quality should be in the top 10% of cities of its size; community should have slightly higher percentage of college educated. Physical and mental health should be in top 10% of cities of its size; community should have substantially less occupationally related illness; private health services should be in top 25% and public health services should be in top 25% of cities of its size. Personal growth and development should be substantially better than cities of its size and community should have job re-training in top 10% of its size. Habitat should be very pleasant and very healthy. Community should have much less vulnerability; community should greatly reduce its vulnerability on job and income loss, affordable and healthy foods, affordable housing, public health services, and community revenues. Community should produce a wider range of products and services for city of its size, a substantially higher percentage of higher quality manufactured products, a high percentage of healthy and well educated children and a range of recreational activities in the top 10% of cities of its size. Climate should continue to be good to very good. Sustainability should be ensured and no longer be in question in spite of changing national and international economics and potential job outsourcing.

c. What has to change externally and internally to achieve your community's thriving future? What has to change externally (outside your community) and internally (within your community) to progress from your community's current status to achieve your desired surviving and thriving status?[84] In Step 1, you identified what positively and negatively impacts or is likely to impact your community. Update those, including any changes to your future community from Step 2a.

Given those, what has to change to achieve a surviving and thriving future? Use Table 5.4 to describe all that has to change externally and internally for the following. To achieve performing well? Being well-off (financially)? Being well nourished (food and drink)? Being well housed? Being well protected (exposures, crime)? Being well educated? Being physically and mentally well? Personally growing/developing well? Living within good habitat?

---

[84] Uses the Toolkit's "Performance Improvement Model" and "via Model".

Thrive!

Not being vulnerable? Producing personal and public goods? Living within a stable, positive climate? Being sustained?

Good changes improve and/or sustain surviving and thriving. Bad changes prevent and/or limit surviving and thriving.

> ***Example.*** *Internally, community should perform better than it has. Internally, community needs to gain more employers to get to 2 percentage points lower than country; community needs to gain more blue collar workers and light industry; internally, community employers should expand and add jobs. Externally, outside employers should locate new jobs in community. Internally, financial condition of community should be even better managed to be generally stable and sufficient to support public services; community should gain slightly higher percentage of blue collar workers; employers should avoid outsourcing of jobs and reducing union effectiveness. Externally, outside employers should locate new jobs in community. Internally, community, grocers and restaurants should make food and drink available and affordable with prices 5% below average for country; community, grocers and restaurants should have sufficient sources of healthy food; community should ensure low income people have adequate resources for healthy food and for food generally; community should add resources to have sufficient resources to feed very poor. Externally, retail and wholesale food sources should hold down prices and add more healthy foods; country and state should provide resources to ensure food affordability for low and lower middle income persons. Internally, community should make available housing for low and lower middle income people that is affordable, available and adequate. Externally, country and state should provide resources to build affordable housing and resources for lower middle and low income people to rent or buy a house. Internally, community should provide resources and management to ensure police force should be in top 10% for country; neighborhood watch groups should exercise good management to avoid any significant problems. Externally, country and state should provide resources to adequately supplement community police resources. Internally, community should provide resources and management to ensure education availability and quality in the top 10% of cities of its size; community should work to retain and increase the percentage of*

- 60 -

college educated. Externally, country and state should provide resources to adequately supplement community education resources. Internally, community and private and public health services should improve services so that physical and mental health should be in top 10% of cities of its size; community and industry should ensure having substantially less occupationally related illness; community and private health services should ensure private health services in top 25% and community should ensure public health services in top 25% of cities of its size. Externally, country and state should ensure affordability (cost and insurance) of health services. Internally, community should help ensure personal growth and development is substantially better than cities of its size; community should ensure job re-training is in top 10% of its size. Externally, country and state should provide additional re-training resources to supplement community. Internally, community should ensure habitat is very pleasant and very healthy. Externally, country and state should ensure habitat is very pleasant and very healthy. Internally, community should reduce its vulnerabilities with special efforts (as listed for other areas) to greatly reduce its vulnerability on job and income loss, affordable and healthy foods, affordable housing, public health services, and community revenues. Externally, country and state should reduce vulnerability country and state-wide with special efforts (as listed for other areas) to greatly reduce its vulnerability on job and income loss, affordable and healthy foods, affordable housing, public health services, and community revenues. Internally, community should ensure a wider range of products and services than other cities of its size, a substantially higher percentage of higher quality manufactured products, a high percentage of healthy and well educated children and a range of recreational activities in the top 10% of cities of its size. Externally, employers should bring more and a wider range of jobs and higher quality manufacturing; country and state provide added education resources; country and state add recreational resources to community. Externally, country and state work to ensure climate is good to very good. Internally, community ensures sustainability is no longer in question in spite of changing national and international economics and potential job outsourcing. Externally, country and state support policies that reduce outsourcing and protect jobs in community.

d. What actions by your community are needed to achieve its thriving future? What internal actions (by you and your community) and external actions (by others) are needed to bring about the needed external and internal changes (identified in "c") that improve your community's current status enough to achieve the desired surviving and thriving status?[85] [See Figure 5.1] [86]

External actions by others. There are very important <u>external</u> actions that are needed to support the *Thrive!* strategy. You already identified what has to change externally to achieve your community's surviving and thriving future. What external actions by others will bring about the needed changes?

Use Table 5.4 to describe all the external actions to be taken.

Identify external actions by others that support <u>good</u> changes that will help improve and/or sustain surviving and thriving. If good changes are likely to occur, together with others support them. If good changes are not likely to occur, together with others support them and develop other good changes to compensate.

Identify external actions by others that stop <u>bad</u> changes that prevent or limit surviving and thriving. If bad changes are not likely to occur, together with others ensure they do not. If bad changes are likely to occur, together with others change them, stop them or avoid/reduce their impact.

---

[85] Uses the Toolkit's "Strategy Model".
[86] An action is defined as "who will do what to/with whom, where, when, and with what result."

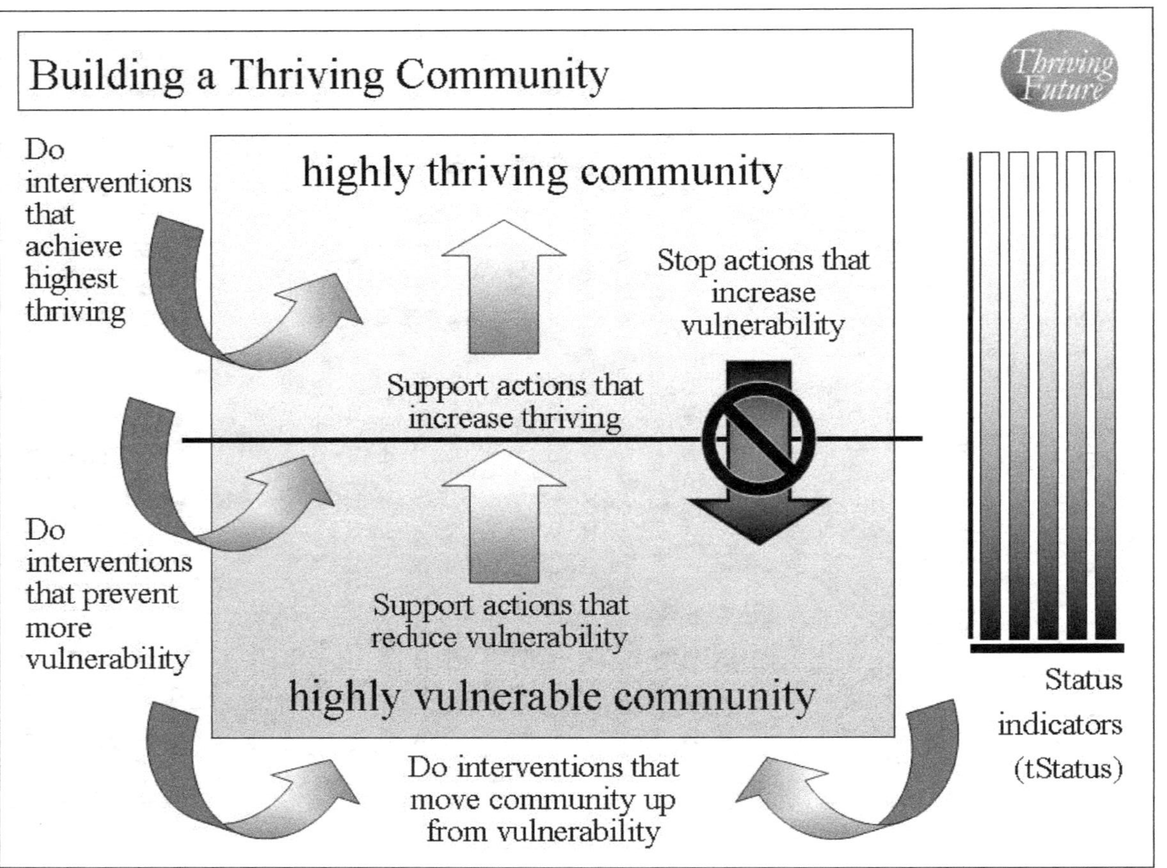

Figure 5.1. Building a Thriving Community.

* **Example.** Outside employers locate new jobs in community. Retail and wholesale food sources hold down prices and add more healthy foods; country and state provide resources to ensure food affordability for low and lower middle income persons. Country and state provide resources to build affordable housing and resources for lower middle and low income people to rent or buy a house. Country and state provide resources to adequately supplement community police resources. Country and state provide resources to adequately supplement community education resources. Country and state ensure affordability (cost and insurance) of health services by instituting cost constraints and providing affordable health insurance. Country and state provide additional re-training resources to supplement community. Country and state ensure habitat is very pleasant and very healthy by adding funding for public parks and preventive health programs. Country and state policies and programs reduce vulnerability country and state-wide with special efforts (as listed for other areas) to greatly reduce its vulnerability on job and income loss, affordable and healthy foods, affordable housing, public health services, and community revenues. Employers bring more and a wider range of jobs and higher quality manufacturing; country and state provide added education resources; country and state add recreational resources to community. Country and state work to ensure climate is good to very good through environmental policy and international agreements. Country and state execute policies that reduce outsourcing and protect jobs in community.*

Internal actions by your community. There are very important <u>internal</u> actions by you and your community that support the ***Thrive!*** strategy. Individual community members and your community as a whole should support your strategy to ensure your community and each community member are performing well. Being well-off (financially). Being well nourished (food and drink). Being well housed. Being well protected (exposures, crime). Being well educated. Being physically and mentally well. Personally growing/developing well. Living within good habitat. Not being vulnerable. Producing personal and public goods. Living within a stable, positive climate. Being sustained.

Thrive!

Use Table 5.4 to describe all the internal actions to be taken.

Identify internal actions by your community that support <u>good</u> changes that will help improve and/or sustain surviving and thriving. If good changes are likely to occur, support them. If good changes are not likely to occur, support them and develop other good changes to compensate.

Identify internal actions by your community that stop <u>bad</u> changes that prevent or limit surviving and thriving. If bad changes are not likely to occur, ensure they do not. If bad changes are likely to occur, change them, stop them or avoid/reduce their impact.

> ***Example.*** *Community provides incentives and community support to gain more employers to get to 2 percentage points lower than country and to gain more blue collar workers and light industry; internally, community employers expand and add jobs. Community recruits outside employers to locate new jobs in community. Community better manages financial condition to be generally stable and sufficient to support public services; community retains and recruits employers to gain slightly higher percentage of blue collar workers; employers avoid outsourcing of jobs and reducing union effectiveness. Community provides incentives to outside employers to locate new jobs in community. Community, grocers and restaurants make food and drink available and affordable with prices 5% below average for country; community, grocers and restaurants provide sufficient sources of healthy food; community provides support to low income people to ensure adequate resources for healthy food and for food generally; community adds resources to have sufficient resources to feed very poor. Community with other communities presses retail and wholesale food sources to hold down prices and add more healthy foods; community with other communities presses country and state to provide resources to ensure food affordability for low and lower middle income persons. Community should make available housing for low and lower middle income people that is affordable, available and adequate. Community presses country and state to provide resources to build affordable housing and resources for lower middle and low income people to rent or buy a house. Community provides*

resources and management to ensure police force is in top 10% for country; neighborhood watch groups exercise good management to avoid any significant problems. Community presses country and state to provide resources to adequately supplement community police resources. Community provides resources and management to ensure education availability and quality in the top 10% of cities of its size; community works to retain and increase the percentage of college educated. Community presses country and state to provide resources to adequately supplement community education resources. Community and private and public health services improve services so that physical and mental health should be in top 10% of cities of its size; community and industry ensure having substantially less occupationally related illness; community and private health services ensure private health services in top 25%; community manages and provides resources to ensure public health services in top 25% of cities of its size. Community presses country and state to ensure affordability (cost and insurance) of health services. Internally, community helps ensure personal growth and development is substantially better than cities of its size; community adds resources to ensure job re-training is in top 10% of its size. Community presses country and state to provide additional re-training resources to supplement community. Community implements policies to ensure habitat is very pleasant and very healthy. Community presses country and state to ensure habitat is very pleasant and very healthy. Community reduces its vulnerabilities with special efforts (as listed for other areas) to greatly reduce its vulnerability on job and income loss, affordable and healthy foods, affordable housing, public health services, and community revenues. Community presses country and state to institute policies and programs that reduce vulnerability country and state-wide with special efforts (as listed for other areas) to greatly reduce its vulnerability on job and income loss, affordable and healthy foods, affordable housing, public health services, and community revenues. Community and private sector ensure a wider range of products and services than other cities of its size and a substantially higher percentage of higher quality manufactured products; community ensures supportive resources to help ensure a high percentage of healthy and well educated children; and community provides resources to ensure a range of recreational activities in the top 10% of cities of its size.

> *Community recruits employers to bring more and a wider range of jobs and higher quality manufacturing; community presses country and state to provide added education resources; community presses country and state to add recreational resources to community. Community presses country and state to ensure climate is good to very good. Community ensures sustainability is no longer in question in spite of changing national and international economics and potential job outsourcing. Community presses country and state to support policies that reduce outsourcing and protect jobs in community.*

e. Overall *Thrive!* strategy and actions. Your overall *Thrive!* strategy and actions need to be documented and agreed to by your community. This will be your community's *Thrive!* **Strategy and Action Plan**. Different members of your community will take on different responsibilities. For each action, designate who of your community will do what to/with whom, where, when, and with what result. [See example below.] Use Table 5.4 to document these actions and responsibilities. [See example table below.] Make sure you have all the actions that are needed to build, achieve and sustain a surviving and thriving community.

As the strategy is executed, you strategy, actions and results should be updated in your *Thrive!* **Strategy and Action Plan**.

Periodically, you and your community should do an evaluation - assessing your strategies/actions near and long term impact on near and long term surviving and thriving. When a) your strategies and actions are not building and sustaining a thriving future and/or b) there are changes in the external world and in your community, you and your community should adjust your overall *Thrive!* **Strategy and Action Plan**.

The key is to successfully execute your community's ***Thrive! Strategy and Action Plan*** and to build a near and long term surviving and thriving future.[87] Each and all must successfully carry out the assigned action. That is, each/all must successfully do what is required to/with whoever is required, where required, when required, and with what needed/desired result. A ***Thrive! Strategy and Action Plan*** is only as good as its successful execution and successful achievement of the desired outcome - a surviving and thriving future.

>*__Example of a community surviving and somewhat thriving.__ [Who will do what to/with whom, where, when, and with what result?] See Example **Thrive! Strategy and Action Plan** in list and table below. With these actions, community would be surviving and doing better but would not yet have achieved full thriving.*
>
>>*__External Actions:__ Outside employers locate new jobs in community within 12 months. Retail and wholesale food sources hold down prices to 1% increase for next 12 months and add more healthy foods on trial basis starting within 6 months; country and state provide resources this fiscal year to ensure food affordability for low and lower middle income persons. Country and state provide resources to build affordable housing and resources for lower middle and low income people to rent or buy a house. Country and state provide resources this fiscal year to adequately supplement community police resources. Country and state*

---

[87] At this point, you may have enough good information to execute you and your country's *Thrive!* strategy and actions. If you want to develop your strategy and actions further, you may want to use more of the tools and models already mentioned and the *Thrive!* **Next Generation Toolkit.**

The full *Thrive!* **Next Generation Toolkit** (Appendix) includes strategy, policy and tools for creating and sustaining large, positive change and building a thriving future. Your community might also want to use ***Thrive! - Building a Thriving Future*** - a manual providing greater depth on strategy and tools and available via www.Amazon.com or free download from www.ThrivingFuture.org.

For example, if you want to develop and assess more in-depth strategies and actions, you may want to use the Behavioral Effectiveness Model (BEM). BEM helps assess a) how your community's and individual community member's motivation and ability will impact future behavior and b) how actions by people outside your community will impact your community's and individual community member's future motivation, ability and behavior. A description of BEM and how to use it is included in the Appendix.

provide resources this fiscal year to adequately supplement community education resources. Country and state ensure affordability (cost and insurance) of health services by instituting cost constraints to less than 3% increase and providing affordable health insurance within 12 months. Country and state provide additional re-training resources this fiscal year to supplement community. Within 2 years, country and state policies and programs substantially reduce vulnerability country and state-wide with special efforts (as listed for other areas) to greatly reduce its vulnerability on job and income loss, affordable and healthy foods, affordable housing, public health services, and community revenues. Country and state ensure habitat is very pleasant and very healthy by adding 25% more funding this fiscal year for public parks and preventive health programs. Employers bring more and a wider range of jobs and higher quality manufacturing within 12 months; country and state provide added education resources this fiscal year; country and state add recreational resources this fiscal year to community. Country and state work to ensure climate is good to very good through environmental policy within 18 months and international agreements within 2 years. Country and state execute policies that reduce outsourcing and protect jobs in community within 12 months.

Internal Actions: *Community provides property tax incentives and community support within 12 months to gain more employers to get to 2 percentage points lower than country and to gain more blue collar workers and light industry; community employers expand and add 10% more jobs within 1 year. Community recruits outside 5 new employers to locate new jobs in community within 2 years. Community better manages financial condition to be generally stable and sufficient to support public services starting next fiscal year; community retains and recruits employers to gain slightly higher percentage of blue collar workers (see above); employers avoid outsourcing of jobs and reducing union effectiveness over next 2 years. Community provides incentives to outside employers to locate new jobs in community (see above). Within 12 months, community, grocers and restaurants make food and drink available and affordable with prices 5% below average for country; community, grocers and restaurants provide sufficient sources of healthy food within 12 months; community provides support to low income people to ensure adequate resources for* *healthy food and for food generally within 12 months; community adds resources to have sufficient resources to feed very poor within 12 months. Starting immediately, community with other communities presses retail and wholesale food sources to hold down prices and add more healthy foods; starting immediately, community with other communities presses country and state to provide resources to ensure food affordability for low and lower middle income persons. Within 2 years, community should make available housing for low and lower middle income people that is affordable, available and adequate. Starting immediately, community presses country and state to provide resources to build affordable housing and resources for lower middle and low income people to rent or buy a house. Community provides resources and management this fiscal year to ensure police force is in top 10% for country; neighborhood watch groups exercise good management to avoid any significant problems starting within 30 days. Starting immediately, community presses country and state to provide resources to adequately supplement community police resources. Community provides resources and management this fiscal year to ensure education availability and quality in the top 10% of cities of its size; starting immediately, community works to retain and increase the percentage of college educated. Starting immediately, community presses country and state to provide resources to adequately supplement community education resources. Within 2 years, community and private and public health services improve services so that physical and mental health should be in top 10% of cities of its size; community and industry ensure having substantially less occupationally related illness within 2 years; community and private health services ensure private health services in top 25% within 2 years; community manages and provides resources this fiscal year to ensure public health services in top 25% of cities of its size. Starting immediately, community presses country and state to ensure affordability (cost and insurance) of health services. Community helps ensure personal growth and development is substantially better than cities of its size within 18 months; community adds resources this fiscal year to ensure job re-training is in top 10% of its size. Starting immediately, community presses country and state to provide additional re-training resources to supplement community. Within 1 year, community implements policies to ensure habitat is very pleasant and very healthy.*

Starting immediately, community presses country and state to ensure habitat is very pleasant and very healthy. Within 2 years, community substantially reduces its vulnerabilities with special efforts (as listed for other areas) to greatly reduce its vulnerability on job and income loss, affordable and healthy foods, affordable housing, public health services, and community revenues. Starting immediately, community presses country and state to institute policies and programs that reduce vulnerability country and state-wide with special efforts (as listed for other areas) to greatly reduce its vulnerability on job and income loss, affordable and healthy foods, affordable housing, public health services, and community revenues. Community and private sector ensure a wider range of products and services than other cities of its size and a substantially higher percentage of higher quality manufactured products within 12 months; community ensures supportive resources this fiscal year to help ensure a high percentage of healthy and well educated children; and community provides resources this fiscal year to ensure a range of recreational activities in the top 10% of cities of its size. Community recruits employers to bring more and a wider range of jobs and higher quality manufacturing within 12 months; starting immediately, community presses country and state to provide added education resources; starting immediately, community presses country and state to add recreational resources to community. Starting immediately, community presses country and state to ensure climate is good to very good. Within 2 years, community ensures sustainability is no longer in question in spite of changing national and international economics and potential job outsourcing. Starting immediately, community presses country and state to support policies that reduce outsourcing and protect jobs in community.

But, we want a <u>thriving</u> future for you and your community. To build, achieve and sustain a surviving <u>and</u> thriving future, the ***Thrive!* Strategy and Action Plan** should be more like the following example:

Example of you and your community surviving and thriving. *[Who will do what to/with whom, where, when, and with what result?] Starting immediately for you and your community, people, business/industry, private organizations (local, country), governments (local, country) and international organizations) build, achieve, and* *sustain a surviving and thriving future for you and your community, including:*[88]

- Performing well. *Starting immediately for you and your community, people, business/industry, private organizations (local, country), governments (local, country) and international organizations act to ensure, within the next 10 years, a) all (who are able and not appropriately retired) can work and earn a living income sufficient to survive and thrive and b) all have sufficient resources for and are living, recreating, learning so that they are surviving and thriving to maximum extent feasible.*

- Being well-off (financially). *Starting immediately for you and your community, people, business/industry, private organizations (local, country), governments (local, country) and international organizations act to ensure, within the next 10 years, a) all have sufficient income/resources to survive and thrive and b) all governments have sufficient resources to provide needed (supporting surviving) and desired (supporting thriving) public programs and policies.*

- Being well nourished (food and drink). *Starting immediately for you and your community, people, business/industry, private organizations (local, country), governments (local, country) and international organizations act to ensure, within the next 10 years, that all have access to, be able to afford and consume healthy foods enough to survive and thrive.*

- Being well housed. *Starting immediately for you and your community, people, business/industry, private organizations (local, country), governments (local, country) and international organizations act to ensure, within the next 20 years, all have access to, be able to afford and live in adequate and preferably high performing housing that supports surviving and thriving.*

- Being well protected (exposures, crime). *Starting immediately for you and your community, people, business/industry, private organizations (local, country), governments (local, country) and international organizations act to ensure, within the next 10 years, a) environmental exposures in home, workplace and elsewhere are minimized so as to not prevent surviving and thriving and b) crimes are minimized to the extent feasible in terms of frequency and impact so as to not prevent surviving and thriving.*

---

[88] International organizations could be a major resource, especially if the community extends beyond a single country's boundaries.

- Being well educated. *Starting immediately for you and your community, people, business/industry, private organizations (local, country), governments (local, country) and international organizations act to ensure, within the next 20 years, all are educated to the full extent of their abilities, needs and desires and to support their surviving and thriving.*
- Being physically and mentally well. *Starting immediately for you and your community, people, business/industry, private organizations (local, country), governments (local, country) and international organizations act to ensure, within the next 20 years, a) all receive the optimal health support to ensure, within the next 10 years, surviving and thriving and b) physical and mental health is optimized to best ensure surviving and thriving.*
- Personally growing/developing well. *Starting immediately for you and your community, people, business/industry, private organizations (local, country), governments (local, country) and international organizations act to ensure, within the next 10 years, all are personally growing and developing to best ensure surviving and thriving.*
- Living within good habitat. *Starting immediately for you and your community, people, business/industry, private organizations (local, country), governments (local, country) and international organizations act to ensure, within the next 10 years, a) all have access to habitat that best supports their surviving and thriving and b) your community has the optimal mix, quantity and quality of habitat to best support its inhabitants' surviving and thriving.*
- Not being vulnerable. *Starting immediately for you and your community, people, business/industry, private organizations (local, country), governments (local, country) and international organizations act to ensure, within the next 10 years, that all, if vulnerable, are vulnerable only to the minimum extent feasible.*
- Producing personal and public goods. *Starting immediately for you and your community, people, business/industry, private organizations (local, country), governments (local, country) and international organizations act to ensure, within the next 10 years, your community produces personal and public goods (including personal income/resources, housing, food and drink, energy, education, health, protection, personal growth and development, and habitat) so as to support surviving and thriving for all.*
- Living within a stable, positive climate. *Starting immediately for you and your community, people, business/industry, private*

organizations (local, country), governments (local, country) and international organizations act to ensure, within the next 10 years, all behave so as to avoid negative impacts and support positive impacts so as to help ensure a stable, positive climate.
- Being sustained. *Starting immediately for you and your community, people, business/industry, private organizations (local, country), governments (local, country) and international organizations act to ensure, within the next 5 years, all people behave so as to ensure the sustainability of your community <u>and</u> its people.*

***Thrive!* Strategy and Action Plan** (Example of surviving and somewhat thriving).

Thriving and Surviving	How well (surviving/ thriving) should your community be in near/long term future?	External/internal changes needed to achieve surviving and thriving future	Actions by your community and others - Who will do what to/with whom, where, when, and with what result?
Performing (live/work/ play) well?	*Community should perform well with close to country's average mix lifestyles for city of its size. Unemployment should be 2 percentage points lower than country; mix of work should be similar to that of country as a whole and continue with a slightly larger percentage of blue collar workers and light industry.*	**External**: *Externally, outside employers should locate new jobs in community.*	**External by others**: *Outside employers locate new jobs in community within 12 months.*
			Internal by your community:
		Internal: *Internally, community should perform better than it has. Internally, community needs to gain more employers to get to 2 percentage points lower than country; community needs to gain more blue collar workers and light industry; internally, community employers should expand and add jobs.*	**Internal by your community**: *Community provides property tax incentives and community support within 12 months to gain more employers to get to 2 percentage points lower than country and to gain more blue collar workers and light industry; community employers expand and add 10% more jobs within 1 year. Community recruits outside 5 new employers to locate new jobs in community within 2 years.*
Well-off?	*Financial condition of community should be generally stable and sufficient to support public services; community should have slightly higher percentage of blue collar workers but who are no longer facing potential outsourcing of jobs and declining*	**External**: *Externally, outside employers should locate new jobs in community. .*	**External by others**: *Outside employers locate new jobs in community within 12 months.*
			Internal by your community: *Community provides incentives to outside employers to locate new jobs in community (see above).*

		Internal: *Internally, financial condition of community should be even better managed to be generally stable and sufficient to support public services; community should gain slightly higher percentage of blue collar workers; employers should avoid outsourcing of jobs and reducing union effectiveness*	**Internal by your community**: *Community better manages financial condition to be generally stable and sufficient to support public services starting next fiscal year; community retains and recruits employers to gain slightly higher percentage of blue collar workers (see above); employers avoid outsourcing of jobs and reducing union effectiveness over next 2 years.*
Well nourished?	*Food and drink should be available and affordable with prices 5% below average for country; community should have sufficient sources of healthy food; low income people should have adequate resources for healthy food and for food generally; community should have sufficient resources to feed very poor.*	**External**: *Externally, retail and wholesale food sources should hold down prices and add more healthy foods; country and state should provide resources to ensure food affordability for low and lower middle income persons.*	**External by others**: *Retail and wholesale food sources hold down prices to 1% increase for next 12 months and add more healthy foods on trial basis starting within 6 months; country and state provide resources this fiscal year to ensure food affordability for low and lower middle income persons.*
			Internal by your community: *Starting immediately, community with other communities presses retail and wholesale food sources to hold down prices and add more healthy foods; starting immediately, community with other communities presses country and state to provide resources to ensure food affordability for low and lower middle income persons.*

		Internal: *Internally, community, grocers and restaurants should make food and drink available and affordable with prices 5% below average for country; community, grocers and restaurants should have sufficient sources of healthy food; community should ensure low income people have adequate resources for healthy food and for food generally; community should add resources to have sufficient resources to feed very poor.*	**Internal by your community**: *Within 12 months, community, grocers and restaurants make food and drink available and affordable with prices 5% below average for country; community, grocers and restaurants provide sufficient sources of healthy food within 12 months; community provides support to low income people to ensure adequate resources for healthy food and for food generally within 12 months; community adds resources to have sufficient resources to feed very poor within 12 months.*
Well housed	*Housing for upper and middle income people should be available and affordable; housing for low and lower middle income people should be affordable, available and adequate.*	**External**: *Externally country and state should provide resources to build affordable housing and resources for lower middle and low income people to rent or buy a house.*	**External by others**: *Country and state provide resources to build affordable housing and resources for lower middle and low income people to rent or buy a house.*
			Internal by your community: *Starting immediately, community presses country and state to provide resources to build affordable housing and resources for lower middle and low income people to rent or buy a house.*

		Internal: *Internally, community should make available housing for low and lower middle income people that is affordable, available and adequate.*	Internal by your community: *Within 2 years, community should make available housing for low and lower middle income people that is affordable, available and adequate.*
Well protected?	*Community police force should be in top 10% for country; some neighborhood watch groups should exist but without any significant problems.*	External: *Externally, country and state should provide resources to adequately supplement community police resources.*	External by others: *Country and state provide resources this fiscal year to adequately supplement community police resources.*
			Internal by your community: *Starting immediately, community presses country and state to provide resources to adequately supplement community police resources.*
		Internal: *Internally, community should provide resources and management to ensure police force should be in top 10% for country; neighborhood watch groups should exercise good management to avoid any significant problems.*	Internal by your community: *Community provides resources and management this fiscal year to ensure police force is in top 10% for country; neighborhood watch groups exercise good management to avoid any significant problems starting within 30 days.*
Well educated?	*Education availability and quality should be in the top 10% of cities of its size; community should have slightly higher percentage of college educated.*	External: *Externally, country and state should provide resources to adequately supplement community education resources.*	External by others: *Country and state provide resources this fiscal year to adequately supplement community education resources.*
			Internal by your community: *Starting immediately, community presses country and state to provide resources to adequately supplement community education resources.*

		Internal: *Internally, community should provide resources and management to ensure education availability and quality in the top 10% of cities of its size; community should work to retain and increase the percentage of college educated.*	Internal by your community: *Community provides resources and management this fiscal year to ensure education availability and quality in the top 10% of cities of its size; starting immediately, community works to retain and increase the percentage of college educated.*
Physically/ mentally well?	*Physical and mental health should be in top 10% of cities of its size; community should have substantially less occupationally related illness; private health services should be in top 25% and public health services should be in top 25% of cities of its size.*	External: *Externally, country and state should ensure affordability (cost and insurance) of health services.*	External by others: *Country and state ensure affordability (cost and insurance) of health services by instituting cost constraints to less than 3% increase and providing affordable health insurance within 12 months.*
			Internal by your community: *Starting immediately, community presses country and state to ensure affordability (cost and insurance) of health services.*

		Internal: *Internally, community and private and public health services should improve services so that physical and mental health should be in top 10% of cities of its size; community and industry should ensure having substantially less occupationally related illness; community and private health services should ensure private health services in top 25% and community should ensure public health services in top 25% of cities of its size.*	**Internal by your community**: *Within 2 years, community and private and public health services improve services so that physical and mental health should be in top 10% of cities of its size; community and industry ensure having substantially less occupationally related illness within 2 years; community and private health services ensure private health services in top 25% within 2 years; community manages and provides resources this fiscal year to ensure public health services in top 25% of cities of its size.*
Growing/ developing well?	*Personal growth and development should be substantially better than cities of its size and community should have job re-training in top 10% of its size.*	**External**: *Externally, country and state should provide additional re-training resources to supplement community.*	**External by others**: *Country and state provide additional re-training resources this fiscal year to supplement community.*
			Internal by your community: *Starting immediately, community presses country and state to provide additional re-training resources to supplement community.*

		Internal: *Internally, community should help ensure personal growth and development is substantially better than cities of its size; community should ensure job re-training is in top 10% of its size.*	Internal by your community: *Community helps ensure personal growth and development is substantially better than cities of its size within 18 months; community adds resources this fiscal year to ensure job re-training is in top 10% of its size.*
Living in good habitat?	*Habitat should be very pleasant and very healthy.*	External: *Externally, country and state should ensure habitat is very pleasant and very healthy.*	External by others: *Country and state ensure habitat is very pleasant and very healthy by adding 25% more funding this fiscal year for public parks and preventive health programs.*
			Internal by your community: *Starting immediately, community presses country and state to ensure habitat is very pleasant and very healthy.*
		Internal: *Internally, community should ensure habitat is very pleasant and very healthy.*	Internal by your community: *Within 1 year, community implements policies to ensure habitat is very pleasant and very healthy.*

Not vulnerable?	*Community should have much less vulnerability; community should greatly reduce its vulnerability on job and income loss, affordable and healthy foods, affordable housing, public health services, and community revenues.*	**External**: *Externally, country and state should reduce vulnerability country and state-wide with special efforts (as listed for other areas) to greatly reduce its vulnerability on job and income loss, affordable and healthy foods, affordable housing, public health services, and community revenues.*	**External by others**: *Within 2 years, country and state policies and programs substantially reduce vulnerability country and state-wide with special efforts (as listed for other areas) to greatly reduce its vulnerability on job and income loss, affordable and healthy foods, affordable housing, public health services, and community revenues.*
			Internal by your community: *Starting immediately, community presses country and state to institute policies and programs that reduce vulnerability country and state-wide with special efforts (as listed for other areas) to greatly reduce its vulnerability on job and income loss, affordable and healthy foods, affordable housing, public health services, and community revenues.*
		Internal: *Internally, community should reduce its vulnerabilities with special efforts (as listed for other areas) to greatly reduce its vulnerability on job and income loss, affordable and healthy foods, affordable housing, public health services, and community revenues.*	**Internal by your community**: *Within 2 years, community substantially reduces its vulnerabilities with special efforts (as listed for other areas) to greatly reduce its vulnerability on job and income loss, affordable and healthy foods, affordable housing, public health services, and community revenues.*

Producing personal/ public goods?	*Community should produce a wider range of products and services for city of its size, a substantially higher percentage of higher quality manufactured products, a high percentage of healthy and well educated children and a range of recreational activities in the top 10% of cities of its size.*	**External**: *Externally, employers should bring more and a wider range of jobs and higher quality manufacturing; country and state provide added education resources; country and state add recreational resources to community.*	**External by others**: *Employers bring more and a wider range of jobs and higher quality manufacturing within 12 months; country and state provide added education resources this fiscal year; country and state add recreational resources this fiscal year to community.*
			Internal by your community: *Community recruits employers to bring more and a wider range of jobs and higher quality manufacturing within 12 months; starting immediately, community presses country and state to provide added education resources; starting immediately, community presses country and state to add recreational resources to community.*

		Internal: *Internally, community should ensure a wider range of products and services than other cities of its size, a substantially higher percentage of higher quality manufactured products, a high percentage of healthy and well educated children and a range of recreational activities in the top 10% of cities of its size.*	Internal by your community: *Community and private sector ensure a wider range of products and services than other cities of its size and a substantially higher percentage of higher quality manufactured products within 12 months; community ensures supportive resources this fiscal year to help ensure a high percentage of healthy and well educated children; and community provides resources this fiscal year to ensure a range of recreational activities in the top 10% of cities of its size.*
Stable, positive climate?	*Climate should continue to be good to very good.*	External: *Externally, country and state work to ensure climate is good to very good.*	External by others: *Country and state work to ensure climate is good to very good through environmental policy within 18 months and international agreements within 2 years.*
			Internal by your community:
		Internal:	Internal by your community:
Sustainable?	*Sustainability should be ensured and no longer be in question in spite of changing national and international economics and potential job outsourcing.*	External: *Externally, country and state support policies that reduce outsourcing and protect jobs in community.*	External by others: *Country and state execute policies that reduce outsourcing and protect jobs in community within 12 months.*

			Internal by your community: *Starting immediately, community presses country and state to support policies that reduce outsourcing and protect jobs in community*
		Internal: *Internally, community ensures sustainability is no longer in question in spite of changing national and international economics and potential job outsourcing.*	Internal by your community: *Starting immediately, community presses country and state to ensure climate is good to very good. Within 2 years, community ensures sustainability is no longer in question in spite of changing national and international economics and potential job outsourcing.*

Table 5.4. *Thrive!* **Strategy and Action Plan.** How well (surviving/thriving) should your community be in near/long term future? What external/internal changes are needed to achieve your community's thriving future? To make this happen, what external/internal actions are needed?

Community Characteristics	What is your community today?
Geographic boundaries	
Gender make-up	
Age make-up	
Racial make-up	
Ethnic make-up	
Lifestyle	
Type of work	
Financial situation	
Food/drink	
Housing	
Protection	
Education	
Physical / mental health	
Personal growth / development	
Habitat	
Producing what	
Climate	
Sustainability	

Table 5.1. What is your community today?

Thriving and Surviving	How well (surviving/ thriving) is your community?	What positively/ negatively impacts its thriving/ surviving?	What is its near/ long term behavior as to thriving/ surviving?
Performing (live/work/play) well?			
Well-off?			
Well nourished?			
Well housed?			
Well protected?			
Well educated?			
Physically/ mentally well?			
Growing/ developing well?			
Living in good habitat?			
Not vulnerable?			
Producing personal/ public goods?			
Stable, positive climate?			
Sustainable?			

Table 5.2. How well (surviving/thriving) is your community? What positively/ negatively impacts it? If no change, what is its near/long term future behavior?

Community Characteristics	What is your desired and/or likely future community?
Type of work/how people live	
Financial situation	
Food/drink	
Housing	
Protection	
Education	
Physical / mental health	
Personal growth / development	
Habitat	
Producing what	
Climate	
Sustainability	

Table 5.3. What is your desired and/or likely future community?

Thriving and Surviving	How well (surviving/ thriving) should your community be in near/long term future?	External/internal changes needed to achieve surviving and thriving future	Actions by your community and others - Who will do what to/with whom, where, when, and with what result?
Performing (live/work/ play) well?		External:	External by others:
			Internal by your community:
		Internal:	Internal by your community:
Well-off?		External:	External by others:
			Internal by your community:
		Internal:	Internal by your community:
Well nourished?		External:	External by others:
			Internal by your community:
		Internal:	Internal by your community:
Well housed		External:	External by others:
			Internal by your community:
		Internal:	Internal by your community:
Well protected?		External:	External by others:
			Internal by your community:
		Internal:	Internal by your community:
Well educated?		External:	External by others:
			Internal by your community:
		Internal:	Internal by your community:
Physically/ mentally well?		External:	External by others:
			Internal by your community:
		Internal:	Internal by your community:

Growing/ developing well?		External:	External by others:
			Internal by your community:
		Internal:	Internal by your community:
Living in good habitat?		External:	External by others:
			Internal by your community:
		Internal:	Internal by your community:
Not vulnerable?		External:	External by others:
			Internal by your community:
		Internal:	Internal by your community:
Producing personal/ public goods?		External:	External by others:
			Internal by your community:
		Internal:	Internal by your community:
Stable, positive climate?		External:	External by others:
			Internal by your community:
		Internal:	Internal by your community:
Sustainable?		External:	External by others:
			Internal by your community:
		Internal:	Internal by your community:

Table 5.4. *Thrive!* **Strategy and Action Plan.** How well (surviving/thriving) should your community be in near/long term future? What external/internal changes are needed to achieve your community's thriving future? To make this happen, what external/internal actions are needed?

Chapter 6: How <u>you and your country</u> can thrive.

How to build, achieve and sustain a surviving and thriving future for you and your country.

Why you and your country <u>can.</u>

You and your country can have a surviving and thriving future. To get to that future, keep in mind that each country is different with a different future already beginning. Whether that future appears bad or good, each country can do better. To build a better future, the *Thrive!* strategy and tools has been used successfully at the personal level and on larger scales (community, country). They can work for you and the country you care about. As they have for others, this strategy and these tools can help you and your country build, achieve and sustain a surviving and thriving future.

Thrive!
Keep in mind that we are more capable than any time in human history. We can build a thriving future by effectively and collaboratively using all available knowledge and tools, including "next generation" *Thrive!* strategy and tools. Next generation *Thrive!* is different and better than anything in human history. It is <u>achieving</u> a thriving future at each level. It understands that <u>people's behavior,</u> including yours, makes (or breaks) a thriving future. It helps people, including you, achieve the behavior that in turn achieves a thriving future at each level and for all forever.

Why you and your country <u>must</u>.

You and your country <u>must</u> have a surviving and thriving future.
Each country <u>must</u> do better whether that future appears bad or good.
Why? Even those countries that have a good future are not fully
thriving, are not likely to be fully thriving in the future, and are still
facing uncertainties about the long term future.   You and your
country want and need a surviving and thriving future because your
country's future is endangered and because of our human need to
survive and desire to thrive. What drives your country and its people
is our human need to survive and desire to thrive now and in a
sustainable future. Further, because your country's people (past and
present) have broken some part of your country and endangered its
future, you and your country's people (present and future) must help
fix what is broken and build a survivable and thriving future for your
country.

Why we all must and can do it together.

To build this better future, your country's people and leadership
should be partners in this endeavor from the beginning and through
each step. Success is dependent on positive leadership from the
country's people and leaders. How that leadership comes about is
the subject of some debate. Some people argue for a leader driven
approach where the leader creates the vision and motivation and the
people join and/or follow. Some argue for bottom-up or self-
organizing approaches where the people lead and the traditional
leaders may or may not join and/or follow. Some argue for a
collaborative approach where the traditional leaders and the people
(also serving as leaders) jointly provide leadership, vision,
motivation, strategy and successful execution. In general, the latter
approach probably has the greater potential to create <u>and</u> sustain
large, positive change and a surviving and thriving country.

When feasible and when your country's national, state and local
governments are a positive force, your governments should be part
of the leadership and be partners in building a surviving and thriving
country. However, it is not sufficient for government to be the only

leader in this endeavor. Non-governmental organizations need to be leaders. Private businesses need to be leaders. Individual people need to be leaders. To be successful, this needs to be a whole country (people and leaders) endeavor.

Key to success is the strong desire by you and your country's people to move your country from its current vulnerabilities through and beyond surviving to a sustained thriving future.

How to build, achieve, and sustain a surviving and thriving future for you and your country.

To build a surviving and thriving future for you and your country, *Thrive!* can be helpful to you and is laid out in the following "how-to".[89,90] The strategy, models and tools apply to countries from small size and low complexity to very large size and very high complexity.

The following "how-to", by design, is simple but powerful. It is a relatively basic how-to providing the framework if not necessarily all the details for doing "your country" strategy.

This "your country" how-to is adapted from the *Thrive!* **Next Generation Toolkit** contained in the Appendix. More is available in *Thrive!* - **Building a Thriving Future** - a manual providing greater depth on strategy and tools and available via www.Amazon.com or free download from www.ThrivingFuture.org. The optimal approach is to use the following how-to framework and

---

[89] Note that for each step, an example is provided to give a sense of how to do that step. The example provides highlights but not the full working of a step.
[90] Note that using *Thrive!* for a country is very similar to using it for a community. In many ways, a country is a community. Here a country is handled separately because of the likely increased size, larger number of governments, and the likely increased complexity and diversity of its people, its politics, its geography, its resources and its habitat.

also use the strategies, models and tools in the Appendix and in
Thrive! - Building a Thriving Future.

Step 1.

Step 1. Current state of you and your country. The first major
step is to understand the current state of your country.

a. What is your country? Let's first go through what is your
country today.[91] A country is defined by its geography, political
boundaries, or population characteristics (e.g. racial/ethnic, gender,
economics, political view, similar mission, religion, labor,
profession, business).

For your country, what are its geographic boundaries and
characteristics? Use Table 6.1 (end of chapter) to describe all of the
following for your country.[92] Its gender, age, racial, ethnic make-up.
Lifestyle. Type of work. Financial situation. Food and drink.
Housing. Protection (crime, environmental hazards). Education.
Physical and mental health. Personal growth and development.
Habitat (living environment, neighboring communities, part of what
state, country, continent). Producing what. Climate. Sustainability.

> ***Example.*** *Country is has about 50 million people occupying 300*
> *square miles on continent X. Gender mix is 51/49 female/male;*
> *age mix approximates that of the world as a whole but with slightly*
> *higher percentage under age 18; racial mix approximates that of*
> *its continent but with a slightly higher percentage of all minorities.*
> *Lifestyle mix is similar to most countries on its continent. Mix of*
> *work is similar to that of world as a whole but with a slightly*
> *larger percentage of blue collar workers, agriculture and light*
> *industry. Financial basis is similar to most countries on its*
> *continent but with slightly higher resources coming from*
> *agriculture and light industry. Food and drink is similar to most*
> *countries on its continent. A good range of housing is available*

---

[91] Uses the Toolkit's "Systems Model (including Ideal Systems)".
[92] Free download of larger, fillable worksheets at www.ThrivingFuture.org

for those with the means to purchase or rent; community has inadequate housing supply. Protection comes primarily from local police force, state police force and country's military. Education is similar to most countries on its continent but with much lower college education level. Physical and mental health is similar to most countries on its continent but with slightly higher occupationally related illness. Personal growth and development is similar to most countries on its continent but with slightly more job training. Habitat consists of many rivers and lakes, widely varying terrain, and moderate deciduous tree cover; located on continent X. Country produces usual range of products and services for country on its continent, slightly higher percentage of manufactured products, wide mix of unhealthy/healthy and poorly/well educated children and a very limited range of developed recreational activities. Climate is moderate with slightly higher percentage of rainfall, slightly higher percentage of sunlight, slightly higher temperatures than other countries on its continent. Sustainability is in question due to low country revenues, under developed natural resources and changing national and international economics.

b. How well is your country? How well (surviving and thriving) is your country?[93] Use Table 6.2 (end of chapter) to describe how well is your country.[94] How well is your country in terms of performing well? Being well-off (financially)? Being well nourished (food and drink)? Being well housed? Being well protected (exposures, crime)? Being well educated? Being physically and mentally well? Personally growing/developing well? Living within good habitat? Not being vulnerable? Producing personal and public goods? Living within a stable, positive climate? Being sustained?

Answering "yes" to all indicates current surviving and thriving. Though the "yes" answers are good, there is still future work to make sure this continues. "No" answers are bad and mean there is current and future work to be done.

---

[93] Uses the Toolkit's "Status Model".

[94] Free download of larger, fillable worksheets at www.ThrivingFuture.org

Thrive!

__Example.__ Country is performing lower than average for countries on its continent with close to continent's average mix of lifestyles for country of its size. Unemployment is 1 percentage point higher than its continent; mix of work is similar to that of its continent but with a slightly larger percentage of blue collar and of agricultural workers and light industry. Financial condition of country is not sufficiently stable and is not sufficient to support needed public services; community has slightly higher percentage of blue collar workers who are facing potential moving of jobs out of country. Food and drink is available and prices are 5% below average for its continent; country lacks sufficient sources of healthy food; low income people lack resources for healthy food and for food generally; country lacks sufficient resources to feed very poor. Housing for upper and middle income people is available and affordable; housing for low and lower middle income people is unavailable, unaffordable and inadequate. Country local police force, state police force and country military are slightly below average for its continent. Education availability and quality is slightly less than other countries on its continent; country has 10 percent less college educated. Physical and mental health is slightly below average as compared to other countries on its continent; country has slightly more occupationally related illness; private health services are substantially below average and public health services are only 75% of other countries on its continent. Personal growth and development is about the same as most countries on its continent but it has slightly more job training. Habitat is about an equal mix of pleasant and harsh and healthy and unhealthy. While country has much vulnerability, it is most vulnerable on job loss, limited income, lack of affordable and healthy foods, lack of affordable and adequate housing for poorer people, inadequate private and public health services, and low country revenues. Country produces usual range of products and services for country on its continent, slightly higher percentage of medium quality manufactured products, slightly below average percentage of healthy and well educated children and an average range of recreational activities. Climate is okay. Sustainability is in question due to potential job losses, limited income and country revenues, lower education and health, under developed natural resources and changing national and international economics.

c. What positively or negatively impacts your country? What positively or negatively impacts or is likely to impact you and your country's surviving and thriving? Use Table 6.2 to describe all of the following impacts (positive and negative; current and future). What impacts your country's performing well? Being well-off (financially)? Being well nourished (food and drink)? Being well housed? Being well protected (exposures, crime)? Being well educated? Being physically and mentally well? Personally growing/developing well? Living within good habitat? Not being vulnerable? Producing personal and public goods? Living within a stable, positive climate? Being sustained?

Positive impacts improve and/or sustain surviving and thriving. If they will continue, you probably can focus on other things. If they may or may not continue, your action is needed to make them continue and/or to develop other things to compensate. Bad impacts prevent or limit surviving and thriving. If they will not continue, you probably can focus on other things. If they may or may not continue, your action is needed to stop them or to avoid or minimize their impact.

> ***Example.*** *Country leadership negatively impacts its performing and results in lower than average performance for countries on its continent. Employers have negative impact by being reluctant to locate or expand blue collar jobs due to lower educated workforce and slightly unstable government; agriculture jobs could be a positive impact if produce more food to feed country and then export rest. Financial condition of country is not sufficiently stable and is negatively impacted by conflicts within government and with private sector; lower education and training negatively impacts blue collar workforce's ability to compete and keep jobs from moving of jobs out of country. Food and drink is somewhat of a positive impact because it is available and prices are 5% below average for its continent; country is negatively impacted because it lacks sufficient sources of healthy food; retail and wholesale food suppliers being resistant to lowering prices and providing healthier food has a negative impact; low income people are negatively impacted because they lack resources for healthy food and for food generally; country is negatively impacted because it lacks sufficient resources to feed very poor. Housing*

for upper and middle income people being available and affordable has a positive impact; housing for low and lower middle income people being unavailable, unaffordable and inadequate has a negative impact; country's low revenues and general resistance to ensuring affordable housing have a negative impact. Country local police force, state police force and country military being slightly below average for its continent has a small negative impact. Education availability and quality being slightly less than other countries on its continent has a negative impact; country being 10 percent less college educated produces a negative impact. Physical and mental health being slightly below average as compared to other countries on its continent has a negative impact; country having slightly more occupationally related illness has a negative impact; a negative impact comes from private health services being substantially below average and public health services being only 75% of other countries on its continent; country's low revenue and lack of any public insurance negatively impact health. Personal growth and development being about the same as most countries on its continent has little impact; having slightly more job training has a positive impact. Habitat being about an equal mix of pleasant and harsh and healthy and unhealthy creates both positive and negative impacts. While country has much vulnerability, the most negative impacts come from job loss, limited income, lack of affordable and healthy foods, lack of affordable and adequate housing for poorer people, inadequate private and public health services, and low country revenues. Country producing usual range of products and services for country on its continent (little impact), slightly higher percentage of medium quality manufactured products (negative impact), slightly below average percentage of healthy and well educated children (negative impact) and an average range of recreational activities (little impact). Climate being okay has little impact near term. Sustainability being in question (due to potential job losses, limited income and country revenues, lower education and health, under developed natural resources and changing national and international economics) has a large negative impact.

d. What is near and long term future behavior of your country? How is your country likely to behave in the near and long term future.[95] Use Table 6.2 to describe all of the following behaviors.

Thrive!

How will your country behave with respect to performing well?
Being well-off (financially). Being well nourished (food and drink)?
Being well housed? Being well protected (exposures, crime)?
Being well educated? Being physically and mentally well?
Personally growing/developing well? Living within good habitat?
Not being vulnerable? Producing personal and public goods?
Living within a stable, positive climate? Being sustained?

> ***Example.*** *Country leadership will try to improve its performing to above the average performance for countries on its continent. Employers will continue to refuse to locate or expand blue collar jobs due to lower educated workforce and slightly unstable government; agriculture producers inside and outside country will try to increase agriculture production and jobs to produce more food to feed country and then export rest. Government and private leaders will continue conflict that results in poor financial and unstable condition of country; governments continue low investment in education an training but private sector may offer some job training to increase blue collar workforce's ability to compete and keep jobs from moving of jobs out of country. Country will work with food and drink producers, wholesalers and retailers to increase sources of healthy food; retail and wholesale food suppliers may try lowering prices and providing healthier food; low income people will struggle to survive because they lack resources for healthy food and for food generally; country may try to find way to get sufficient resources to feed very poor. Bankers and builders will continue supporting housing for upper and middle income people that is available and affordable; government, bankers and builders may continue to not support housing for low and lower middle income people being available, affordable and adequate; country will try to find way to increase low revenues and be more open to ensuring affordable housing. Country will continue to support local police force, state police force and country military to be slightly below average for its continent. Governments at all levels will try to determine how to improve education availability and quality above other countries on its continent; country will try to improve college availability and affordability and to recruit college educated. Country and private and public sector health services will explore how to*

---

[95] Uses the Toolkit's "Population Model".

improve physical and mental health to be above average as compared to other countries on its continent; country and employers will consider efforts to reduce occupationally related illness; private health services may seek government and sources outside country to improve services; country and local governments will try to figure out how to increase public revenues and improve public health services above 75% of other countries on its continent; country will try to figure out how to increase revenue and remove lack of any public insurance. Country will likely continue current levels of personal growth and development being about the same as most countries on its continent; employers explore more job training. Country may do little about habitat though being about an equal mix of pleasant and harsh and healthy and unhealthy has both positive and negative impacts. Because the country has much vulnerability as noted earlier, the country will explore how to reduce vulnerability but will need to increase revenues. Country will likely continue producing usual range of products and services for country on its continent, slightly higher percentage of medium quality manufactured products, slightly below average percentage of healthy and well educated children and an average range of recreational activities. Country will be less likely to act on climate being it is okay now and has little impact near term. Because sustainability is in question (due to potential job losses, limited income and country revenues, lower education and health, under developed natural resources and changing national and international economics), country will explore how best to survive and is unlikely to explore how best to thrive.

e. Want more on your country's future and behavior? At this point, you have a basic baseline with which to measure progress for your country. Your country may have enough good information to move to Step 2 and to develop strategy for you and your country. If your country wants more information before moving to strategy, your country may want to use more of the tools and models already mentioned and the ***Thrive!* Next Generation Toolkit** (Appendix). This is encouraged and may be necessary for very large, complex countries.

Using the full ***Thrive!* Next Generation Toolkit** (Appendix) is recommended because it includes more strategy, policy and tools for creating and sustaining large, positive change and building a surviving and thriving future.[96] Using the manual ***Thrive! - Building a Thriving Future*** is recommended because it provides even greater depth on strategy and tools. It is available via www.Amazon.com or free download from www.ThrivingFuture.org.

Step 2.

Step 2. Strategy to achieve you and your country's surviving and thriving future. The next major step is to develop the strategy that will help you and your country build and achieve a surviving and thriving future.

a. What will your country be in the future? What will be your likely future country?[97]   Use Table 6.3 (end of chapter) to describe the likely future. [98] If there are any changes to your country that are desired or likely, take them into account. What will be its characteristics? Type of work/how people live. Financial situation. Food and drink. Housing. Protection (crime, environmental hazards). Education. Physical and mental health. Personal growth and development. Habitat (living environment, neighboring communities, part of what state, country, continent). Producing what. Climate. Sustainability.

> ***Example.*** *Country will change very little. It will still be about 50 million people occupying 300 square miles on continent X. Gender mix will continue at about 51/49 female/male; age mix will*

---

[96] For example, if you want to develop and assess more in-depth strategies and actions, you may want to use the Behavioral Effectiveness Model (BEM). BEM helps assess a) how your country's and individual country member's motivation and ability will impact future behavior and b) how actions by people outside your country will impact your country's and individual country member's future motivation, ability and behavior. A description of BEM and how to use it is included in the Appendix.

[97] Uses the Toolkit's "Systems Model (including Ideal Systems)".

[98] Free download of larger, fillable worksheets at www.ThrivingFuture.org

approximate that of the world as a whole but with slightly higher percentage under age 21; racial mix will approximate that of its continent but with a slightly higher percentage of all minorities. Lifestyle mix will be similar to most countries on its continent. Mix of work will be similar to that of world as a whole but with a smaller percentage of blue collar workers, a higher percentage of agriculture workers and a smaller percentage of light industry. Financial basis will weaker and be lower than most countries on its continent but with substantially higher percentage of resources coming from agriculture. Food and drink will be similar to most countries on its continent. A good range of housing will be available for those with the means to purchase or rent; community will have inadequate housing supply. Protection will come primarily from local police force, state police force and country's military. Education will be lower than most countries on its continent and with much lower college education level. Physical and mental health will be slightly lower than most countries on its continent and it no longer has higher occupationally related illness. Personal growth and development will be similar to most countries on its continent but with slightly more job training. Habitat will consist of many rivers and lakes, widely varying terrain, and moderate deciduous tree cover; located on continent X. Country will produce usual range of products and services for country on its continent, the same or lower higher percentage of manufactured products, wide mix of unhealthy/healthy and poorly/well educated children and a very limited range of developed recreational activities. Climate will be moderate in the near term with slightly higher percentage of rainfall, slightly higher percentage of sunlight, slightly higher temperatures than other countries on its continent. Sustainability will be in question due to low country revenues, under developed natural resources and changing national and international economics.

b. How well should your country be in the near and long term future? How well should your country as a whole be in the future?[99] Overall, it should be <u>surviving and thriving</u>. With this as a guide, you and your country choose the surviving and thriving future your community wants to build and achieve. The "***Thrive!* strategy**" will help you accomplish that.

----

[99] Uses the Toolkit's "Status Model".

Use Table 6.4 (end of chapter) to describe how well your country should be.[100] From you and your country's view and to be surviving and thriving, indicate to what extent your country should be performing well. Be well-off (financially). Be well nourished (food and drink). Be well housed. Be well protected (exposures, crime). Be well educated. Be physically and mentally well. Be personally growing/developing well. Be living within good habitat. Not be vulnerable. Be producing personal and public goods. Be living within a stable, positive climate. Be sustained. Again, your country should be surviving and thriving.

> **Example.** *Country should perform better than countries on its continent with close to continent's average mix of lifestyles for country of its size. Unemployment should be lower than its continent; mix of work should be similar to that of its continent but with a larger percentage of blue collar and of agricultural workers and light industry. Financial condition of country should be stable and sufficient to support needed public services; community has slightly higher percentage of blue collar workers who should not face potential moving of jobs out of country. Food and drink should be available and prices should be 10% below average for its continent; country should have sufficient sources of healthy food; low income people should have resources for healthy food and for food generally; country should have sufficient resources to feed very poor. Housing for upper and middle income people should be available and affordable; housing for low and lower middle income people should be available, affordable and adequate. Country local police force, state police force and country military should be best for its continent. Education availability and quality should be best on its continent; country should have 10 percent more college educated than its continent. Physical and mental health should be best compared to other countries on its continent; country should have substantially less occupationally related illness; private and public health services should be best on its continent. Personal growth and development should be better than countries on its continent and have substantially more job training. Habitat should have the best mix*

---

[100] Free download of larger, fillable worksheets at www.ThrivingFuture.org

of pleasant and harsh and healthy and unhealthy on its continent. While country has had much vulnerability, it should no longer be vulnerable on job loss, limited income, lack of affordable and healthy foods, lack of affordable and adequate housing for poorer people, inadequate private and public health services, and low country revenues. Compared to its continent, country should produce an optimal range of products and services for its continent, a substantially higher percentage of high quality manufactured products, the best percentage of healthy and well educated children and a wide range of recreational activities. Climate should be very good and stay that way. Sustainability should be ensured and no longer be in question due to potential job losses, limited income and country revenues, lower education and health, under developed natural resources and changing national and international economics.

c. What has to change externally and internally to achieve your country's thriving future? What has to change externally (outside your country) and internally (within your country) to progress from your country's current status to achieve your desired surviving and thriving status?[101] In Step 1, you identified what positively and negatively impacts or is likely to impact your country. Update those, including any changes to your future country.

Given those, what has to change externally and internally to achieve a surviving and thriving future? Use Table 6.4 to describe all that has to change for the following. To achieve performing well? Being well-off (financially)? Being well nourished (food and drink)? Being well housed? Being well protected (exposures, crime)? Being well educated? Being physically and mentally well? Personally growing/developing well? Living within good habitat? Not being vulnerable? Producing personal and public goods? Living within a stable, positive climate? Being sustained?

Good changes improve and/or sustain surviving and thriving. Bad changes prevent and/or limit surviving and thriving.

---

[101] Uses the Toolkit's "Performance Improvement Model" and "via Model".

Example. *Internally, country should have a better, more collaborative government with a collaborative partnership with the private sector committed to perform better than countries on its continent. Internally, more business, agriculture and light industry should stay in country with more employment for blue collar and agriculture workers. Externally, more business, agriculture and light industry should move into country with more employment for blue collar and agriculture workers. Internally, government and private sector should collaborate and ensure financial condition is stable and sufficient to support needed public services; employers should be committed to blue collar workers and not moving their jobs out of country; country and employers should have expanded job training. Internally, food and drink producers, wholesalers and retailers should ensure food and drink is available and 10% below average cost for its continent; country and food industry should ensure sufficient sources of healthy food; country should ensure low income people have resources for healthy food and for food generally; country should ensure sufficient resources to feed very poor. Internally, banks and housing industry should ensure housing for upper and middle income people is available and affordable; government, bankers and builders should ensure housing for low and lower middle income people is available, affordable and adequate. Internally, country and its local police force, state police force and country military should ensure it is best of its continent, including adequate resourcing. Internally, country and its education people should ensure education availability and quality is best on its continent and should ensure country has 10 percent more college educated than its continent. Internally, country and its private and public health services should ensure physical and mental health is best compared to other countries on its continent; country and employers should ensure workers have substantially less occupationally related illness; country and private and public health services should ensure services are best on its continent; country should ensure every person without private insurance has financial access to needed health services; country and its people should ensure each person is improving personal and family health. Internally, country and its people should ensure personal growth and development is better than countries on its continent; country and employers should ensure substantially more job training. Internally, country and its people should ensure habitat* *has the best mix of pleasant and harsh and healthy and unhealthy on its continent. Externally, country and its neighboring countries should jointly ensure habitat has the best mix of pleasant and harsh and healthy and unhealthy. Internally, while country has had much vulnerability, country and its people should ensure it is no longer vulnerable on job loss, limited income, lack of affordable and healthy foods, lack of affordable and adequate housing for poorer people, inadequate private and public health services, and low country revenues. Internally and compared to its continent, country and its people should ensure it produces an optimal range of products and services for its continent, a substantially higher percentage of high quality manufactured products, the best percentage of healthy and well educated children on its continent and a wide range of recreational activities. Externally, country should join with international community to ensure climate is very good and stays that way. Internally, country and its people should ensure sustainability and that there is no longer job losses, limited income and country revenues, lower education and health, under developed natural resources and no negative impact from changing national and international economics. Externally, country should join with neighboring countries and international community to ensure no negative impact from changing national and international economics.*

d. What actions by your country are needed to achieve its thriving future? What internal actions (by you and your country) and external actions (by others) are needed to bring about the needed external and internal changes (identified in "c") that improve your country's current status enough to achieve the desired surviving and thriving status?[102] [Figure 6.1] [103]

---

[102] Uses the Toolkit's "Strategy Model".
[103] An action is defined as "who will do what to/with whom, where, when, and with what result."

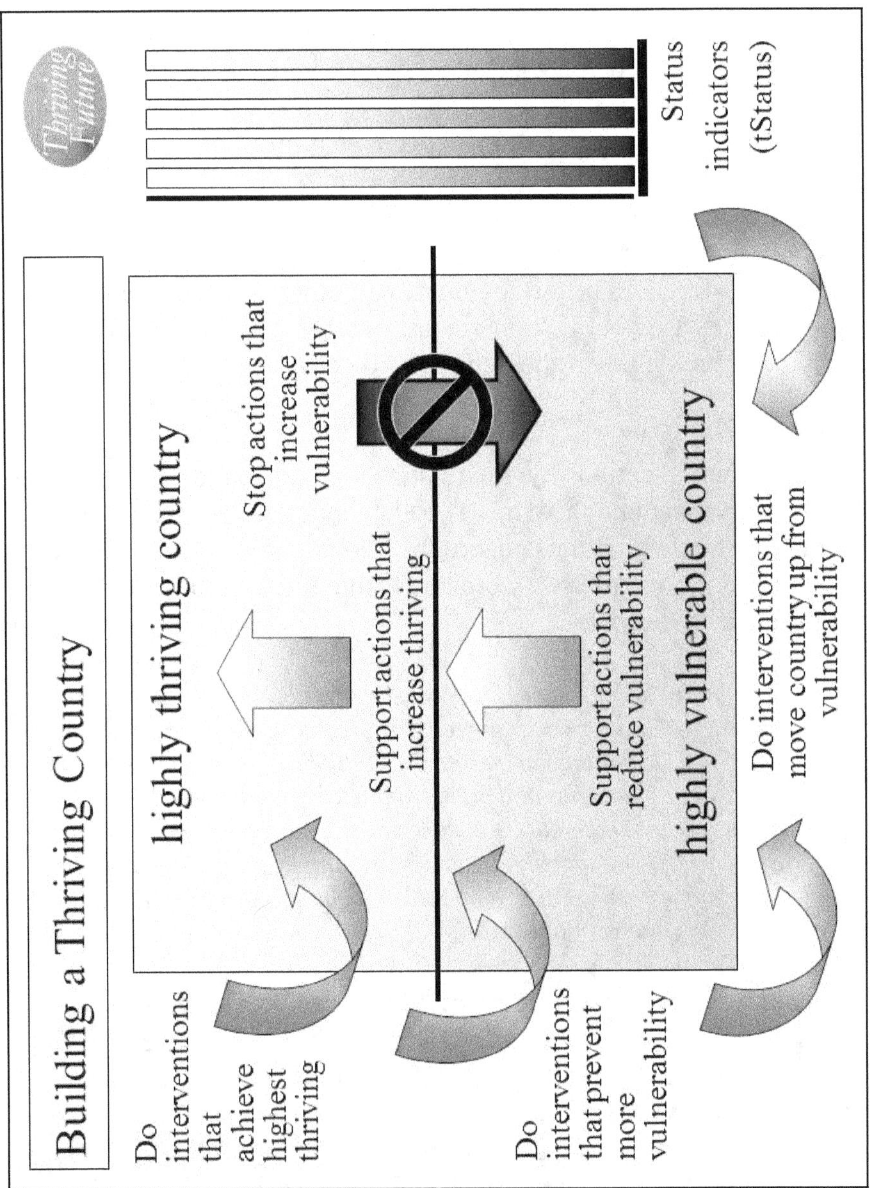

Figure 6.1. Building a Thriving Country.

External actions by others. There are very important <u>external</u> actions that are needed to support the ***Thrive!*** strategy. You already identified what has to change externally to achieve your country's surviving and thriving future. What external actions by others will bring about the needed changes?

Use Table 6.4 to describe all the external actions to be taken.

Identify external actions by others that support <u>good</u> changes that will help improve and/or sustain surviving and thriving. If good changes are likely to occur, together with others support them. If good changes are not likely to occur, together with others support them and develop other good changes to compensate. [Use Table 6.4]

Identify external actions by others that stop <u>bad</u> changes that prevent or limit surviving and thriving. If bad changes are not likely to occur, together with others ensure they do not. If bad changes are likely to occur, together with others change them, stop them or avoid/reduce their impact.

> *Example. More business, agriculture and light industry move into country with more employment for blue collar and agriculture workers. Neighboring countries jointly help ensure habitat has the best mix of pleasant and harsh and healthy and unhealthy. International community ensures climate is very good and stays that way. Neighboring countries and international community help ensure no negative impact from changing national and international economics.*

Internal actions by your country. There are very important <u>internal</u> actions by you and your country that support the *Thrive!* strategy. Individual country members and your country as a whole should support your country's strategy to ensure your country and each country member are performing well. Being well-off (financially). Being well nourished (food and drink). Being well housed. Being well protected (exposures, crime). Being well educated. Being physically and mentally well. Personally growing/developing well. Living within good habitat. Not being vulnerable. Producing personal and public goods. Living within a stable, positive climate. Being sustained.

Use Table 6.4 to describe all the internal actions to be taken.

Identify internal actions by your country that support <u>good</u> changes that will help improve and/or sustain surviving and thriving. If good changes are likely to occur, support them. If good changes are not likely to occur, support them and develop other good changes to compensate.

Identify internal actions by your country that stop <u>bad</u> changes that prevent or limit surviving and thriving. If bad changes are not likely to occur, ensure they do not. If bad changes are likely to occur, change them, stop them or avoid/reduce their impact.

> ***Example.*** *Country builds and sustains a better, more collaborative government with a collaborative partnership with the private sector committed to perform better than countries on its continent. With small incentives added by government, more business, agriculture and light industry stay in country with more employment for blue collar and agriculture workers. With small incentives added by government, more business, agriculture and light industry move into country with more employment for blue collar and agriculture workers. Government and private sector collaborate and ensure financial condition is stable and sufficient to support needed public services; employers commit to blue collar workers and to not moving their jobs out of country; country and employers expand job training. Food and drink producers, wholesalers and retailers ensure food and drink is available and 10% below average cost for its continent; country and food industry ensure sufficient sources of healthy food; country helps ensure low income people have resources for healthy food and for food generally; country ensures sufficient resources to feed very poor. Banks and housing industry ensure housing for upper and middle income people is available and affordable; government, bankers and builders ensure housing for low and lower middle income people is available, affordable and adequate. Country and its local police force, state police force and country military ensure it is best of its continent, including adequate resourcing. Country and its education people ensure education availability and quality is best on its continent and ensure country has 10 percent more college educated than its continent. Country and its private and*

public health services ensure physical and mental health is best compared to other countries on its continent; country and employers ensure workers have substantially less occupationally related illness; country and private and public health services ensure services are best on its continent; country ensures every person without private insurance has financial access to needed health services; country and its people ensure each person is improving personal and family health. Country and its people ensure personal growth and development is better than countries on its continent; country and employers ensure substantially more job training. Country and its people ensure habitat has the best mix of pleasant and harsh and healthy and unhealthy on its continent. Country joins with its neighboring countries to jointly ensure habitat has the best mix of pleasant and harsh and healthy and unhealthy. While country has had much vulnerability, country and its people ensure it is no longer vulnerable on job loss, limited income, lack of affordable and healthy foods, lack of affordable and adequate housing for poorer people, inadequate private and public health services, and low country revenues. Compared to its continent, country and its people ensure it produces an optimal range of products and services for its continent, a substantially higher percentage of high quality manufactured products, the best percentage of healthy and well educated children on its continent and a wide range of recreational activities. Country joins with international community to ensure climate is very good and stays that way. Country and its people ensure sustainability and that there is no longer job losses, limited income and country revenues, lower education and health, under developed natural resources and negative impact from changing national and international economics. Country joins with neighboring countries and international community to ensure no negative impact from changing national and international economics.

Overall *Thrive!* strategy and actions. Your country's overall *Thrive!* strategy and actions need to be documented and agreed to by your country. This will be your country's ***Thrive!* Strategy and Action Plan**. Different members of your country will take on different responsibilities. For each action, designate who of your country will do what to/with whom, where, when, and with what result. [See example below.] Use Table 6.4 to document these actions and responsibilities. [See example table below.] Make sure your country has all the actions that are needed to build, achieve and sustain a surviving and thriving country.

As the strategy is executed, your country's strategy, actions and results should be updated in your *Thrive!* **Strategy and Action Plan**.

Periodically, you and your country should do an evaluation - assessing your country's strategies/actions near and long term impact on near and long term surviving and thriving. When a) your country's strategies and actions are not building and sustaining a thriving future and/or b) there are changes in the external world and in your country, you and your country should adjust your overall *Thrive!* strategy and actions.

The key is to successfully execute your country's *Thrive!* **Strategy and Action Plan** and to build a near and long term surviving and thriving future.[104] Each and all must successfully carry out the assigned action. That is, each/all must successfully do what is required to/with whoever is required, where required, when required, and with what needed/desired result. A *Thrive!* **Strategy and**

---

[104] At this point, you and your country should have enough good information to execute you and your country's *Thrive!* Strategy and Action Plan. If you and your country want to develop strategy and actions further, you and your country may want to use more of the tools and models already mentioned and the *Thrive!* **Next Generation Toolkit.** This is encouraged and may be necessary for very large, complex countries.

As stated earlier, this "how-to", by design, is simple but powerful. It is relatively basic providing the framework for doing "your country" strategy. The optimal approach is to use this how-to framework <u>and</u> use the more extensive strategy, models and tools in a) the *Thrive!* **Next Generation Toolkit** contained in the Appendix and b) *Thrive!* **- Building a Thriving Future** available via www.Amazon.com or free download from www.ThrivingFuture.org.

For example, if you want to develop and assess more in-depth strategies and actions, you may want to use the Behavioral Effectiveness Model (BEM). BEM helps assess a) how your country's and individual country member's motivation and ability will impact future behavior and b) how actions by people outside your country will impact your country's and individual country member's future motivation, ability and behavior. A description of BEM and how to use it is included in the Appendix.

Thrive!

Action Plan is only as good as its successful execution and successful achievement of the desired outcome - a surviving and thriving future.

Example of a country surviving and somewhat thriving. [Who will do what to/with whom, where, when, and with what result?] See Example **Thrive! Strategy and Action Plan** *in list and table below. With these actions, country would be surviving and doing better but would not yet have achieved full thriving.*

External Actions: Twenty-five percent more business, agriculture and light industry move into country with more employment for blue collar and agriculture workers within 2 years. Neighboring countries agree within 1 year and jointly help ensure habitat has the best mix of pleasant and harsh and healthy and unhealthy with phased plan over next 5 years. International community comes to agreement within 2 years and ensures climate is very good and stays that way for centuries to come. Neighboring countries and international community come to agreement within 1 year and help ensure no negative impact from changing national and international economics for at least next 10 years.

Internal Actions: Within 1 year, country builds and sustains a better, more collaborative government with a collaborative partnership with the private sector committed to perform better than countries on its continent. With small incentives added by government, 95% of business, agriculture and light industry stay in country with more employment for blue collar and agriculture workers. With small incentives added by government, 25 percent more business, agriculture and light industry move into country within 2 years with more employment for blue collar and agriculture workers. Government and private sector collaborate and come to agreement this year and ensure financial condition is stable and sufficient to support needed public services for at least next 5 years; employers commit to blue collar workers and not moving their jobs out of country for at least next 5 years; country and employers expand job training by 50% within 1 year with 50/50 funding. Food and drink producers, wholesalers and retailers ensure food and drink is available and 10% below average cost for its continent for at least next 3 years; country and food industry agree to and ensure sufficient sources of healthy food for at least next 3 years; country comes to agreement, provides funding and helps ensure low income people have resources for healthy food and for food generally for at least next 5 years; country comes to agreement, provides funding and ensures sufficient resources to feed very poor for at least next 5 years. Banks and housing industry continue to ensure housing for upper and middle income people is available and affordable for at least next 5 years; government, bankers and builders come to agreement, government provides incentive funding and all ensure housing for low and lower middle income people is available, affordable and adequate within 5 years. Country and its local police force, state police force and country military ensure it is best of its continent, including strong management and adequate resourcing for at least next 5 years. Country and its education people come to agreement within 1 year; government provides funding; and all ensure education availability and quality is best on its continent and ensure country has 10 percent more college educated than its continent for at least next 5 years. Country and its private and public health services agree and within 2 years ensure physical and mental health is best compared to other countries on its continent; country and employers agree within 1 year and ensure workers have substantially less occupationally related illness; country and private and public health services agree within 1 year and ensure services are best on its continent within 2 years; country agrees within 1 year, provides funding for at least 5 years, and ensures every person without private insurance has financial access to needed health services for at least the next 5 years; country and its people begin collaborative effort this year and ensure each person is improving personal and family health starting within 2 years. Country and its people begin collaborative effort this year and ensure personal growth and development is better than countries on its continent within 2 years; country and employers agree within 1 year and agree to 50/50 funding ensure substantially more job training within 1 year. Country and its people develop collaborative effort and strategy and, within 5 years, ensure habitat has the best mix of pleasant and harsh and healthy and unhealthy on its continent. Starting immediately, country joins with neighboring countries, agree within 1 year, and jointly help ensure habitat has the best mix of pleasant and harsh and healthy and unhealthy with phased plan over next 5 years. While country has had much vulnerability, country and its people collaborate, develop strategy and, within 1 year start to ensure it is no longer vulnerable on job loss, limited income, lack of affordable and healthy foods, lack of affordable and adequate housing for poorer people, inadequate private and public health services, and low country revenues. Within 5 years and compared to its continent, country and its people work together to ensure it produces an optimal range of products and services for its continent, a substantially higher percentage of high quality manufactured products, the best percentage of healthy and well educated children on its continent and a wide range of recreational activities. Starting immediately, country joins with international community, comes to agreement within 2 years and ensures climate is very good and stays that way for centuries to come.   Country and its people collaborate, develop strategy and, within 1 year work to ensure sustainability and that there is no longer job losses, limited income and country revenues, lower education and health, under developed natural resources and negative impact from changing national and international economics for at least next 10 years.   Starting immediately, country joins with neighboring countries and international community, comes to agreement within 1 year and helps ensure no negative impact from changing national and international economics for at least the next 10 years.

But, we want a <u>thriving</u> future for you and your country. To build, achieve and sustain a surviving <u>and</u> thriving future, the ***Thrive!* Strategy and Action Plan** should be more like the following example:

Example of you and your country surviving and thriving. *[Who will do what to/with whom, where, when, and with what result?] Starting immediately for you and your country, people, business/industry, private organizations (local, country), governments (local, country) and international organizations build, achieve, and sustain a surviving and thriving future for you and your country, including:*

- Performing well. *Starting immediately for you and your country, people, business/industry, private organizations (local, country), governments (local, country) and international organizations act to ensure, within the next 20 years, a) all (who are able and not appropriately retired) can work and earn a living income sufficient to survive and thrive and b) all have sufficient resources for and are living, recreating, learning so that they are surviving and thriving to maximum extent feasible.*

- Being well-off (financially). *Starting immediately for you and your country, people, business/industry, private organizations (local, country), governments (local, country) and international organizations act to ensure, within the next 20 years, a) all have sufficient income/resources to survive and thrive and b) all governments have sufficient resources to provide needed (supporting surviving) and desired (supporting thriving) public programs and policies.*

- Being well nourished (food and drink). *Starting immediately for you and your country, people, business/industry, private organizations (local, country), governments (local, country) and international organizations act to ensure, within the next 20 years, that all have access to, be able to afford and consume healthy foods enough to survive and thrive.*

- Being well housed. *Starting immediately for you and your country, people, business/industry, private organizations (local, country), governments (local, country) and international organizations act to ensure, within the next 20 years, all have access to, be able to afford and live in adequate and preferably high performing housing that supports surviving and thriving.*

- Being well protected (exposures, crime). *Starting immediately for you and your country, people, business/industry, private organizations (local, country), governments (local, country) and international organizations act to ensure, within the next 20 years, a) environmental exposures in home, workplace and elsewhere are minimized so as to not prevent surviving and thriving and b) crimes are minimized to the extent feasible in terms of frequency and impact so as to not prevent surviving and thriving.*

- Being well educated. *Starting immediately for you and your country, people, business/industry, private organizations (local, country), governments (local, country) and international organizations act to ensure, within the next 20 years, all people are educated to the full extent of their abilities, needs and desires and to support their surviving and thriving.*

- Being physically and mentally well. *Starting immediately for you and your country, people, business/industry, private organizations (local, country), governments (local, country) and international organizations act to ensure, within the next 20 years, a) all receive the optimal health support to ensure, within the next 20 years, surviving and thriving and b) physical and mental health is optimized to best ensure surviving and thriving.*

Thrive!

- Personally growing/developing well. *Starting immediately for you and your country, people, business/industry, private organizations (local, country), governments (local, country) and international organizations act to ensure, within the next 20 years, all are personally growing and developing to best ensure surviving and thriving.*
- Living within good habitat. *Starting immediately for you and your country, people, business/industry, private organizations (local, country), governments (local, country) and international organizations act to ensure, within the next 20 years, a) all have access to habitat that best supports their surviving and thriving and b) your country has the optimal mix, quantity and quality of habitat to best support its inhabitants' surviving and thriving.*
- Not being vulnerable. *Starting immediately for you and your country, people, business/industry, private organizations (local, country), governments (local, country) and international organizations act to ensure, within the next 20 years, your country and all of its people, if vulnerable, are vulnerable only to the minimum extent feasible.*
- Producing personal and public goods. *Starting immediately for you and your country, people, business/industry, private organizations (local, country), governments (local, country) and international organizations act to ensure, within the next 20 years, your country produces personal and public goods (including personal income/resources, housing, food and drink, energy, education, health, protection, personal growth and development, and habitat) so as to support surviving and thriving for all persons and for our world overall.*
- Living within a stable, positive climate. *Starting immediately for you and your country, people, business/industry, private organizations (local, country), governments (local, country) and international organizations act to ensure, within the next 10 years, all behave so as to avoid negative impacts and support positive impacts so as to help ensure a stable, positive climate.*
- Being sustained. *Starting immediately for you and your country, people, business/industry, private organizations (local, country), governments (local, country) and international organizations act to ensure, within the next 5 years, all behave so as to ensure the sustainability of your country <u>and</u> its people.*

***Thrive!* Strategy and Action Plan** (Example of surviving and somewhat thriving).

Thriving and Surviving	How well (surviving/ thriving) should your country be in near/long term future?	External/internal changes needed to achieve surviving and thriving future	Actions by your country and others - Who will do what to/with whom, where, when, and with what result?
Performing (live/work/ play) well?	*Country should perform better than countries on its continent with close to continent's average mix of lifestyles for country of its size. Unemployment should be lower than its continent; mix of work should be similar to that of its continent but with a larger percentage of blue collar and of agricultural workers and light industry.*	**External**: *Externally, more business, agriculture and light industry should move into country with more employment for blue collar and agriculture workers.*	**External by others**: *Twenty-five percent more business, agriculture and light industry move into country with more employment for blue collar and agriculture workers within 2 years.* **Internal by your country**:
		Internal: *Internally, country should have a better, more collaborative government with a collaborative partnership with the private sector committed to perform better than countries on its continent. Internally, more business, agriculture and light industry should stay in country with more employment for blue collar and agriculture workers.*	**Internal by your country**: *Within 1 year, country builds and sustains a better, more collaborative government with a collaborative partnership with the private sector committed to perform better than countries on its continent. With small incentives added by government, 95% of business, agriculture and light industry stay in country with more employment for blue collar and agriculture workers. With small incentives added by government, 25 percent more business, agriculture and light industry move into country within 2 years with more employment for blue collar and agriculture workers.*
Well-off?	*Financial condition of country should*	**External**:	**External by others**: **Internal by your country**:

	percentage of blue collar workers who should not face potential moving of jobs out of country.	**Internal**: *Internally, government and private sector should collaborate and ensure financial condition is stable and sufficient to support needed public services; employers should be committed to blue collar workers and not moving their jobs out of country; country and employers should have expanded job training.*	**Internal by your country**: *Government and private sector collaborate and come to agreement this year and ensure financial condition is stable and sufficient to support needed public services for at least next 5 years; employers commit to blue collar workers and not moving their jobs out of country for at least next 5 years; country and employers expand job training by 50% within 1 year with 50/50 funding.*
Well nourished?	*Food and drink should be available and prices should be 10% below average for its continent; country should have sufficient sources of healthy food; low income people should have resources for healthy food and for food generally; country should have sufficient resources to feed very poor.*	**External**:	**External by others**:
			Internal by your country:
		Internal: *Internally, food and drink producers, wholesalers and retailers should ensure food and drink is available and 10% below average cost for its continent; country and food industry should ensure sufficient sources of healthy food; country should ensure low income people have resources for healthy food and for food generally; country should ensure sufficient resources to feed very poor.*	**Internal by your country**: *Food and drink producers, wholesalers and retailers ensure food and drink is available and 10% below average cost for its continent for at least next 3 years; country and food industry agree to and ensure sufficient sources of healthy food for at least next 3 years; country comes to agreement, provides funding and helps ensure low income people have resources for healthy food and for food generally for at least next 5 years; country comes to agreement, provides funding and ensures sufficient resources to feed very poor for at least next 5 years.*
Well housed	*Housing for upper and middle income*	**External**:	**External by others**:
			Internal by your country:

	and lower middle income people should be available, affordable and adequate.	**Internal**: *Internally, banks and housing industry should ensure housing for upper and middle income people is available and affordable; government, bankers and builders should ensure housing for low and lower middle income people is available, affordable and adequate.*	**Internal by your country**: *Banks and housing industry continue to ensure housing for upper and middle income people is available and affordable for at least next 5 years; government, bankers and builders come to agreement, government provides incentive funding and all ensure housing for low and lower middle income people is available, affordable and adequate within 5 years.*
Well protected?	*Country local police force, state police force and country military should be best for its continent.*	**External**:	**External by others**:
			Internal by your country:
		Internal: *Internally, country and its local police force, state police force and country military should ensure it is best of its continent, including adequate resourcing.*	**Internal by your country**: *Country and its local police force, state police force and country military ensure it is best of its continent, including strong management and adequate resourcing for at least next 5 years.*
Well educated?	*Education availability and quality should be best on its continent; country should have 10 percent more college educated than its continent.*	**External**:	**External by others**:
			Internal by your country:
		Internal: *Internally, country and its education people should ensure education availability and quality is best on its continent and should ensure country has 10 percent more college educated than its continent.*	**Internal by your country**: *Country and its education people come to agreement within 1 year; government provides funding; and all ensure education availability and quality is best on its continent and ensure country has 10 percent more college educated than its continent for at least next 5 years.*
Physically/ mentally well?	*Physical and mental health should be best*	**External**:	**External by others**:
			Internal by your country:

	substantially less occupationally related illness; private and public health services should be best on its continent.	**Internal**: *Internally, country and its private and public health services should ensure physical and mental health is best compared to other countries on its continent; country and employers should ensure workers have substantially less occupationally related illness; country and private and public health services should ensure services are best on its continent; country should ensure every person without private insurance has financial access to needed health services; country and its people should ensure each person is improving personal and family health.*	**Internal by your country**: *Country and its private and public health services agree and within 2 years ensure physical and mental health is best compared to other countries on its continent; country and employers agree within 1 year and ensure workers have substantially less occupationally related illness; country and private and public health services agree within 1 year and ensure services are best on its continent within 2 years; country agrees within 1 year, provides funding for at least 5 years, and ensures every person without private insurance has financial access to needed health services for at least the next 5 years; country and its people begin collaborative effort this year and ensure each person is improving personal and family health starting within 2 years.*
Growing/ developing well?	*Personal growth and development should be better than countries on its continent and have substantially more job training.*	**External**: **Internal**: *Internally, country and its people should ensure personal growth and development is better than countries on its continent; country and employers should ensure substantially more job training.*	**External by others**: **Internal by your country**: **Internal by your country**: *Country and its people begin collaborative effort this year and ensure personal growth and development is better than countries on its continent within 2 years; country and employers agree within 1 year and agree to 50/50 funding ensure substantially more job training within 1 year.*

Living in good habitat?	*Habitat should have the best mix of pleasant and harsh and healthy and unhealthy on its continent.*	**External**: *Externally, country and its neighboring countries should jointly ensure habitat has the best mix of pleasant and harsh and healthy and unhealthy.*	**External by others**: *Neighboring countries agree within 1 year and jointly help ensure habitat has the best mix of pleasant and harsh and healthy and unhealthy with phased plan over next 5 years.*
			Internal by your country: *Starting immediately, country joins with neighboring countries, agree within 1 year, and jointly help ensure habitat has the best mix of pleasant and harsh and healthy and unhealthy with phased plan over next 5 years.*
		Internal: *Internally, country and its people should ensure habitat has the best mix of pleasant and harsh and healthy and unhealthy on its continent.*	**Internal by your country**: *Country and its people develop collaborative effort and strategy and, within 5 years, ensure habitat has the best mix of pleasant and harsh and healthy and unhealthy on its continent.*
Not vulnerable?	*While country has had much vulnerability, it should no longer be vulnerable on job loss, limited income, lack of affordable and healthy foods, lack of affordable and adequate housing for poorer people, inadequate private and public health services, and low country revenues.*	**External**:	**External by others**:
			Internal by your country:
		Internal: *Internally, while country has had much vulnerability, country and its people should ensure it is no longer vulnerable on job loss, limited income, lack of affordable and healthy foods, lack of affordable and adequate housing for poorer people, inadequate private and public health services, and low country revenues.*	**Internal by your country**: *While country has had much vulnerability, country and its people collaborate, develop strategy and, within 1 year start to ensure it is no longer vulnerable on job loss, limited income, lack of affordable and healthy foods, lack of affordable and adequate housing for poorer people, inadequate private and public health services, and low country revenues.*
Producing personal/ public	*Compared to its continent, country should*	**External**:	**External by others**:
			Internal by your country:

		Internal / External	Internal / External by country / others
	products and services for its continent, a substantially higher percentage of high quality manufactured products, the best percentage of healthy and well educated children and a wide range of recreational activities.	**Internal**: *Internally and compared to its continent, country and its people should ensure it produces an optimal range of products and services for its continent, a substantially higher percentage of high quality manufactured products, the best percentage of healthy and well educated children and a wide range of recreational activities.*	**Internal by your country**: *Within 5 years and compared to its continent, country and its people work together to ensure it produces an optimal range of products and services for its continent, a substantially higher percentage of high quality manufactured products, the best percentage of healthy and well educated children on its continent and a wide range of recreational activities.*
Stable, positive climate?	*Climate should be very good and stay that way.*	**External**: *Externally, country should join with international community to ensure climate is very good and stays that way.*	**External by others**: *International community comes to agreement within 2 years and ensures climate is very good and stays that way for centuries to come.*
			Internal by your country: *Starting immediately, country joins with international community, comes to agreement within 2 years and ensures climate is very good and stays that way for centuries to come.*
		Internal:	**Internal by your country**:
Sustainable?	*Sustainability should be ensured and no longer be in question due to potential job losses, limited income and country revenues, lower education and health, under developed natural resources and changing national and international*	**External**: *Externally, country should join with neighboring countries and international community to ensure no negative impact from changing national and international economics.*	**External by others**: *Neighboring countries and international community come to agreement within 1 year and help ensure no negative impact from changing national and international economics for at least next 10 years.*
			Internal by your country: *Starting immediately, country joins with neighboring countries and international community, comes to agreement within 1 year and helps ensure no negative impact from changing national and international economics for at least the next 10 years.*

	economics.	**Internal**: *Internally, country and its people should ensure sustainability and that there is no longer job losses, limited income and country revenues, lower education and health, under developed natural resources and no negative impact from changing national and international economics.*	**Internal by your country**: *Country and its people collaborate, develop strategy and, within 1 year work to ensure sustainability and that there is no longer job losses, limited income and country revenues, lower education and health, under developed natural resources and negative impact from changing national and international economics for at least next 10 years.*

Table 6.4. *Thrive!* **Strategy and Action Plan.** How well (surviving/thriving) should your country be in near/long term future? What external/internal changes are needed to achieve your country's thriving future? To make this happen, what external/internal actions are needed?

Thrive!

Country Characteristics	What is your country today?
Geographic boundaries	
Gender make-up	
Age make-up	
Racial make-up	
Ethnic make-up	
Lifestyle	
Type of work	
Financial situation	
Food/drink	
Housing	
Protection	
Education	
Physical / mental health	
Personal growth / development	
Habitat	
Producing what	
Climate	
Sustainability	

Table 6.1. What is your country today?

Thrive!

Thriving and Surviving	How well (surviving/ thriving) is your country?	What positively/ negatively impacts its thriving/ surviving?	What is its near/ long term behavior as to thriving/ surviving?
Performing (live/work/play) well?			
Well-off?			
Well nourished?			
Well housed?			
Well protected?			
Well educated?			
Physically/ mentally well?			
Growing/ developing well?			
Living in good habitat?			
Not vulnerable?			
Producing personal/ public goods?			
Stable, positive climate?			
Sustainable?			

Table 6.2. How well (surviving/thriving) is your country? What positively/ negatively impacts it? What is its near/long term future behavior?

Country Characteristics	What is your desired and/or likely future country?
Type of work/how people live	
Financial situation	
Food/drink	
Housing	
Protection	
Education	
Physical / mental health	
Personal growth / development	
Habitat	
Producing what	
Climate	
Sustainability	

Table 6.3. What is your desired and/or likely future country?

Thriving and Surviving	How well (surviving/ thriving) should your country be in near/long term future?	External/internal changes needed to achieve surviving and thriving future	Actions by your country and others - Who will do what to/with whom, where, when, and with what result?
Performing (live/work/ play) well?		External:	External by others:
			Internal by your country:
		Internal:	Internal by your country:
Well-off?		External:	External by others:
			Internal by your country:
		Internal:	Internal by your country:
Well nourished?		External:	External by others:
			Internal by your country:
		Internal:	Internal by your country:
Well housed		External:	External by others:
			Internal by your country:
		Internal:	Internal by your country:
Well protected?		External:	External by others:
			Internal by your country:
		Internal:	Internal by your country:
Well educated?		External:	External by others:
			Internal by your country:
		Internal:	Internal by your country:
Physically/ mentally well?		External:	External by others:
			Internal by your country:
		Internal:	Internal by your country:

Growing/ developing well?		External:	External by others:
			Internal by your country:
		Internal:	Internal by your country:
Living in good habitat?		External:	External by others:
			Internal by your country:
		Internal:	Internal by your country:
Not vulnerable?		External:	External by others:
			Internal by your country:
		Internal:	Internal by your country:
Producing personal/ public goods?		External:	External by others:
			Internal by your country:
		Internal:	Internal by your country:
Stable, positive climate?		External:	External by others:
			Internal by your country:
		Internal:	Internal by your country:
Sustainable?		External:	External by others:
			Internal by your country:
		Internal:	Internal by your country:

Table 6.4. *Thrive!* **Strategy and Action Plan.** How well (surviving/thriving) should your country be in near/long term future? What external/internal changes are needed to achieve your country's thriving future? To make this happen, what external/internal actions are needed?

Chapter 7: How <u>our world</u> can thrive.

How to build, achieve and sustain a surviving and thriving future for our world. [105,106]

Why our world <u>can</u>.
Our world can have a surviving and thriving future. To get to that future, keep in mind that our world has a future already beginning. Whether that future appears bad or good, our world can do better. To build a better future, the *Thrive!* strategy and tools has been used successfully at the personal level and on larger scales (community, country). They can work for the world we all care about. As they have for others, this strategy and these tools can help our world build, achieve and sustain a surviving and thriving future.

Thrive!
Keep in mind that we are more capable than any time in human history. We can build a thriving future by effectively and collaboratively using all available knowledge and tools, including "next generation" *Thrive!* strategy and tools. Next generation *Thrive!* is different and better than anything in human history. It is <u>achieving</u> a thriving future at each level. It understands that <u>people's behavior</u>, including yours, makes (or breaks) a thriving future. It helps people, including you, achieve the behavior that in turn achieves a thriving future at each level and for all forever.

---

[105] In working through "how our world can thrive", the focus shifts from "you and family, friends, community and country" to "we" and "our world" in keeping with the all inclusive context. Also, in this context, the word "we" means essentially all of us, including future generations, joined together.

[106] We must keep in mind that "our world" is expanding as we explore and move beyond earth to other parts of our universe. For that reason, "a thriving future for all forever" reaches at least as far as we touch or ever hope to touch.

Why our world <u>must</u>.

Our world <u>must</u> have a surviving and thriving future. Our world <u>must</u> do better whether that future appears bad or good. Why? Even if we believe that our world has a good future, we are not fully thriving, are not likely to be fully thriving in the future, and are still facing uncertainties about the long term future. We want and need a surviving and thriving future because our world's future is endangered and because of our human need to survive and desire to thrive. What drives our world and all of us is our human need to survive and desire to thrive now and in a sustainable future. Further, because we (past and present) have broken parts of our world and endangered its future, we (present and future) must help fix what is broken and build a survivable and thriving future for our world.

Why we all must and can do it together.

To build this better future, we (our world's current and future people and leadership) should be partners in this endeavor from the beginning and through each step. Success is dependent on positive leadership from us - our world's people and leaders. How that leadership comes about is the subject of some debate. Some people argue for a leader driven approach where the leader creates the vision and motivation and the people join and/or follow. Some argue for bottom-up or self-organizing approaches where the people lead and the traditional leaders may or may not join and/or follow. Some argue for a collaborative approach where the traditional leaders and the people (also serving as leaders) jointly provide leadership, vision, motivation, strategy and successful execution. In general, the latter approach probably has the greater potential to create <u>and</u> sustain large, positive change and a surviving and thriving world.

For a world or global endeavor, international organizations (e.g. the United Nations, multi-country regional organizations) and country governments should be part of the leadership and be partners in building a surviving and thriving world. However, it is not sufficient for government-based international organizations and country governments to be the only leaders in this endeavor. Non-governmental international and national organizations need to be leaders. Private businesses need to be leaders. Individual people need to be leaders. To be successful, this needs to be a whole world (people and leaders) endeavor.

Key to success is the strong desire by all of us (our world's leaders and people) to move our world from its current vulnerabilities through and beyond surviving to a sustained thriving future.

How to build, achieve, and sustain a surviving and thriving future for our world.

To build a surviving and thriving future for our world, *Thrive!* can be helpful and is laid out in the following "how-to".[107,108]

The following "how-to", by design, is simple but powerful. It is a relatively basic how-to providing the framework if not necessarily all the details for doing "our world" strategy.

This "our world" how-to is adapted from the *Thrive!* **Next Generation Toolkit** contained in the Appendix. More is available in *Thrive!* **- Building a Thriving Future** - a manual providing greater depth on strategy and tools and available via www.Amazon.com or free download from www.ThrivingFuture.org. The optimal approach is to use the following how-to framework and also use the strategies, models and tools in the Appendix and in *Thrive!* **- Building a Thriving Future**.

---

[107] Note that for each step, an example is provided to give a sense of how to do that step. The example provides highlights but not the full working of a step.

[108] Note that using *Thrive!* for our world has some similarities to using it for your community or your country. Our world has some of the characteristics of a community and a country but is much, much larger in terms of land/water, people, and governments and is much, much more complex and diverse in terms of its people, its politics, its geography, its resources and its habitat.

Step 1.

Step 1. Current state of our world. The first major step for us is to understand the current state of our world.

a. What is our world? We first define and understand what our world is today.[109] Our world is defined by its geography, political boundaries, and population characteristics (including racial/ethnic, gender, economics, political view, similar mission, religion, labor, profession, business).

We need to understand our world's geographic boundaries and characteristics. Use Table 7.1 (end of chapter) to describe all of the following for our world.[110] Its gender, age, racial, ethnic make-up. Lifestyle. Type of work. Financial situation. Food and drink. Housing. Protection (crime, environmental hazards). Education. Physical and mental health. Personal growth and development. Habitat (living environment). Producing what. Climate. Sustainability.

Example.
- Gender, age, racial, ethnic make-up. Lifestyle. Type of work. *Our world has 7 billion people, about equal numbers of females and males, a population growth rate of 1.1%, a literacy rate of 84% and 197 million sq mi (57 million sq mi of land). Type of work is 6% agriculture, 31% industry and 63% services.*
- Financial situation. *Financial situation includes slowing growth in gross world product, very uneven per capita income and uneven growth, unemployment rate of 9% and growing, poverty being primary cause of hunger, and as many as 3.5 billion people living in poverty.*
- Food and drink. *Over 800 million do not eat enough to be healthy; 1/3 of child deaths are due to hunger; over 100 million children are underweight; world produces enough food to feed everyone; concerns are increasing about food safety; healthy food is not*

---

[109] Uses the Toolkit's "Systems Model (including Ideal Systems)".
[110] Free download of larger, fillable worksheets at www.ThrivingFuture.org

sufficiently affordable or available; and climate change may reduce food production.

- Housing. *Housing continues to be unavailable, unaffordable and inadequate for low and lower middle income people worldwide.*
- Protection (crime, environmental hazards). *Crimes total over 63 million; intentional homicides total around 500 million; police protection is getting more effective; and military spending is over $1.8 trillion (about 2.2% of gross domestic product) and some country militaries are growing and some shrinking. Protection against environmental hazards in workplace, homes and elsewhere remains inadequate.*
- Education. *Education has drop-out rates of 25%, out-of-school children of over 59 million, public expenditures of 5% of gross domestic product, and 30% of adults with college degree.*
- Physical and mental health. *Health has a life expectancy at birth of 70 years, infant mortality rate of 37, significant progress in reducing child deaths, 1/10 of adults have diabetes, decline in new HIV infections, 2.5 billion lack improved sanitation facilities, depression being leading disability cause, and medicines unaffordable for many.*
- Personal growth and development. *Personal growth and development occurs but often not at the level to survive and seldom at the level for thriving.*
- Habitat (living environment). *Habitat is partly reflected in housing adequacy/inadequacy; many ecosystems are under threat due to urbanization; development and harvesting depletes limited natural resources; parks and other recreational facilities are insufficient for growing population; and drinking water more available but inadequate in developing countries.*
- Producing what. *Producing wide range of products and services; producing sufficient amount of food; not producing a high enough percentage of educated people; and increasing stress on public services due to increased need and decreased resources.*
- Climate. *Climate is 2 polar climates, 2 rather narrow temperate zones and a wide equatorial band of tropical to subtropical climates and is warming with an extremely high probability most warming is due to human influence.*
- Sustainability. *Global sustainability is in question due to global warming, income inequality and inadequate incomes for many, unaffordability of food, using up non-renewable resources, not adequately conserving energy, over-developing available land,*

many people not surviving that should, and most people not thriving that could.

b. How well is our world? How well (surviving and thriving) is our world?[111] How well is our world in terms of performing well? Being well-off (financially)? Being well nourished (food and drink)? Being well housed? Being well protected (exposures, crime)? Being well educated? Being physically and mentally well? Personally growing/developing well? Living within good habitat? Not being vulnerable? Producing personal and public goods? Living within a stable, positive climate? Being sustained?

Answering "yes" indicates current surviving and thriving. Though the "yes" answers are good, there is still future work to make sure this continues. "No" answers are bad and mean there is current and future work to be done.

For our world, there are relatively few "yes" answers when it comes to thriving and very many no answers when it comes to surviving.

So how well is our world?
- Our world and our people are not performing (living, working, recreating, learning) well enough to survive and thrive. *For example, our world has a population problem with 7 billion people, too many already for earth's capacity and a too high growth rate of 1.1%. Type of work varies widely to fit country and global needs.*
- Our world and our people are not well-off (financially) enough to survive and thrive. *For example, financial situation is not good and includes slowing growth in gross world product, very uneven per capita income and uneven growth, unemployment rate of 9% and growing, poverty being primary cause of hunger, and as many as 3.5 billion people living in poverty.*
- Our world and our people are not well nourished (food and drink) enough to survive and thrive. *For example, food and drink is not good enough with over 800 million who do not eat enough to be healthy, 1/3 of child deaths due to hunger, over 100 million children underweight, there are increasing concerns about food*

---

[111] Uses the Toolkit's "Status Model".

safety, healthy food not being sufficiently affordable or available, and climate change potentially reducing food production.

- Our world and our people are not well housed enough to survive and thrive. *For example, housing continues to be unavailable, unaffordable and inadequate for low and lower middle income people worldwide.*

- Our world and our people are not well protected (exposures, crime) enough to survive and thrive. *For example, crimes total of over 63 million; intentional homicides total around 500 million; police protection is getting more effective; and large amount of resources are going to military spending of over \$1.8 trillion (about 2.2% of gross domestic product) with some country militaries growing and some shrinking. Protection against environmental hazards in workplace, homes and elsewhere remains inadequate.*

- Our world and our people are not well educated enough to survive and thrive. *For example, education has drop-out rates of 25%, out-of-school children of over 59 million, public expenditures (5% of gross domestic product) probably too low with some countries spending much less, and a too low percentage of 30% of adults with college degree.*

- Our world and our people are not physically and mentally well enough to survive and thrive. *For example, health has too high infant mortality rate of 37, significant progress in reducing child deaths, too high rate of 1 in 10 adults having diabetes, positive decline in new HIV infections, too many people (2.5 billion) lacking improved sanitation facilities, preventable/treatable depression being inadequately prevented/treated making it the leading disability cause, and medicines being unaffordable for many.*

- Our world and our people are not personally growing/developing well enough to survive and thrive. *For example, personal growth and development occurs but often not at the level to survive (for example, too little or poor job training/re-training) and seldom at the level for thriving.*

- Our world is not good enough habitat to survive and thrive. *For example, habitat is problematic in terms of housing inadequacy; many ecosystems are under threat due to urbanization, development; harvesting depletes limited natural resources; parks and other recreational facilities are insufficient for growing population; and drinking water is more available than past but inadequate in developing countries.*

- Our world and our people are too vulnerable. *For example, vulnerability too high in terms of frequency, level, duration and impact.*
- Our world and our people are not producing personal and public goods enough to survive and thrive. *For example, producing wide range of products and services is good; producing sufficient amount of food is good; food not being affordable or healthy is bad; not producing a high enough percentage of educated people is bad; and increasing stress on public services due to increased need and decreased resources is bad.*
- Our world does not have a stable, positive climate. *For example, climate consists of wide variance to meet personal preferences; climate changes and warming create living and agriculture problems.*
- Our world and our people are not being sustained. *For example, global sustainability is a problem due to global warming, income inequality and inadequate incomes for many, unaffordability of food, using up non-renewable resources, not adequately conserving energy, over-developing available land, many people not surviving that should, and most people not thriving that could.*

Based on these over arching measures, use Table 7.2 (end of chapter) to more specifically describe how well is our world.[112]

c. What positively or negatively impacts our world? What positively or negatively impacts or is likely to impact our world's surviving and thriving? Use Table 7.2 to describe all of the following impacts (positive and negative; current and future). What impacts our world's performing well? Being well-off (financially)? Being well nourished (food and drink)? Being well housed? Being well protected (exposures, crime)? Being well educated? Being physically and mentally well? Personally growing/developing well? Living within good habitat? Not being vulnerable? Producing personal and public goods? Living within a stable, positive climate? Being sustained?

Positive impacts improve and/or sustain surviving and thriving. If they will continue, we probably can focus on other things. If they

---

[112] Free download of larger, fillable worksheets at www.ThrivingFuture.org

may or may not continue, our action is needed to make them continue and/or to develop other things to compensate. Bad impacts prevent or limit surviving and thriving. If they will not continue, we probably can focus on other things. If they may or may not continue, our action is needed to stop them or to avoid or minimize their impact.

Example.

- Performing well? *A negative impact is due to too many people already for earth's capacity and a too high growth rate of 1.1% is a negative impact. A positive impact is due to the type of work varies widely to fit country and global needs.*
- Being well-off (financially)? *A negative impact on the financial situation comes from slowing growth in gross world product, very uneven per capita income and uneven growth, unemployment rate of 9% and growing, poverty being primary cause of hunger, and as many as 3.5 billion people living in poverty.*
- Being well nourished (food and drink)? *A negative impact is due to over 800 million who do not eat enough to be healthy, 1/3 of child deaths due to hunger, over 100 million children underweight, increasing concerns about food safety, healthy food not being sufficiently affordable or available, and climate change potentially reducing food production.*
- Being well housed? *A negative impact is due to it continuing to be unavailable, unaffordable and inadequate for low and lower middle income people worldwide.*
- Being well protected (exposures, crime)? *Crimes have a negative impact with a total of over 63 million crimes and intentional homicides totaling around 500 million. Police protection can have a negative or positive impact depending on the circumstances as it gets more effective; and military can have a negative or positive impact as large amount of resources are going to military spending of over $1.8 trillion (about 2.2% of gross domestic product) with some country militaries growing and some shrinking. A negative impact comes when protection against environmental hazards in workplace, homes and elsewhere remains inadequate.*
- Being well educated? *A negative impact is due to drop-out rates of 25%, out-of-school children of over 59 million, public expenditures (5% of gross domestic product) probably too low*

with some countries spending much less, and a too low percentage of 30% of adults with college degree.

- Being physically and mentally well? *A negative impact is due to too high infant mortality rate of 37, too many people (2.5 billion) lacking improved sanitation facilities, too high rate of 1 in 10 adults having diabetes, preventable/treatable depression being inadequately prevented/treated making it the leading disability cause, and medicines being unaffordable for many. A positive impact on health is due to significant progress in reducing child death, and positive decline in new HIV infections.*

- Personally growing/developing well? *Personal growth and development occurs which has a positive impact but the negative impact comes when it is not at the level to survive (for example, too little or poor job training/re-training) and seldom at the level for thriving.*

- Living within good habitat? *A negative impact comes when housing is inadequate; many ecosystems are under threat due to urbanization, development; harvesting depletes limited natural resources; parks and other recreational facilities are insufficient for growing population; and drinking water is more available (somewhat positive) than past but inadequate in developing countries.*

- Producing personal and public goods? *A positive impact comes from producing wide range of products and services and producing sufficient amount of food. A negative impact comes from food not being affordable or healthy, not producing a high enough percentage of educated people, and increasing stress on public services due to increased need and decreased resources is bad.*

- Living within a stable, positive climate? *A positive impact comes when climate consists of wide variance to meet personal preferences. A negative impact comes when climate changes and warming create living and agriculture problems.*

- Being sustained? *Global sustainability suffers a negative impact from global warming, income inequality and inadequate incomes for many, unaffordability of food, using up non-renewable resources, not adequately conserving energy, over-developing available land, many people not surviving that should, and most people not thriving that could.*

d. What is near and long term future behavior of our world?

How is our world (including international and country organizations, countries, business/industry, people) likely to behave in the near and long term future.[113] Use Table 7.2 to describe all of the following behaviors. How will our world behave with respect to performing well? Being well-off (financially)? Being well nourished (food and drink)? Being well housed? Being well protected (exposures, crime)? Being well educated? Being physically and mentally well? Personally growing/developing well? Living within good habitat? Not being vulnerable? Producing personal and public goods? Living within a stable, positive climate? Being sustained?

Example.

- Performing well? *Our world (including international and country organizations, countries, business/industry, people) will increase population beyond Earth's capacity. Our world will continue work that varies widely to fit country and global needs.*
- Being well-off (financially)? *Our world will behave in a way that continues very uneven per capita income and uneven growth, high unemployment rates, and high and growing poverty (causing hunger and other problems).*
- Being well nourished (food and drink)? *Our world will continue providing food and drink that results in too many who do not eat enough to be healthy, too many child deaths due to hunger, too many children underweight, increasing concerns about food safety, healthy food not being sufficiently affordable or available, and climate change potentially reducing food production.*
- Being well housed? *Our world will continue housing that is unavailable, unaffordable and inadequate for low and lower middle income people worldwide.*
- Being well protected (exposures, crime)? *Our world will continue to commit too many crimes (including intentional homicides), to provide increasingly effective police protection, and to provide large and powerful militaries. Our world will continue to provide inadequate protection against environmental hazards in workplace, homes and elsewhere.*
- Being well educated? *Our world will continue inadequate education (in part due to too low public expenditures and not*

---

[113] Uses the Toolkit's "Population Model".

sufficiently effective schools) resulting in too high drop-out rates, too many out-of-school children, and a too low percentage of adults with college degree.

- Being physically and mentally well? *Our world will continue inadequate health support resulting in too high infant mortality rate, too high rate of adults having diabetes, too many people lacking improved sanitation facilities, too much preventable/treatable depression being inadequately prevented/treated, and medicines being unaffordable for many.*

- Personally growing/developing well? *Our world will continue personal growth and development but often not at the level for surviving (for example, too little or poor job training/re-training) and seldom at the level for thriving.*

- Living within good habitat? *Our world will continue to not ensure good habitat, including housing inadequacy, many ecosystems threatened due to urbanization, over development, depletion of limited natural resources, insufficient parks and other recreational facilities for growing population, and inadequate drinking water in developing and developed countries.*

- Producing personal and public goods? *Our world will continue producing wide range of products and services, producing sufficient amount of food, not ensuring affordable and healthy food, not producing a high enough percentage of educated people, and increasing stress on public services due to increased need and decreased resources.*

- Living within a stable, positive climate? *Our world will continue to produce climate changes and warming that creates living and agriculture problems.*

- Being sustained? *Our world will continue not ensuring global sustainability that is threatened by global warming, income inequality and inadequate incomes for many, unaffordability of food, using up non-renewable resources, not adequately conserving energy, over-developing available land, too many people not surviving that should, and most people not thriving that could.*

e. More on our world's future and behavior? At this point, we have a basic baseline with which to measure progress for our world. We may have enough good information to move to Step 2 and to develop strategy for our world. But using more of the tools and models already mentioned would greatly improve our chances of success and our outcome in terms of surviving and thriving.

Using the full *Thrive!* **Next Generation Toolkit** (Appendix) is very highly recommended because it includes more strategy, policy and tools for creating and sustaining large, positive change and building a surviving and thriving future.[114] Using ***Thrive!* - Building a Thriving Future** is very highly recommended because it provides much greater depth on strategy and. It is available via www.Amazon.com or free download from www.ThrivingFuture.org.

Step 2.

Step 2. Strategy to achieve our world's surviving and thriving future. The next major step is to develop the strategy that will help us build and achieve a surviving and thriving future.

a. What will our world be in the future? What will be our likely future world?[115] Population characteristics. Type of work/how people live. Financial situation. Food and drink. Housing. Protection (crime, environmental hazards). Education. Physical and mental health. Personal growth and development. Habitat (living environment, neighboring communities, part of what state, country, continent).
Producing what. Climate. Sustainability.

If there are any changes to our world that are desired or likely, take them into account. Use Table 7.3 (end of chapter) to describe the likely future.[116]

---

[114] For example, if you want to develop and assess more in-depth strategies and actions, you may want to use the Behavioral Effectiveness Model (BEM). BEM helps assess how our world's and individual world member's motivation and ability will impact future behavior. A description of BEM and how to use it is included in the Appendix.

[115] Uses the Toolkit's "Systems Model (including Ideal Systems)".

[116] Free download of larger, fillable worksheets at www.ThrivingFuture.org

Example: *Unless we build, achieve, and sustain a surviving and thriving future for all forever, our world will be in trouble, including:*

- Population characteristics. *Our world will have too many people for Earth's carrying capacity and will have 197 million sq mi (57 million sq mi of land).*

- Type of work. *Mix of work will include agriculture, industry and services.*

- Financial situation. *Financial situation will include slowing growth in gross world product, very uneven per capita income and uneven growth, high unemployment rate and growing, poverty being primary cause of hunger, and too many people living in poverty.*

- Food and drink. *Too many will not eat enough to be healthy; too many child deaths will be due to hunger; too many children will be underweight; world may or may not produce enough food to feed everyone; concerns will increase about food safety; healthy food will not be sufficiently affordable or available; and climate change may reduce food production.*

- Housing. *Housing will continue to be unavailable, unaffordable and inadequate for low and lower middle income people worldwide.*

- Protection (crime, environmental hazards). *Crimes (including intentional homicides) will be too many; police protection will be more effective; and militaries will be relatively large. Protection against environmental hazards in workplace, in homes and elsewhere will remain inadequate.*

- Education. *Education will continue too high drop-out rates, too many out-of-school children, too low public expenditures, insufficiently effective schools, and too few adults with college degree or adequate job training.*

- Physical and mental health. *Health will continue to be problematic with too high infant mortality rate, too many adults with diabetes, too many lacking improved sanitation facilities, too much un-prevented and untreated depression, and unaffordable medicine for too many. Health will continue progress with lower child death rates, higher life expectancy and lower HIV morbidity and morality.*

- Personal growth and development. *Personal growth and development will continue but too often not at the level to survive and seldom at the level for thriving.*

- Habitat (living environment, neighboring communities, part of what state, country, continent). *Habitat will continue to be stressed due to housing inadequacy; many ecosystems threatened by urbanization, limited natural resources depleted by development and harvesting, parks and other recreational facilities insufficient for growing population, and inadequate drinking water inadequate developing and possibly developed countries.*
- Producing what. *Will continue producing wide range of products and services, producing sufficient amount of food, not producing a high enough percentage of educated people and increasing stress on public services due to increased need and decreased resources.*
- Climate. *Climate will continue to have 2 polar climates, 2 rather narrow temperate zones and a wide equatorial band of tropical to subtropical climates and will continue warming with an extremely high probability most warming is due to human influence.*
- Sustainability. *Global sustainability will remain in question due to global warming, income inequality and inadequate incomes for many, unaffordability of food, using up non-renewable resources, not adequately conserving energy, over-developing available land, too many people not surviving that should, and most people not thriving that could.*

b. How well should our world be in the near and long term future? How well should our world as a whole be in the future?[117] Overall, it should be <u>surviving and thriving</u>. The "*Thrive!* strategy" will help us accomplish that. From our world's view and to be surviving and thriving, indicate to what extent our world should be performing well. Be well-off (financially). Be well nourished (food and drink). Be well housed. Be well protected (exposures, crime). Be well educated. Be physically and mentally well. Be personally growing/developing well. Be living within good habitat. Not be vulnerable. Be producing personal and public goods. Be living within a stable, positive climate. Be sustained. Again, your country should be surviving and thriving.

To be surviving and thriving, our world and our people should, in general, be this well:

---

[117] Uses the Toolkit's "Status Model".

- Our world and our people should be performing (living, working, recreating, learning) well enough to survive and thrive. *For example. All live, work, recreate and learn well.*
- Our world and our people should be well-off (financially) enough to survive and thrive. *For example. A living income for all, eliminate poverty.*
- Our world and our people should be well nourished (food and drink) enough to survive and thrive. *For example. Affordable and healthy food for all.*
- Our world and our people should be well housed enough to survive and thrive. *For example. Affordable and adequate housing for all.*
- Our world and our people should be well protected (exposures, crime) enough to survive and thrive. *For example. All are protected from crime and environmental threats.*
- Our world and our people should be well educated enough to survive and thrive. *For example. All are well educated with all reaching optimum educational levels.*
- Our world and our people should be physically and mentally well enough to survive and thrive. *For example. All are physically and mentally healthy.*
- Our world and our people should be personally growing/developing well enough to survive and thrive. *For example. All are growing and developing to their full potential.*
- Our world should be good habitat enough to survive and thrive. *For example. All live in good, sustainable habitat including housing, community, and natural environment.*
- Our world and our people should not be vulnerable. *For example. Vulnerability is minimized in terms of frequency, level, duration and impact.*
- Our world and our people should be producing personal and public goods enough to survive and thrive. *For example. Should produce optimal personal income/resources, housing, food and drink, energy, education, health, protection, personal growth and development, and habitat.*

- Our world should have a stable, positive climate. *For example. Our climate should help support all human, animal and plant life forever.*
- Our world and our people should be sustained. *For example. Our people and our earth are sustained for all forever.*

Based on these over arching measures, use Table 7.4 (end of chapter) to describe more specifically how well our world should be.[118]

c. What has to change to achieve our world's thriving future?
What has to change to progress from our world's current status to achieve our desired surviving and thriving status?[119] In Step 1, we identified what positively and negatively impacts or is likely to impact our world. We include any changes to our future world.

Given those, what has to change to achieve a surviving and thriving future? To achieve performing well? Being well-off (financially)? Being well nourished (food and drink)? Being well housed? Being well protected (exposures, crime)? Being well educated? Being physically and mentally well? Personally growing/developing well? Living within good habitat? Not being vulnerable? Producing personal and public goods? Living within a stable, positive climate? Being sustained?

Good changes improve and/or sustain surviving and thriving. Bad changes prevent and/or limit surviving and thriving.

Given those, what has to change to achieve a surviving and thriving future? Good changes improve and/or sustain surviving and thriving. Bad changes prevent and/or limit surviving and thriving.

These should be the overarching changes:
- Our world and our people should be performing (living, working, recreating, learning) well enough to survive and thrive. *For example. All (who are able and not*

---

[118] Free download of larger, fillable worksheets at www.ThrivingFuture.org
[119] Uses the Toolkit's "Performance Improvement Model" and "via Model".

appropriately retired) should work and earn a living income sufficient to survive and thrive. All should be living, recreating, learning so that they are surviving and thriving to maximum extent feasible.

- Our world and our people should be well-off (financially) enough to survive and thrive. *For example. All should have sufficient income/resources to survive and thrive. All governments should have sufficient resources to provide needed (supporting surviving) and desired (supporting thriving) public programs and policies.*
- Our world and our people should be well nourished (food and drink) enough to survive and thrive. *For example. All people should have access to, be able to afford and consume healthy foods enough to survive and thrive.*
- Our world and our people should be well housed enough to survive and thrive. *For example. All should have access to, be able to afford and live in adequate and preferably high performing housing that supports surviving and thriving.*
- Our world and our people should be well protected (exposures, crime) enough to survive and thrive. *For example. All environmental exposures in home, workplace and elsewhere should be minimized so as to support surviving and thriving. Crimes should be minimized in terms of frequency and impact so as to not prevent surviving and thriving.*
- Our world and our people should be well educated enough to survive and thrive. *For example. All people should be educated to the full extent of their abilities, needs and desires and to support their surviving and thriving.*
- Our world and our people should be physically and mentally well enough to survive and thrive. *For example. All people should receive the optimal health support to ensure surviving and thriving. All people's physical and mental health should be optimized to best ensure surviving and thriving.*
- Our world and our people should be personally growing/developing well enough to survive and thrive. *For example. All people should be personally growing and developing to best ensure their surviving and thriving.*

- Our world should be good habitat enough to survive and thrive. *For example. All people should have access to habitat that best supports their surviving and thriving. Our world should have the optimal mix, quantity and quality of habitat to best support our world and its inhabitants' surviving and thriving.*
- Our world and our people should not be vulnerable. *For example. Our world and all of its people, if vulnerable, should be vulnerable only to the minimum extent feasible.*
- Our world and our people should be producing personal and public goods enough to survive and thrive. *For example. Our people should produce optimal personal and public goods (including personal income/resources, housing, food and drink, energy, education, health, protection, personal growth and development, and habitat) so as to support surviving and thriving for all persons and for our world overall.*
- Our world should have a stable, positive climate. *For example. All people should behave so as to avoid negative impacts and support positive impacts so as to help ensure a stable, positive climate.*
- Our world and our people should be sustained. *For example. All people should behave so as to ensure the sustainability of our world <u>and</u> its people.*

Based on these overarching changes, use Table 7.4 to describe more specifically what all that has to change to progress from our world's current status to achieve our desired surviving and thriving status.

d. What actions are needed to achieve its thriving future? What actions are needed to bring about the needed changes (identified in "c") that improve our world's current status enough to achieve the desired surviving and thriving status?[120] [Figure 7.1] [121]

As individual people, private business, interest groups/organizations, countries and international organizations, together we should support our jointly developed strategy and successfully take the actions to ensure our world and each person in our world are performing well. Being well-off (financially). Being well nourished (food and drink). Being well housed. Being well protected (exposures, crime). Being well educated. Being physically and mentally well. Personally growing/developing well. Living within good habitat. Not being vulnerable. Producing personal and public goods. Living within a stable, positive climate. Being sustained.

We identify actions that support <u>good</u> changes that will help improve and/or sustain surviving and thriving. If good changes are likely to occur, together we support them. If good changes are not likely to occur, together we support them and develop other good changes to compensate.

We identify actions that stop <u>bad</u> changes that prevent or limit surviving and thriving. If bad changes are not likely to occur, together we ensure they do not. If bad changes are likely to occur, together we change them, stop them or avoid/reduce their impact.

Use Table 7.4 to describe all the actions to be taken.

---

[120] Uses the Toolkit's "Strategy Model".
[121] An action is defined as "who will do what to/with whom, where, when, and with what result."

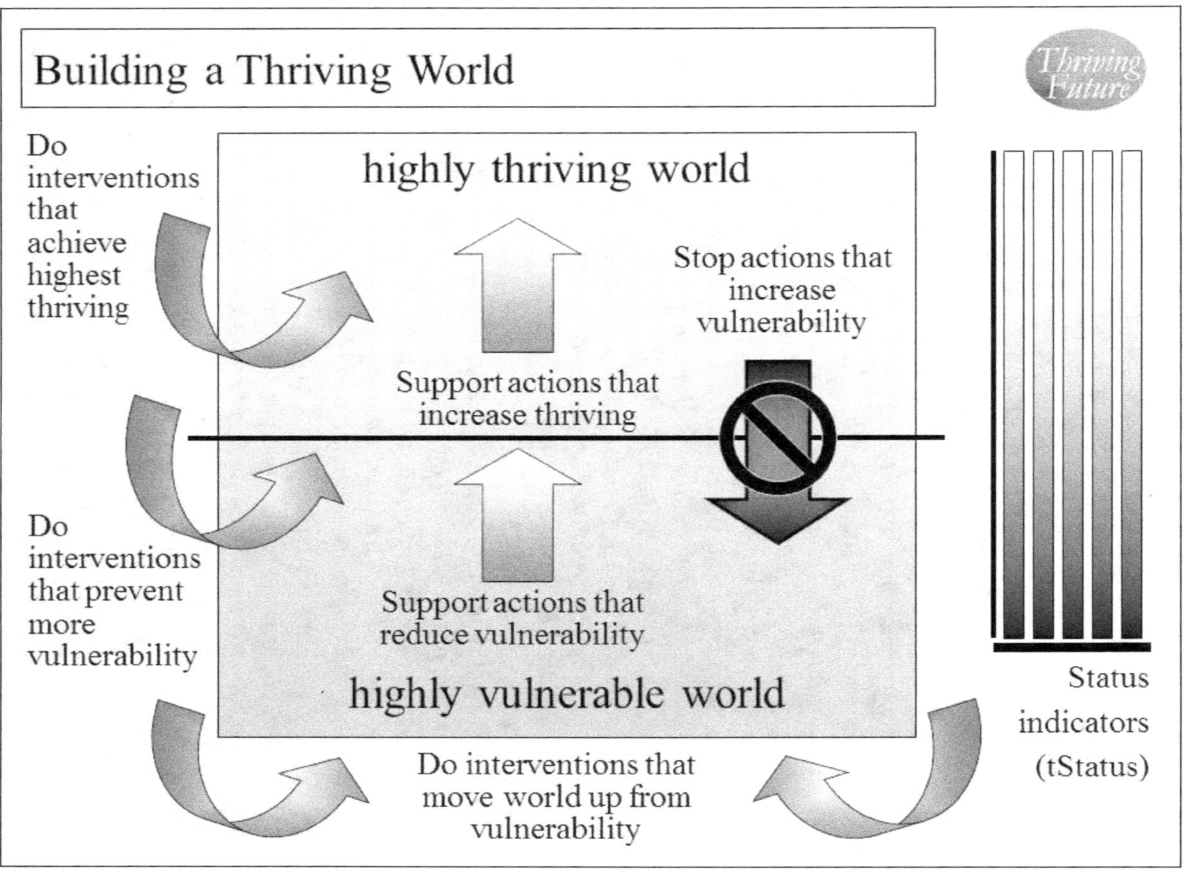

Figure 7.1. Building a Thriving World.

Thrive!

Example: *We together build, achieve, and sustain a surviving and thriving future for all forever:*

- Performing well. *People, business/industry, private organizations (local, country), governments (local, country) and international organizations act to ensure a) all (who are able and not appropriately retired) can work and earn a living income sufficient to survive and thrive and b) all have sufficient resources for and are living, recreating, learning so that they are surviving and thriving to maximum extent feasible.*
- Being well-off (financially). *People, business/industry, private organizations (local, country), governments (local, country) and international organizations act to ensure a) all have sufficient income/resources to survive and thrive and b) all governments have sufficient resources to provide needed (supporting surviving) and desired (supporting thriving) public programs and policies.*
- Being well nourished (food and drink). *People, business/industry, private organizations (local, country), governments (local, country) and international organizations act to ensure that all people have access to, be able to afford and consume healthy foods enough to survive and thrive.*
- Being well housed. *People, business/industry, private organizations (local, country), governments (local, country) and international organizations act to ensure all have access to, be able to afford and live in adequate and preferably high performing housing that supports surviving and thriving.*
- Being well protected (exposures, crime). *People, business/industry, private organizations (local, country), governments (local, country) and international organizations act to ensure a) environmental exposures in home, workplace and elsewhere are minimized so as to not prevent surviving and thriving and b) crimes are minimized in terms of frequency and impact so as to not prevent surviving and thriving.*
- Being well educated. *People, business/industry, private organizations (local, country), governments (local, country) and international organizations act to ensure all people are educated to the full extent of their abilities, needs and desires and to support their surviving and thriving.*
- Being physically and mentally well. *People, business/industry, private organizations (local, country), governments (local, country) and international organizations act to ensure a) all people receive the optimal health support to ensure surviving and*

thriving and b) all people's physical and mental health is optimized to best ensure surviving and thriving.

- Personally growing/developing well. *People, business/industry, private organizations (local, country), governments (local, country) and international organizations act to ensure all people are personally growing and developing to best ensure surviving and thriving.*

- Living within good habitat. *People, business/industry, private organizations (local, country), governments (local, country) and international organizations act to ensure a) all people have access to habitat that best supports their surviving and thriving and b) our world has the optimal mix, quantity and quality of habitat to best support our world and its inhabitants' surviving and thriving.*

- Not being vulnerable. *People, business/industry, private organizations (local, country), governments (local, country) and international organizations act to ensure our world and all of its people, if vulnerable, are vulnerable only to the minimum extent feasible.*

- Producing personal and public goods. *People, business/industry, private organizations (local, country), governments (local, country) and international organizations act to ensure our people produce personal and public goods (including personal income/resources, housing, food and drink, energy, education, health, protection, personal growth and development, and habitat) so as to support surviving and thriving for all persons and for our world overall.*

- Living within a stable, positive climate. *People, business/industry, private organizations (local, country), governments (local, country) and international organizations act to ensure all people behave so as to avoid negative impacts and support positive impacts so as to help ensure a stable, positive climate.*

- Being sustained. *People, business/industry, private organizations (local, country), governments (local, country) and international organizations act to ensure all people behave so as to ensure the sustainability of our world <u>and</u> its people.*

Overall *Thrive!* strategy and actions. Our overall *Thrive!* strategy and actions need to be documented and agreed to by all of us - our world's people and leaders. This will be our world's ***Thrive!* Strategy and Action Plan**.

Different individual people, interest groups/organizations, countries and international organizations will take on different responsibilities. For each action, we designate who will do what to/with whom, where, when, and with what result. [See example below.] Use Table 7.4 to document these actions and responsibilities. [See example table below.] We make sure we have all the actions that are needed to build, achieve and sustain our surviving and thriving world.

As the strategy is executed, our strategy, actions and results should be updated in our *Thrive!* **Strategy and Action Plan**.

Periodically, we should do an evaluation that assesses our world's strategies/actions near and long term impact on near and long term surviving and thriving. When a) our world's strategies and actions are not building and sustaining a thriving future and/or b) there are changes in our world, we should adjust our overall *Thrive!* strategy and actions.

The key is to successfully execute our world's *Thrive!* **Strategy and Action Plan** and to build a near and long term surviving and thriving future.[122]

> ***Example of our world surviving and thriving.*** *[Who will do what to/with whom, where, when, and with what result?] See Example*

---

[122] At this point, we have good information to execute our world's *Thrive!* Strategy and Action Plan. We can make progress. But, if feasible, we should develop our strategy and actions further using more of the tools and models already mentioned. This is very highly encouraged and is necessary because of our very, very complex world.

As stated earlier, this "how-to", by design, is simple but powerful. It is relatively basic providing the framework for doing "our world" strategy. The optimal approach is to use this how-to framework <u>and</u> use the more extensive strategy, models and tools in a) the *Thrive!* **Next Generation Toolkit** contained in the Appendix and b) ***Thrive! - Building a Thriving Future*** available via <u>www.Amazon.com</u> or free download from <u>www.ThrivingFuture.org</u>.

For example, if you want to develop and assess more in-depth strategies and actions, you may want to use the Behavioral Effectiveness Model (BEM). BEM helps assess how our world's and individual world member's motivation and ability will impact future behavior. A description of BEM and how to use it is included in the Appendix.

Thrive!

Thrive! Strategy and Action Plan *in list and table below. Starting immediately, we (people, business/industry, private organizations (local, country), governments (local, country) and international organizations) build, achieve, and sustain a surviving and thriving future for our world and for all forever, including:*

- Performing well. *Starting immediately, people, business/industry, private organizations (local, country), governments (local, country) and international organizations act to ensure, within the next 20 years, a) all (who are able and not appropriately retired) can work and earn a living income sufficient to survive and thrive and b) all have sufficient resources for and are living, recreating, learning so that they are surviving and thriving to maximum extent feasible.*

- Being well-off (financially). *Starting immediately, people, business/industry, private organizations (local, country), governments (local, country) and international organizations act to ensure, within the next 20 years, a) all have sufficient income/resources to survive and thrive and b) all governments have sufficient resources to provide needed (supporting surviving) and desired (supporting thriving) public programs and policies.*

- Being well nourished (food and drink). *Starting immediately, people, business/industry, private organizations (local, country), governments (local, country) and international organizations act to ensure, within the next 20 years, that all people have access to, be able to afford and consume healthy foods enough to survive and thrive.*

- Being well housed. *Starting immediately, people, business/industry, private organizations (local, country), governments (local, country) and international organizations act to ensure, within the next 20 years, all have access to, be able to afford and live in adequate and preferably high performing housing that supports surviving and thriving.*

- Being well protected (exposures, crime). *Starting immediately, people, business/industry, private organizations (local, country), governments (local, country) and international organizations act to ensure, within the next 20 years, a) environmental exposures in home, workplace and elsewhere are minimized so as to not prevent surviving and thriving and b) crimes are minimized to the extent feasible in terms of frequency and impact so as to not prevent surviving and thriving.*

- 153 -

- Being well educated. *Starting immediately, people, business/industry, private organizations (local, country), governments (local, country) and international organizations act to ensure, within the next 20 years, all people are educated to the full extent of their abilities, needs and desires and to support their surviving and thriving.*
- Being physically and mentally well. *Starting immediately, people, business/industry, private organizations (local, country), governments (local, country) and international organizations act to ensure, within the next 20 years, a) all people receive the optimal health support to ensure, within the next 20 years, surviving and thriving and b) all people's physical and mental health is optimized to best ensure surviving and thriving.*
- Personally growing/developing well. *Starting immediately, people, business/industry, private organizations (local, country), governments (local, country) and international organizations act to ensure, within the next 20 years, all people are personally growing and developing to best ensure surviving and thriving.*
- Living within good habitat. *Starting immediately, people, business/industry, private organizations (local, country), governments (local, country) and international organizations act to ensure, within the next 20 years, a) all people have access to habitat that best supports their surviving and thriving and b) our world has the optimal mix, quantity and quality of habitat to best support our world and its inhabitants' surviving and thriving.*
- Not being vulnerable. *Starting immediately, people, business/industry, private organizations (local, country), governments (local, country) and international organizations act to ensure, within the next 20 years, our world and all of its people, if vulnerable, are vulnerable only to the minimum extent feasible.*
- Producing personal and public goods. *Starting immediately, people, business/industry, private organizations (local, country), governments (local, country) and international organizations act to ensure, within the next 20 years, our people produce personal and public goods (including personal income/resources, housing, food and drink, energy, education, health, protection, personal growth and development, and habitat) so as to support surviving and thriving for all persons and for our world overall.*
- Living within a stable, positive climate. *Starting immediately, people, business/industry, private organizations (local, country), governments (local, country) and international organizations act*

to ensure, within the next 10 years, all people behave so as to avoid negative impacts and support positive impacts so as to help ensure a stable, positive climate.

- Being sustained. *Starting immediately, people, business/industry, private organizations (local, country), governments (local, country) and international organizations act to ensure, within the next 5 years, all people behave so as to ensure the sustainability of our world <u>and</u> its people.*

Thrive!

Thrive! **Strategy and Action Plan** (Example of surviving and thriving).

Thriving and Surviving	How well (surviving/ thriving) should our world be in near/long term future?	Changes needed to achieve surviving and thriving future	Actions - Who will do what to/with whom, where, when, and with what result?
			Starting immediately, we (people, business/industry, private organizations (local, country), governments (local, country) and international organizations) build, achieve, and sustain a surviving and thriving future for our world and for all forever, including:
Performing (live/work/ play) well?	Our world and our people should be performing (living, working, recreating, learning) well enough to survive and thrive. *For example. All live, work, recreate and learn well.*	*People, business/industry, private organizations (local, country), governments (local, country) and international organizations act to ensure a) all (who are able and not appropriately retired) can work and earn a living income sufficient to survive and thrive and b) all have sufficient resources for and are living, recreating, learning so that they are surviving and thriving to maximum extent feasible.*	*Starting immediately, people, business/industry, private organizations (local, country), governments (local, country) and international organizations act to ensure, within the next 20 years, a) all (who are able and not appropriately retired) can work and earn a living income sufficient to survive and thrive and b) all have sufficient resources for and are living, recreating, learning so that they are surviving and thriving to maximum extent feasible.*
Well-off?	Our world and our people should be well-off (financially) enough to survive and thrive. *For example. A living income for all, eliminate poverty.*	*People, business/industry, private organizations (local, country), governments (local, country) and international organizations act to ensure a) all have sufficient income/resources to survive and thrive and b) all governments have sufficient resources to*	*Starting immediately, people, business/industry, private organizations (local, country), governments (local, country) and international organizations act to ensure, within the next 20 years, a) all have sufficient income/resources to survive and thrive and b) all governments have*

		provide needed (supporting surviving) and desired (supporting thriving) public programs and policies.	*sufficient resources to provide needed (supporting surviving) and desired (supporting thriving) public programs and policies.*
Well nourished?	Our world and our people should be well nourished (food and drink) enough to survive and thrive. *For example, Affordable and healthy food for all.*	*People, business/industry, private organizations (local, country), governments (local, country) and international organizations act to ensure that all people have access to, be able to afford and consume healthy foods enough to survive and thrive.*	*Starting immediately, people, business/industry, private organizations (local, country), governments (local, country) and international organizations act to ensure, within the next 20 years, that all people have access to, be able to afford and consume healthy foods enough to survive and thrive.*
Well housed?	Our world and our people should be well housed enough to survive and thrive. *For example. Affordable and adequate housing for all.*	*People, business/industry, private organizations (local, country), governments (local, country) and international organizations act to ensure all have access to, be able to afford and live in adequate and preferably high performing housing that supports surviving and thriving.*	*Starting immediately, people, business/industry, private organizations (local, country), governments (local, country) and international organizations act to ensure, within the next 20 years, all have access to, be able to afford and live in adequate and preferably high performing housing that supports surviving and thriving.*
Well protected?	Our world and our people should be well protected (exposures, crime) enough to survive and thrive. *For example. All are protected from crime and environmental threats.*	*People, business/industry, private organizations (local, country), governments (local, country) and international organizations act to ensure a) environmental exposures in home, workplace and elsewhere are minimized so as to not prevent surviving and thriving and b) crimes are minimized in terms of frequency and impact so as to not prevent surviving and thriving.*	*Starting immediately, people, business/industry, private organizations (local, country), governments (local, country) and international organizations act to ensure, within the next 20 years, a) environmental exposures in home, workplace and elsewhere are minimized so as to not prevent surviving and thriving and b) crimes are minimized to the extent feasible in terms of frequency and impact so as to not prevent surviving*

			and thriving.
Well educated?	Our world and our people should be well educated enough to survive and thrive. *For example. All are well educated with all reaching optimum educational levels.*	*People, business/industry, private organizations (local, country), governments (local, country) and international organizations act to ensure all people are educated to the full extent of their abilities, needs and desires and to support their surviving and thriving.*	*Starting immediately, people, business/industry, private organizations (local, country), governments (local, country) and international organizations act to ensure, within the next 20 years, all people are educated to the full extent of their abilities, needs and desires and to support their surviving and thriving.*
Physically/ mentally well?	Our world and our people should be physically and mentally well enough to survive and thrive. *For example. All are physically and mentally healthy.*	*People, business/industry, private organizations (local, country), governments (local, country) and international organizations act to ensure a) all people receive the optimal health support to ensure surviving and thriving and b) all people's physical and mental health is optimized to best ensure surviving and thriving.*	*Starting immediately, people, business/industry, private organizations (local, country), governments (local, country) and international organizations act to ensure, within the next 20 years, a) all people receive the optimal health support to ensure, within the next 20 years, surviving and thriving and b) all people's physical and mental health is optimized to best ensure surviving and thriving.*
Growing/ developing well?	Our world and our people should be personally growing/developing well enough to survive and thrive. *For example. All are growing and developing to their full potential.*	*People, business/industry, private organizations (local, country), governments (local, country) and international organizations act to ensure all people are personally growing and developing to best ensure surviving and thriving.*	*Starting immediately, people, business/industry, private organizations (local, country), governments (local, country) and international organizations act to ensure, within the next 20 years, all people are personally growing and developing to best ensure surviving and thriving.*
Living in good habitat?	Our world should be good habitat enough	*People, business/industry, private organizations (local, country),*	*Starting immediately, people, business/industry, private organizations*

	to survive and thrive. *For example. All live in good, sustainable habitat including housing, community, and natural environment.*	*governments (local, country) and international organizations act to ensure a) all people have access to habitat that best supports their surviving and thriving and b) our world has the optimal mix, quantity and quality of habitat to best support our world and its inhabitants' surviving and thriving.*	*(local, country), governments (local, country) and international organizations act to ensure, within the next 20 years, a) all people have access to habitat that best supports their surviving and thriving and b) our world has the optimal mix, quantity and quality of habitat to best support our world and its inhabitants' surviving and thriving.*
Not vulnerable?	Our world and our people should not be vulnerable. *For example. Vulnerability is minimized in terms of frequency, level, duration and impact.*	*People, business/industry, private organizations (local, country), governments (local, country) and international organizations act to ensure our world and all of its people, if vulnerable, are vulnerable only to the minimum extent feasible.*	*Starting immediately, people, business/industry, private organizations (local, country), governments (local, country) and international organizations act to ensure, within the next 20 years, our world and all of its people, if vulnerable, are vulnerable only to the minimum extent feasible.*
Producing personal/ public goods?	Our world and our people should be producing personal and public goods enough to survive and thrive. *For example. Should produce optimal personal income/resourc es, housing, food and drink, energy, education, health, protection, personal growth and development, and habitat.*	*People, business/industry, private organizations (local, country), governments (local, country) and international organizations act to ensure our people produce personal and public goods (including personal income/resources, housing, food and drink, energy, education, health, protection, personal growth and development, and habitat) so as to support surviving and thriving for all persons and for our world overall.*	*Starting immediately, people, business/industry, private organizations (local, country), governments (local, country) and international organizations act to ensure, within the next 20 years, our people produce personal and public goods (including personal income/resources, housing, food and drink, energy, education, health, protection, personal growth and development, and habitat) so as to support surviving and thriving for all persons and for our world overall.*

Stable, positive climate?	Our world should have a stable, positive climate. *For example. Our climate should help support all human, animal and plant life forever.*	*People, business/industry, private organizations (local, country), governments (local, country) and international organizations act to ensure all people behave so as to avoid negative impacts and support positive impacts so as to help ensure a stable, positive climate.*	*Starting immediately, people, business/industry, private organizations (local, country), governments (local, country) and international organizations act to ensure, within the next 10 years, all people behave so as to avoid negative impacts and support positive impacts so as to help ensure a stable, positive climate.*
Sustainable?	Our world and our people should be sustained. *For example. Our people and our earth are sustained for all forever.*	*People, business/industry, private organizations (local, country), governments (local, country) and international organizations act to ensure all people behave so as to ensure the sustainability of our world <u>and</u> its people.*	*Starting immediately, people, business/industry, private organizations (local, country), governments (local, country) and international organizations act to ensure, within the next 5 years, all people behave so as to ensure the sustainability of our world <u>and</u> its people.*

Table 7.4. ***Thrive!* Strategy and Action Plan.** How well (surviving/thriving) should our world be in near/long term future? What changes are needed to achieve our world's thriving future? To make this happen, what actions are needed?

World Characteristics	What is our world today?
Geographic boundaries	
Gender make-up	
Age make-up	
Racial make-up	
Ethnic make-up	
Lifestyle	
Type of work	
Financial situation	
Food/drink	
Housing	
Protection	
Education	
Physical / mental health	
Personal growth / development	
Habitat	
Producing what	
Climate	
Sustainability	

Table 7.1. What is our world today?

Thriving and Surviving	How well (surviving/ thriving) is our world?	What positively/ negatively impacts its thriving/ surviving?	What is its near/ long term behavior as to thriving/ surviving?
Performing (live/work/play) well?			
Well-off?			
Well nourished?			
Well housed?			
Well protected?			
Well educated?			
Physically/ mentally well?			
Growing/ developing well?			
Living in good habitat?			
Not vulnerable?			
Producing personal/ public goods?			
Stable, positive climate?			
Sustainable?			

Table 7.2. How well (surviving/thriving) is our world? What positively/ negatively impacts it? What is its near/long term future behavior?

World Characteristics	What is our desired and/or likely future world?
Type of work/how people live	
Financial situation	
Food/drink	
Housing	
Protection	
Education	
Physical / mental health	
Personal growth / development	
Habitat	
Producing what	
Climate	
Sustainability	

Table 7.3. What is our desired and/or likely future world?

Thriving and Surviving	How well (surviving/ thriving) should our world be in near/long term future?	Changes needed to achieve surviving and thriving future	**Actions** - Who will do what to/with whom, where, when, and with what result?
Performing (live/work/play) well?			
Well-off?			
Well nourished?			
Well housed?			
Well protected?			
Well educated?			
Physically/ mentally well?			
Growing/ developing well?			
Living in good habitat?			
Not vulnerable?			
Producing personal/ public goods?			
Stable, positive climate?			
Sustainable?			

Table 7.4. *Thrive!* **Strategy and Action Plan.** How well (surviving/thriving) should our world be in near/long term future? What changes are needed to achieve our world's thriving future? To make this happen, what actions are needed?

Chapter 8: Thrive! System© (TS). Achieve thriving people and communities with highest levels of thriving for all everywhere.

How **Thrive! Systems** help builds, achieves and sustains <u>a thriving future</u> <u>for people and communities.</u>

In the 1970s, inner city Milwaukee (WI) suffered from a severe shortage of health and related support for its low- and middle-income people. The author, serving as Director of Special Projects for the Milwaukee Health Department, designed and implemented a four-site personal support system providing support to inner city people. It was a rudimentary first instance of a Thrive! System. Bringing together a wide range of public and private organizations, a wide range of personal support was provided together in several sites. They included preventive health, public health, medical care, dental care, mental health care, social services, and financial assistance. This personal support was coordinated for persons by Nurse Coordinators in each site. The community was actively involved and supportive. The system was funded through a collaboration of the City, County, private hospitals, the dental school, The Robert Wood Johnson Foundation, Community Development Funds and waiver from the Medicare and Medicaid programs. This effort operated successfully for decades. While far short of what is described here as a Thrive! System, this effort served as a foundation for Thrive! Systems proposed here.

In previous chapters, vision and strategy for achieving thriving people and communities has been laid out. Also laid out has been the rationale for **Thrive! Systems (TS),** ideal systems that can help achieve that vision.

In our lives, if we survive birth, only two things are sure about our lives. We are born. We die. Everything else varies from person to person and over a person's lifetime.

Better than our current incomplete and inadequate personal support, a Thrive! System (TS) gives us our best chance to survive and thrive throughout our lifetime.[123] Our having a TS for our community ensures we are more thriving people in a more thriving community. (Table 8.1. Thrive! System – Helping Ensure Thriving for All)

A TS has persons and their communities at the center-. At the center with persons are their Primary Personal Support (PPS) surrounded by all needed and wanted Personal Support (PS). A TS adjusts when locations, time, person, and community change. It takes into account all of personal and community characteristics and all of health and well-being. It understands personal and community environment and its impact on thriving. It understands and uses the full range of thriving support to improve and sustain thriving. It connects all of these, with information and other support, into a fully integrated and supportive system for persons and their communities. (Figure 8.1. Thrive! Systems Ensure More Thriving People)

---

[123] Thrive! Systems (TS) are comprehensive systems that can be of almost any size and for any type of community. Community includes legal communities (e.g., village, town, city, county, State, nation), geographic areas (e.g., regions), groups (e.g. families, ethnic groups, affinity groups), and worlds.

Thrive! System – Helping Ensure Thriving For All [1]

Vision	Thriving people and communities with highest levels of thriving for all everywhere.
Mission	Achieve thriving people and communities with highest levels of thriving for all everywhere.
System	<ul><li>Ensures accessible, affordable and high quality Personal Support for everyone in community.</li><li>Supports whole person and whole community's thriving rather than disconnected or partially connected support or supporting only parts of a person (e.g. only health) and a community.</li><li>Operates in partnership with the person and their family and community.</li><li>Provides a person-centered Primary Personal Support as the primary partner with the person to access and coordinate all needed Personal Support to achieve highest levels of thriving.</li><li>Provides a personal support system for persons and their Primary Personal Support.</li><li>Provides directly or indirectly the full range of Personal Support.</li><li>Provides directly and provides collaboratively via affiliations the full range of Personal Support to ensure accessibility for the person and the community.</li><li>Utilizes all payers (public, private and person) and optimizes costs to ensure affordability of Primary Personal Support and Personal Support for the person and the community.</li><li>Utilizes effective quality assurance collaboratively by Thrive! Systems and affiliated organizations to ensure high quality Primary Personal Support and Personal Support.</li><li>Ensures that all people, other creatures and Earth survive and thrive to maximum extent feasible.</li></ul>

[1] Thrive! System is the updated, upgraded and more comprehensive and complete version of system created for and implemented in inner city Milwaukee (WI) in late 1970s and which operated successfully for decades.

Table 8.1. Thrive! System – Helping Ensure Thriving for All.

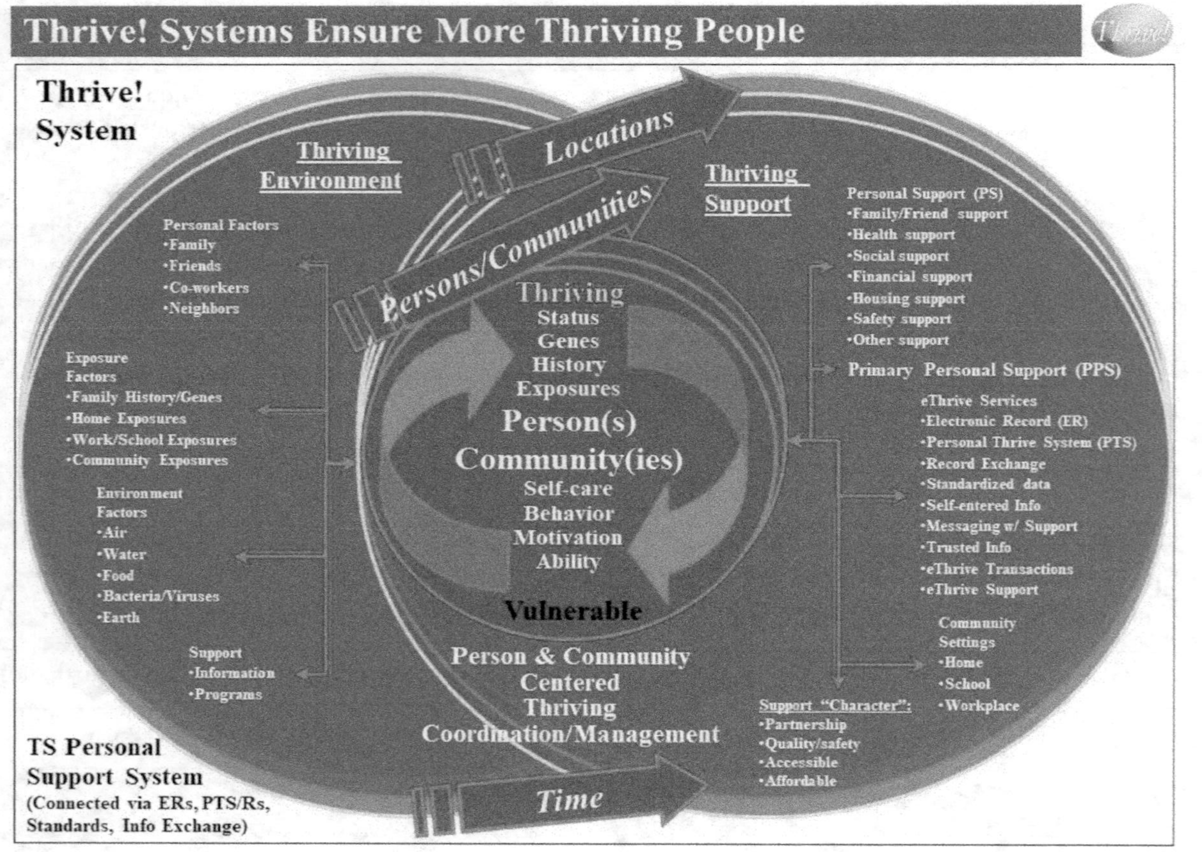

Figure 8.1. Thrive! Systems Ensure More Thriving People.

Thrive!

We want to thrive as much as possible over our lifetime.

We are born. If we live long enough, we are a child, an adult, and an older adult. Then we die. Over our lifetime and depending on how long we live, we may go through early development, may learn, may work, may expand our family, and may have post-work time. Then we die.

If we are fortunate, we live many years through all of these stages until we die a quick and painless death. If we are truly fortunate, we thrive through all of these stages. Very few of us will be that fortunate under the current incomplete and inadequate system.

During our lives after we are born, we may thrive and/or we may be vulnerable. Then we die.

We should want to thrive for as much of our lives as possible. We should do everything reasonable and possible to thrive. While we may be able and willing to do much by ourselves, we will be more successful with truly good partners (Primary Personal Support (PPS)) with all needed and wanted Personal Support (PS) in a truly good system (a Thrive! System (TS)). (Figure 8.2. Persons & Our Lifetime.)

What does it mean for us to thrive?

Very simply, we thrive when we do well throughout our lives. When our families and friends do well throughout their lives. When our communities do well now and for the long term. When our world does well now and for the long term.

More specifically, we, our families and friends, our communities and our world thrive when we are:
- Performing well,
- Well-off (financially),
- Well nourished,
- Well housed,
- Well protected (exposures, crime),
- Well educated,
- Physically and mentally well (people),
- Growing/developing well,
- Living within good habitat,

Thrive!

- Physically well (Earth, plants, animals, environment),
- Not vulnerable,
- Producing personal and public goods,
- Living within a stable, positive climate, and
- Sustained.

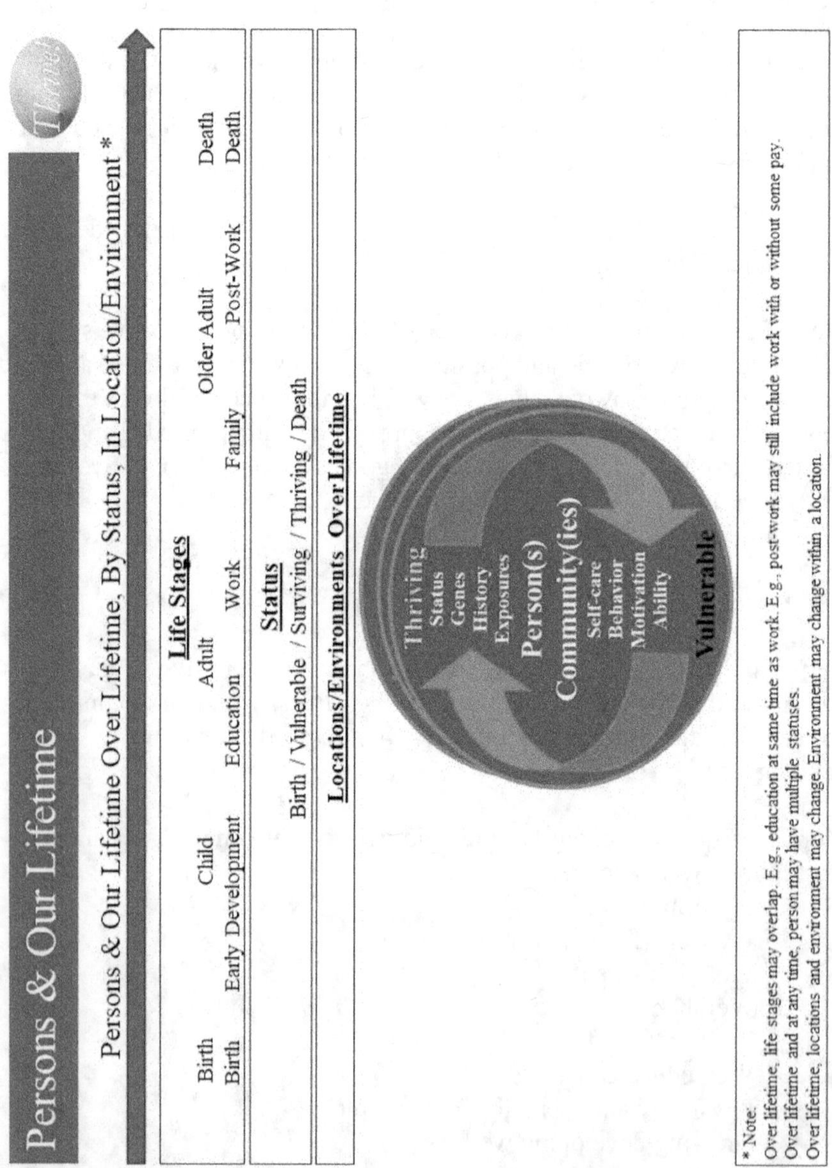

Figure 8.2. Persons & Our Lifetime.

We are more likely to thrive in a Thrive! System© (TS).

The U.S. Institute of Medicine (IOM) [now the National Academy of Medicine] provides a way of viewing a health system's performance through our eyes. What we want from a health system is that we are "staying healthy", "getting better", "living with illness or disability" and/or "coping with the end of life." Only considering health, this is a health system we want and need. This health system, a Thriving Health System, is described in **HealthePeople® - Achieving Health People, Communities & World Via Thrive!®**.

Going beyond health and taking this one more major positive step via a Thrive! System (TS), we "start and stay thriving", "get better (from vulnerable to thriving) faster", "live as well as possible with illness or disability" and/or "cope as well as possible with end of life." Some of us may experience more than one of these at the same time. IOM's quality reports have six aims for a high performing health system. They stress it should be safe, effective, person/patient-centered, timely, efficient, and equitable. Going further, a Thrive! System should be safe, effective, person- and community-centered, efficient and equitable, and should help achieve thriving for both a person and a community.

Building on and going beyond the IOM work, a TS should perform well from the person's perspective and a community's perspective. As depicted in the attached figure, a TS would "check all the boxes." (Figure 8.3. Thrive! System's Six Aims & Person's and Community's Perspective on Thriving) As suggested earlier, a TS can, should and will do much better.

To get to the personal support we truly want and need, we need a TS that has us and our Primary Personal Support (PPS) at the center. Together as partners from birth to death, we access whatever other support is needed to help us start and stay thriving, help us get better (from vulnerable to thriving) faster, help us live as well as possible with illness or disability, and help us cope as well as possible with end of life.

Six Aims & Person/Community's Perspective on Thriving

Supportive of Institute of Medicine principles and aims, a Thrive! System supports persons, communities and their Primary Personal Support, and the rest of Personal Support in continuing to innovate and find better ways to achieve thriving.

Person & Community's Perspective on Needs	Aims for Personal Support Performance/Quality. Achieve Thriving for Both Person and Community.					
	Safe	Effective	Person & Community centered	Timely	Efficient	Equitable
Start & stay thriving	+	+	+	+	+	+
Get better (from vulnerable to thriving) faster	+	+	+	+	+	+
Live as well as possible with illness or disability	+	+	+	+	+	+
Cope as well as possible with end of life	+	+	+	+	+	+

Figure 8.3. Six Aims & Person's and Community's Perspective on Thriving.

Can we transform what we have into TS? Yes, but not easily. Most of the elements exist in our current communities. But they are poorly organized, poorly connected and poorly communicating. The first step is to put in place the Primary Personal Supports (PPS) and connect them to us and the rest of Personal Support (PS). We need to improve and organize the existing PS elements so they better provide and coordinate personal support. We need a lifetime electronic personal support system that tracks and appropriately shares both our interactions with our PPS and all other PS and appropriately and carefully tracks our own personal needs, wants, behaviors and conditions. We need our PPS and ourselves to appropriately share our information carefully and accurately only with whom we want when we want and how we want.

We are more likely to thrive in a Thrive! System© (TS) that addresses the whole person and the whole community.

A Thrive! System (TS) is very different from what we have today. TS addresses the whole person, not just piecemeal parts of the person. TS addresses the whole community, not just piecemeal parts of the community.

What we have today is a piecemeal approach to persons. It is more problem by problem oriented than effectively dealing with the <u>full range</u> of problems experienced by persons at a point in time or over their lifetime. Health is generally addressed separately from housing. Housing from income. Work from school. Public safety from environmental protection. Etc. The same is generally true for a community.

What we have today is more oriented toward solving individual problems rather than being oriented toward solving <u>all</u> problems that a person experiences. The same is generally true for a community.

What we have today is more oriented toward solving problems than <u>helping the whole person thrive</u>. The same is generally true for a community

What we have today is a non-system in which different parts of personal support are poorly coordinated, are disconnected and communicate poorly.

What we have today is a non-system where persons are essentially on their own when it comes to addressing the whole set of factors that reduce vulnerability and increase thriving. Not only is the person not well served but the community is not well served.

Very differently and much more effectively, a TS has a PPS for each person who partners with the person to address all factors that reduce vulnerability and increase thriving.

Very differently and much more effectively, a TS is fully coordinated, is fully connected and communicates well among persons, their Primary Personal Support (PPS), and their total Personal Support (PS). A TS addresses all the factors in a person's life that reduce vulnerability and increase thriving. A TS addresses all the factors in a community that reduce vulnerability and increase thriving.

We are more likely to thrive with a Primary Personal Support (PPS) partner in a Thrive! System© (TS).
A Primary Personal Support (PPS) functions as a partner with us within our community. A partner who brings more knowledge about how to reduce vulnerability and increase thriving than we have and who supports our efforts to thrive. This partner would preferably be a person with specific training and experience to be a PPS. This partner must be well trained and may come from a range of professions, including a social worker or a nurse.

On our behalf, a PPS partners with the rest of Primary Support (PS) across as many life stages and as much of our life as is appropriate and feasible.

Our PPS partner knows us, knows our key thriving and vulnerability factors, knows our needs and wants, knows our behaviors, knows our living and work environment, and provides continuity over as much of our lifetime as possible. Our PPS partner helps us start and stay thriving, helps us get better (from vulnerable to thriving) faster, helps us live as well as possible with illness or disability, and helps us cope as well as possible with end of life. (Figure 8.4. Persons & Our Personal Support)

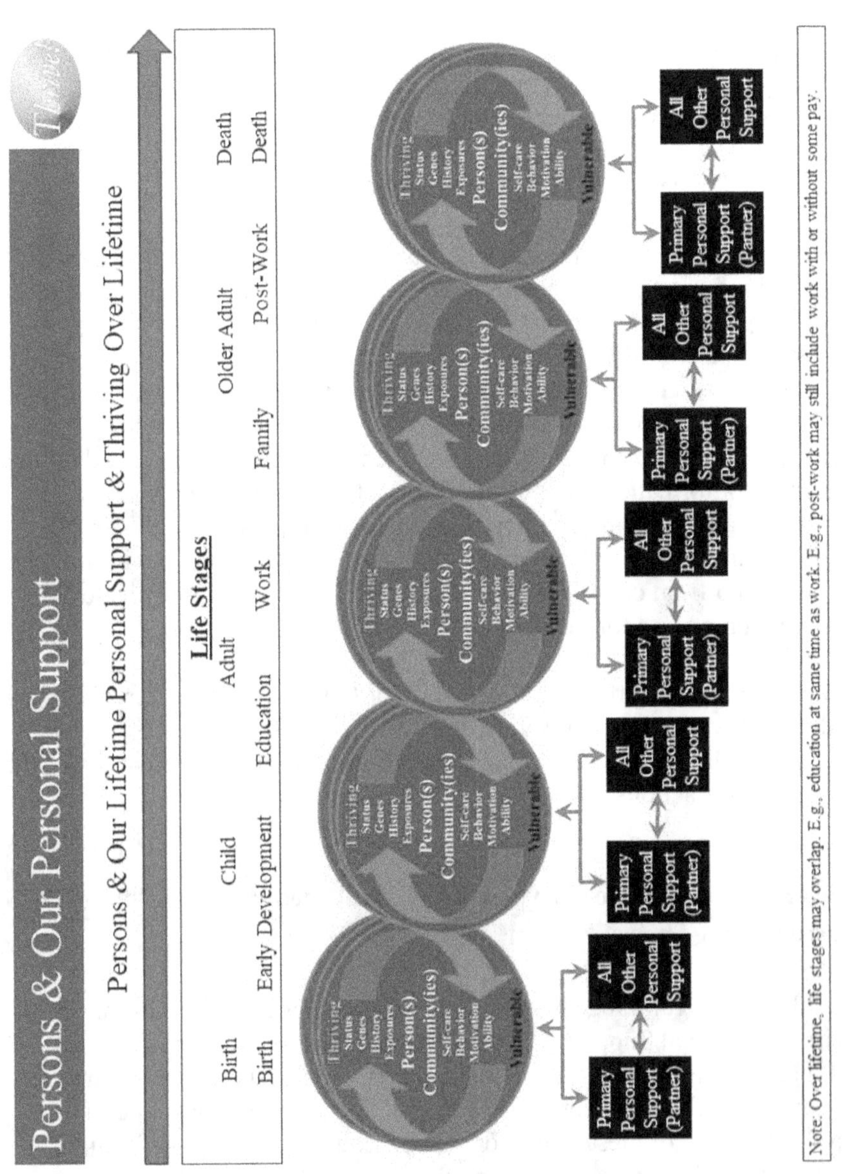

Figure 8.4. Persons & Our Personal Support.

**We are more likely to thrive by having and using Thrive! System©
(TS) personal support systems for persons and their Primary Personal
Support (PPS).** [124]

---

[124] The TS personal support system is also known as a "Thrive! System", a

As is increasingly the case with respect to health, persons and their Primary Personal Support (PPS) need personal support systems to help them collect and store personal information, access electronic support resources (information and tools), and decide and adjust the best path and actions to reduce vulnerability and increase thriving.

These Thrive! System (TS) personal support systems collect and hold the personal information on persons that relate to vulnerability and thriving. They help persons and their PPS assess the current status and develop and adjust the strategy that will achieve the most thriving. They utilize artificial intelligence and other decision support mechanisms to support decision-making. They track progress toward reducing vulnerability and increasing thriving. They help connect to and use the full range of internet and other electronic information and personal support resources. They enable communication and information sharing between persons and their PPS and with any other needed Personal Support (PS). They enable information to be moved from one PPS to a subsequent PPS. They enable connecting information on and for members of a family.

When persons want or need information or to take an action to reduce vulnerability or increase thriving, the TS personal support systems enable them to get the information, make better decisions, and effectively take the best action or actions.

We are more likely to thrive by using all needed Personal Support (PS) partners in a Thrive! System© (TS).

To address the full range of conditions we may face in our lives, our Primary Personal Support (PPS) and we both need all needed Personal Support (PS) as partners. We need partners to help successfully address conditions such as an acute illness or injury, a chronic illness and/or a disability. Each of these conditions often require additional skills and knowledge. Maybe a specialist or subspecialist. Maybe rehabilitation people. Maybe a therapist of one kind or another. Maybe home care or community care people. Maybe a palliative or hospice care team.

---

subsystem of the overall TS.

PS may include family and friends. It may include public social services and financial assistance. May include spiritual healers, public health, and personal assistants. May include schools and employers. May include public safety people. May include food and nutrition people.

PS may be any one of the full range of personal support that can and should be provided when needed. Many different types of people and organizations will have the skills and knowledge to be partners and help address conditions. Depending on our need, any of these people may have an important role as partners in helping us start and stay thriving, helping us get better (from vulnerable to thriving) faster, helping us live as well as possible with illness or disability, and helping us cope as well as possible with end of life.

Our having full "Personal Support (PS)" is more and better than what supports us today.

To keep ourselves thriving, traditional personal support is not enough. While traditional support has a very important role to play, we need more and better support. Full Personal Support (PS) is more complete and is the full range of people, goods and services that can help us thrive as much as possible. This includes the partners described above. But it also includes electronic support (e.g. internet information, apps and devices, messaging, our personal record) and devices, sensors, computers, smartphones, tablets and many more support tools yet to come. A Thrive! System (TS) has the types of personal support we have today plus other important personal support and plus future personal support yet to be available or even developed.

At the center of a TS are persons and their Primary Personal Support (PPS). Together, they access whatever PS is wanted or needed. Traditional PS services may include health care and social services. When needed for a severe or terminal illness, PS may also include hospice and palliative care. When a person has a disability, PS may include personal assistance or home care. When a person has multiple issues, the Primary Personal Support (PPS) is especially important.

In the following figure, many more of the potential PS are detailed. But even this is not a complete PS list. (Figure 8.5. Thrive! Systems – Person and Primary and Other Personal Support.)

- Support For Thriving
- Support Against Vulnerability
- Community Support
- Family/Friends Support
- Financial/Income Support
- Health Support
- Food/Nutrition Support
- Disability Support
- End of Life Support
- Education/Training Support
- Supportive Environment/Habitat
- Housing Support
- Internet Info & Services
- Protection from Crime
- Protection from Exposures
- Growth & Development Support

There are many other types of personal support that are part of a TS. There is information that is provided through understanding a person's history, family history, environmental history, education history, work history and genetic makeup.

There is also indirect support, support that may never touch the person directly but that helps reduce vulnerability and increase thriving for the person. Examples of indirect support include advocacy, government executive and legislative branches, environmental protection, workplace protection, health-related research, food production, regulation, and standards setting.

In a TS, personal support is whatever support a person wants and needs that will improve or maintain thriving or will help a person who is vulnerable with a disability and/or with a terminal illness or injury. The PPS partners with a person to make best use of any or all available personal support.

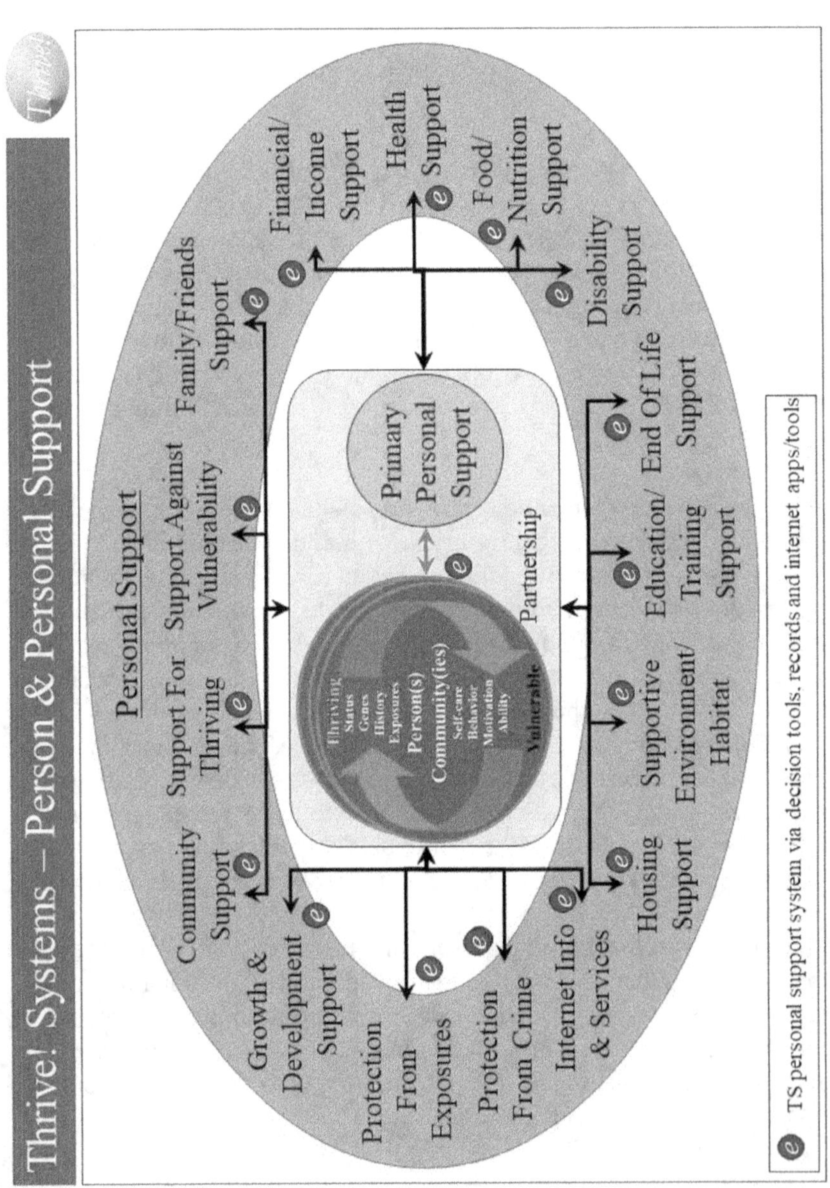

Figure 8.5. Thrive! Systems – Person and Primary and Other Personal Support.

Together in a TS, all of this personal support best supports persons and their PPS as they partner to help start and stay thriving, get better (from vulnerable to thriving) faster, live as well as possible with illness or disability, and cope as well as possible with end of life.

How is a Thrive! System© (TS) best organized to help us?

A Thrive! System (TS) for a community may provide personal support via a fully integrated TS (single organization with Primary Personal Support (PPS) at the center) and/or partially-integrated TS (well-connected multiple organizations with one or more Primary Personal Support at one or more centers). They both can support persons, their PPS and all other Personal Support (PS). (Figure 8.6. Thrive! Systems – Person & Community Centered Organizations.)

Public and private organizations provide personal support that is key to maintaining and improving thriving. Together, they should include PPS and other Personal Support, including health care, skilled nursing home, long term nursing home, home care, personal assistance, rehabilitation, illness/injury specific support, public health, nutrition, emotional support, hospice, palliative, and holistic therapies. They should include social service, food/nutrition, housing, income support, financial services, payment for health care, personal security, justice, education/training, environmental protection, regulation, roads, parks, waste disposal, utilities, libraries, and emergency assistance. Some employers provide personal support in- and/or outside of the workplace. Some schools provide personal support. The Federal government provides national security.

Connecting all of this PS with persons and their PPS are TS personal support systems that can and should hold and process information to be shared carefully and only when needed, appropriate and authorized. They must be able to exchange information in a standardized way that supports effective decision-making for the person, for a person's PPS and for a person and community's PS.

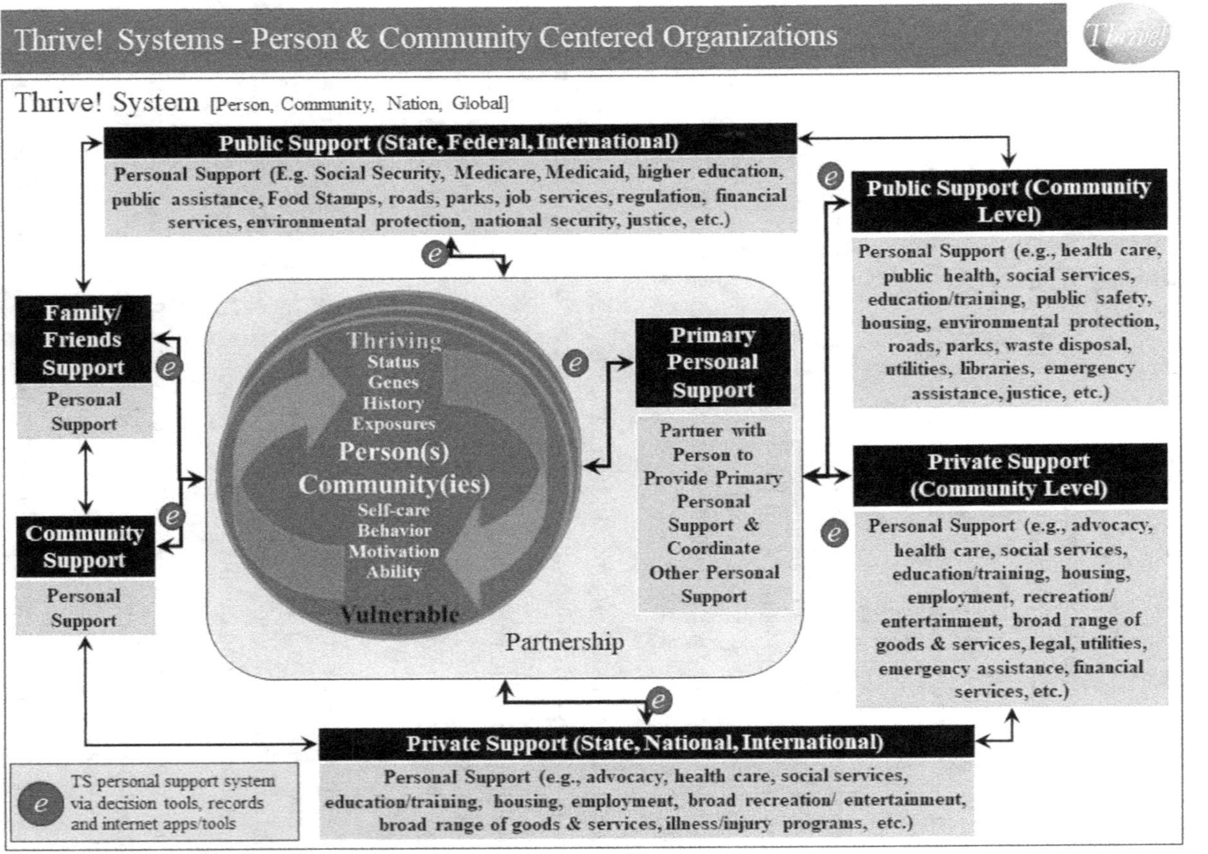

Figure 8.6. Thrive! Systems - Person & Community Centered Organizations.

Thrive!

How does a Thrive! System© (TS) support a person and a community?

A Thrive! System (TS) supports a person or persons from beginning to end. Prior to birth, we, via our family, are partnered with a Primary Personal Support (PPS). Starting with our birth and through childhood, we have a PPS partner. The PPS partners with us as individuals or with us and our family and helps us access all other Personal Support (PS). As children and as we grow, we take an increasing part in our own pursuit of thriving. The more the better.

When we become an adult, we may change our PPS partner. Our respective roles are similar. Our PPS may be one with more skills and knowledge to support our adult lives. As an adult and to the extent we can, we take on a stronger role in our pursuit of thriving. The more the better. If we have a family, we and our family may partner with a PPS as a family unit.

In our later years when any children have moved on to their own lives and we may experience more illness or disabling conditions, we may change our PPS to one who has more skills and knowledge with illness and/or disabling conditions. We and our PPS will need to access the PS that can best help us manage illnesses or disabling conditions. To the extent we are able, we should take a strong role in our pursuit of thriving. The more the better.

If we have a terminal illness or are just nearing the end of our lives as part of normal aging, our PPS may be one who can best help us best cope with end of life. We should live this part of our lives as independently and with as much dignity and quality of life as possible. The more the better.

At any point in our lives, we may experience a major illness or disabling condition that requires us to partner with a PPS with that skill and knowledge.

In a TS, all wanted and needed PS must be physically accessible. This is particularly challenging in rural areas but more doable today with internet and other communication resources. Special provisions must be made for people with physical or cognitive limitations.

Even if all this PS is available, interconnected and accessible, financial access must be ensured. PS must be affordable for all payers, including the person. Today, this is through private support, public support, charity and self-pay. There are possibly better ways a TS can ensure financial access. In a TS, no person fails to receive wanted and needed PS due to financial limitations or inability.

What will our lives be like in a Thrive! System© (TS)?

Starting with our birth and through childhood, we and our families and our Primary Personal Support (PPS) focus on how to increase and sustain thriving in the way we live our daily lives. Eat and drink healthier. Exercise better. Avoid or minimize environmental risks. Get age-appropriate health and well-being exams. Treat illnesses and injuries early and well. Obtain education and training. Track our personal vulnerability and thriving. Use effective Personal Support (PS) partners. Take responsibility for our and our family's thriving and for our community's thriving. Together, these actions help us reduce vulnerability and increase thriving.

When we become an adult, we take more responsibility for our own vulnerability and thriving. But we still do so in partnership with our PPS. We continue to eat and drink healthier. Exercise better. Avoid or minimize environmental risks. Get age-appropriate health and well-being exams. Treat illnesses and injuries early and well. Continue to learn and develop. Ensure our food and housing. Ensure our financial viability now and through the end of our lives. Ensure our personal safety. Track our personal vulnerability and thriving. Learn more about our specific risks from family history, genetic make-up, environmental risks, and how we live our lives. Together, these actions help us reduce vulnerability and increase thriving, help us deal with vulnerabilities earlier and better, and help us reduce vulnerability and increase thriving.

In our later years when any children have moved on to their own lives and we may experience more illness or disabling conditions, we continue with our PPS and with what we have been doing throughout our adulthood. But now we may be experiencing even more vulnerability, more illnesses, more disabling conditions, more of these at the same time and more severe versions of these. Together, we and our PPS help us reduce vulnerability, prevent illness and injury, help us deal with vulnerabilities earlier and better, help us reduce the severity of these, help us better deal with simultaneous vulnerabilities, help us better cope with a chronic or disabling condition, help us better deal with simultaneous and different PS, and help us reduce vulnerability and increase thriving.

If we have a terminal illness or are just nearing the end of our lives as part of normal aging, our PPS may be one who can best help us best cope with end of life. We still try to thrive as best we can given that we are nearing the end. Managing pain better. Prioritizing what PS are done or not done. Addressing emotional issues better for ourselves and our family and friends. Making sure we have our final arrangements in order. Handling the end of our lives as we want and with dignity.

Across and throughout our lives, we effectively use effective PS partners. We take responsibility for our and our family's health and well-being and for our community's health and well-being.

We want our "status" to improve from "worst thriving (highly vulnerable)" to "best thriving (highly thriving)" status. (Figure 8.7. Thriving Status – Move From Vulnerable To Thriving.)

It is worst when we are highly vulnerable and experience low personal and support ability, low personal and support motivation, unsupportive "environment", poor prevention outcomes, poor treatment and intervention outcomes, high risk for adverse events, high morbidity, low quality of life, high mortality, low life expectancy, and low satisfaction with PPS and PS.

It is best when we are highly thriving and experience high personal and support ability, high personal and support motivation, supportive "environment", good prevention outcomes, good treatment and intervention outcomes, low risk for adverse events, low morbidity, high quality of life, low mortality, high life expectancy, and high satisfaction with PPS and PS.

We need to move each element of our lives from being worst (highly vulnerable) to being best (highly thriving). Move to best outcomes and status. Move to thriving. We do that best in a Thrive! System (TS).

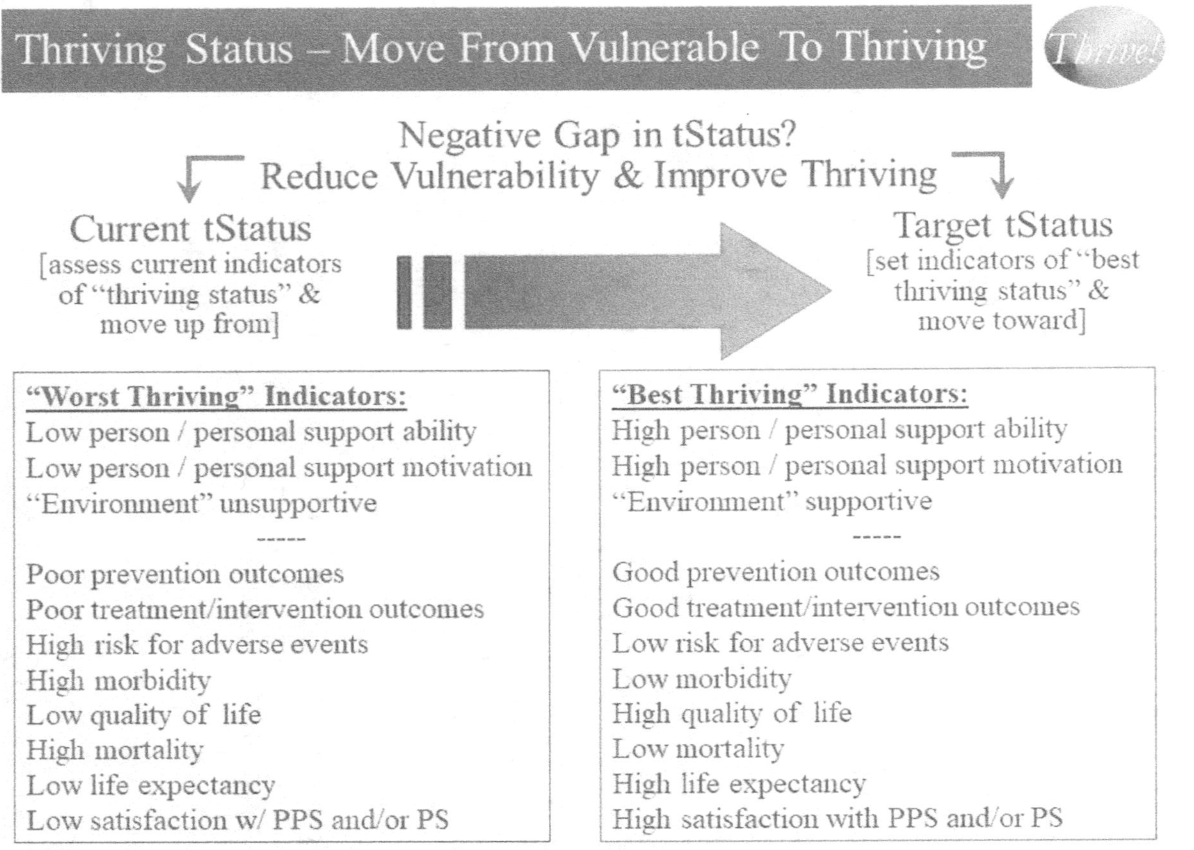

Figure 8.7. Thriving Status – Move From Vulnerable To Thriving.

How will we know when we are successful? When we are thriving? As noted earlier, thriving is when we are: performing well, well-off (financially), well nourished, well housed, well protected (exposures, crime), well educated, physically and mentally well (people), growing/developing well, living within good habitat, physically well (Earth, plants, animals, environment), not vulnerable, producing personal and public goods, living within a stable, positive climate, and sustained.

Our having Thrive! Systems© (TS) can and should achieve thriving people and communities for all everywhere.

Thrive!® and Thrive! Systems (TS) have a vision of thriving people and communities for all everywhere. They have the strategy to achieve that vision. (Figure 8.8. Thrive! Systems – Help Achieve Thriving).

The strategy is for us to thrive as best we can by doing the following:
- Stop actions that increase vulnerability.
- Support actions that increase thriving.
- Support actions that reduce vulnerability.
- Do interventions that best achieve highest thriving.
- Do interventions that best prevent more vulnerability.
- Do interventions that move up from vulnerability.

This is the Thrive!® vision for Thrive! Systems and for us and the communities these systems support.[125] As people, communities, nations and world, we should proceed toward the vision of achieving thriving people and communities for all everywhere.

---

[125] Thrive!® - Vision, mission, strategy and supportive tools help create and sustain large, positive and timely change and build a thriving future for all forever. They help build a thriving and surviving future:
- Vision: All thrive forever. All includes persons, communities, and world.
- Mission: Large, positive, timely change achieving surviving and thriving future for all forever.
- Strategy: A joint Thrive! Endeavor and call to action building a thriving future for all forever.

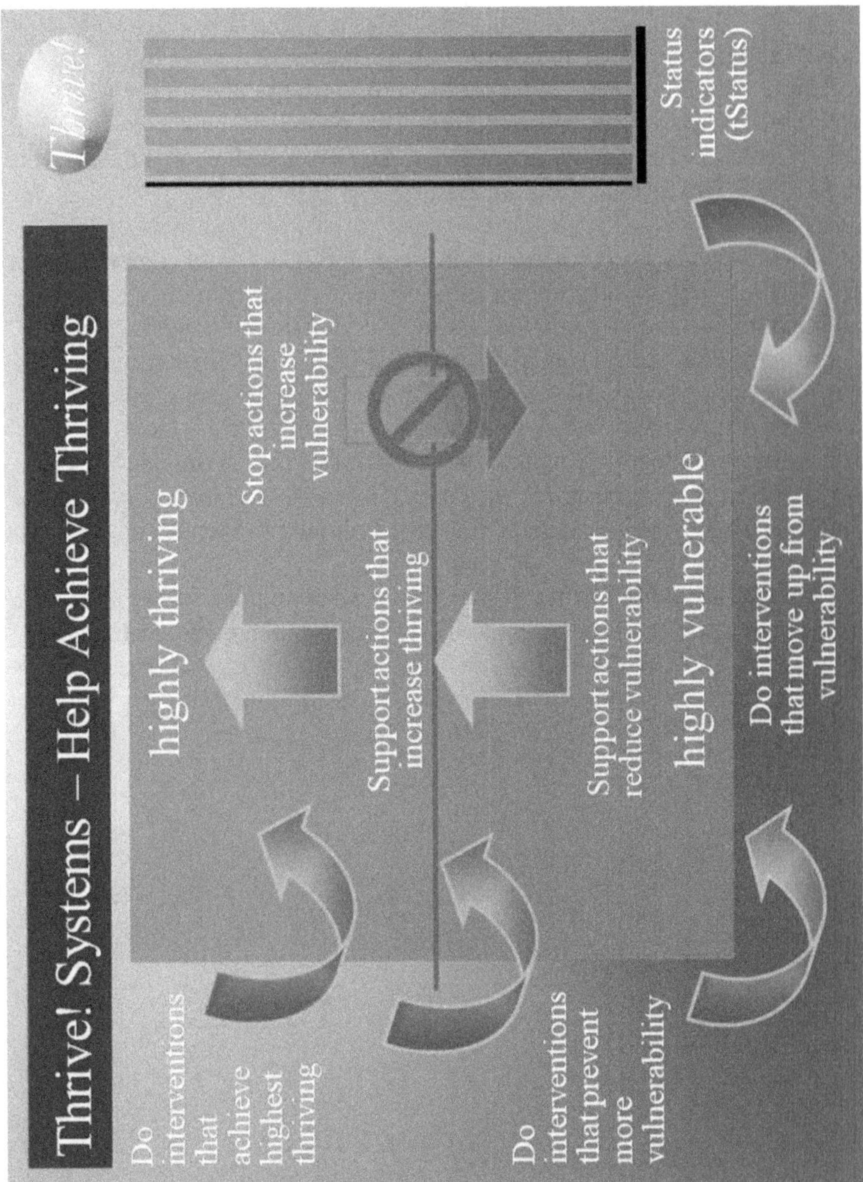

Figure 8.8. Thrive! Systems – Help Achieve Thriving.

We do this via a strategy of TS for all people and communities everywhere. TS are self-perpetuating, very affordable, easily accessible, "e" enabled, person-centered, prevention-oriented, and high quality systems. They produce high outcomes and status (thriving).

Such TS, partly physical and partly virtual and put into place by collaborative private and public partnerships, will greatly improve accessibility, quality and affordability for all people everywhere. They will greatly reduce vulnerability and increase thriving for all people everywhere and for all other creatures and for Earth.

Every community everywhere should have an effective and comprehensive TS. By every community having an effective and comprehensive TS, we can help people and communities thrive everywhere in the world. Every community's TS should effectively connect with every other community's TS. Together, they can best support people as they move amongst the world's communities. Together, they can share valuable resources to most efficiently and effectively support people and their communities. Together, they can best support people, their communities and the world, including the Earth upon which we depend for our continuing existence and thriving.

We can and should build and sustain TS for all people everywhere. We can and should achieve substantially more thriving people, communities, nations and world. We can and should move toward a truly thriving world. All people everywhere deserve and should expect nothing less.

Chapter 9: How the *Thrive!* Endeavor, you and all of us together, builds a thriving future.

How the *Thrive!* **Endeavor**, you and all of us together, builds, achieves and sustains a thriving future for all forever.

Thrive! Survive! Vulnerable! These are the keys to a call for creating and sustaining large, positive and timely change and building a surviving and thriving future. We are all vulnerable to some extent but that can change for the better. *Thrive!* is that call to action and a rallying cry for a better and thriving future. It is a vision and a mission for those wanting to build a better future. To achieve that vision and succeed with the mission, the *Thrive!* **Endeavor**, all of us together, strives to energize and empower people to build a thriving future for our families and friends, communities, countries and world. It strives to build, achieve and sustain a surviving and thriving future for all forever, to the maximum extent possible.[126] This future is *Thrive!* and is a bold vision and mission.

We have laid out why (Chapters 2 and 3) and how (Chapters 4 through 8) to build a surviving and thriving future for you and your family and friends, for you and your community, for you and your country, and for you and our world. But to truly have a thriving future, we need to have it for you and everybody's family and friends and every community and every country and every part of and our entire world. When all this comes together, you and all of us

---

[126] We must keep in mind that "our world" and "all" is expanding as we explore and move beyond earth to other parts of our universe. For that reason, "a thriving future for all forever" reaches as far as we reach or hope to reach.

will have built, achieved and sustained a surviving and thriving future.

How best to do this? We bring all this together with the ***Thrive!* Endeavor** where you and all of us together, build, achieve and sustain <u>a thriving future</u> <u>for all</u> <u>forever</u>. Creating and sustaining this vast human endeavor is the driving purpose and mission of this **People's Guide**.

Why the *Thrive!* Endeavor?

As laid out in Chapters 2 and 3, you and all of us want and need a surviving and thriving future because of our endangered future and our human need to survive and desire to thrive. And <u>only people</u> can and must fix all that is broken. And <u>only people</u> can and must build, achieve and sustain a survivable and thriving future. And <u>only all of us joined together</u> can succeed due to the scope (all), level (surviving and thriving), duration (forever) of the challenge. For these reasons, building, achieving and sustaining a surviving and thriving future requires a vast, sustained ***Thrive!* Endeavor** of all of us together.

What is the *Thrive!* Endeavor?

The ***Thrive!* Endeavor** is all of us together. It is vision, mission, strategy and call to action. Its vision is a surviving and thriving future for all forever. Its mission is to create and sustain large positive and timely change that builds, achieves and sustains a surviving and thriving future for all forever, to the maximum extent possible. Its strategy is to energize and empower all of us together in the vast, sustained human endeavor building and sustaining a thriving future. Its call for action is to motivate all of us (individual people, groups of people, private sector organizations, governments) to seek a thriving future, to create and sustain the necessary large positive change, and to work together to build, achieve and sustain a surviving and thriving future.

In support of this vision and mission, the Endeavor adopts and embraces "<u>A People's Constitution</u>" - "We the people, in order to form a more perfect union, commit to a thriving future for all forever." [127]

Who is and will be the *Thrive!* Endeavor?

The *Thrive!* Endeavor is <u>all of us together</u> building, achieving and sustaining a surviving and thriving future. "All of us together" include individual people, groups of people, private sector organizations and governments. "All of us together" include <u>current and future generations</u>. "All of us together" include <u>you</u>, and <u>everybody's</u> family and friends, and <u>every</u> community, and <u>every</u> country, and <u>every part of and our entire</u> world.

Who does what and how in the *Thrive!* Endeavor?

What the *Thrive!* Endeavor does and how it does it is different than past and current approaches which have major limitations and defects. The Endeavor is unique and better because it:

- Strives to achieve a thriving and sustainable future for all forever, to the maximum extent possible. But it also helps ensure survival, a necessary but not sufficient step to achieving a thriving future
- Enables the building of a surviving and thriving future for you, your family and friends, your community, your country and our world.
- Joins people of all backgrounds/generations together to achieve a thriving future.
- Is able to address every person, community and issue.
- Uses whole "community" (local, regional, state, country, world/global) strategy for creating and sustaining change and building thriving futures. [No longer should we rely on piecemeal strategies.]
- Uses whole "person" strategy for creating and sustaining change and building thriving futures. [No longer is the

---

[127] The **People's Constitution** should be just this brief, understandable and powerful. It should not replace any country's constitution. The intent is for it to be embraced by and acted upon affirmatively by all people forever.

focus only on parts (ill health, hunger, poor education or insufficient income).]

- Uses whole "system" (community, health, education, economy, housing, etc.) strategy for creating and sustaining change and building thriving futures. [No longer should we rely on survival and piecemeal strategies for just parts of a system.]
- Takes an integrated approach to cross-cutting issues.
- Uses an integrated approach to people/environment strategy, change and thriving futures. [No longer is the focus only on people <u>or</u> the environment.]
- Uses a "person-centered" strategic approach that recognizes people's behaviors are the problem and the solution. [No longer should we fail to address "people's behavior".]
- Uses eMedia and social networking to expand communication and joint action and to activate and coordinate a large endeavor in "real time".
- Uses the *Thrive!* **Next Generation Toolkit** of strategy, models and tools to create and sustain change and build thriving futures. [See Appendix.] [No longer should we rely on past approaches that failed or had limited success.]
- Uses strategic/operational planning and combines it with strategic/operational execution.
- Creates a collaborative strategy with the necessary positive actions to build, achieve and sustain a surviving and thriving future.

To improve our chances of success, the ***Thrive!* Endeavor** recognizes and will positively use tipping points, a critical element in positive change efforts historically.[128] Throughout human history, we see moments when "tipping points" exist. Tipping points can enable negative or positive change. We see moments when a positive action is taken at a tipping point and major positive change occurs. We are now at such a tipping point. We are now at an historical moment when government and the private sector are broken in many ways, when our resources are becoming increasingly limited, when our environment is increasingly and negatively impacted, when our future is endangered, and when a failure to act positively dooms us to a failed, potentially non-survivable future. But, it is also a historical moment when we are the most able to change all that for the better. At this tipping point when our future is most endangered and we are most able, carefully developed and positive actions are more necessary and more likely to be effective and successful.

As laid out above in this Chapter and in Chapters 4 through 8, each and all of us should develop and take as many positive actions as we can. The more positive actions taken, the better for all of us. Each

---

[128] Using tipping points can be very helpful in building a thriving future. However, positive change efforts can also occur without an existing tipping point or without any tipping point. It is just more difficult. Where feasible, we should use current, future and creatable tipping points:
- Use current tipping points.
- Partner with families and friends, communities and countries that are broken and/or with clearly endangered futures.
- Partner with families and friends, communities and countries that are positioned to move up from surviving to thriving.
- Build off issue areas and cross-cutting issue areas that are broken and/or with endangered futures.
- Use breakthroughs in knowledge and technology.
- Partner with new, more capable and more motivated leaders emerge.
- Use eMedia and social networking.
- Use grassroots and self-organizing movements.
- Watch for and use new tipping points as they emerge.
- When necessary, appropriate and doable, create new tipping points that are opportunities to build a thriving future.

and all of us should help build, achieve and sustain a surviving and thriving future for <u>our family and friends</u>. Each and all of us should help build, achieve and sustain a surviving and thriving future for <u>our community</u>. Each and all of us should help build, achieve and sustain a surviving and thriving future for <u>our country</u>. Each and all of us should help build, achieve and sustain a surviving and thriving future for <u>our world</u>, including the Earth on which we depend. Via these actions and the ***Thrive!* Endeavor**, <u>each and all of us together</u> should build, achieve and sustain a surviving and thriving future.

What positive actions are needed to bring about the needed changes that improve our current status enough to achieve the desired surviving and thriving status? [Figure 9.1] Each and all of us identify actions that support <u>good</u> changes that will help reduce vulnerability and/or improve and/or sustain surviving and thriving. If good changes are likely to occur, together we support them. If good changes are not likely to occur, together we support them and develop other good changes to compensate.

Each and all of us identify actions that stop <u>bad</u> changes that increase vulnerability and/or prevent or limit surviving and thriving. If bad changes are not likely to occur, together we ensure they do not. If bad changes are likely to occur, together we change them, stop them or avoid/reduce their impact.

Via the Endeavor, all of us together develop our strategy and successfully take the actions to ensure a surviving and thriving future.

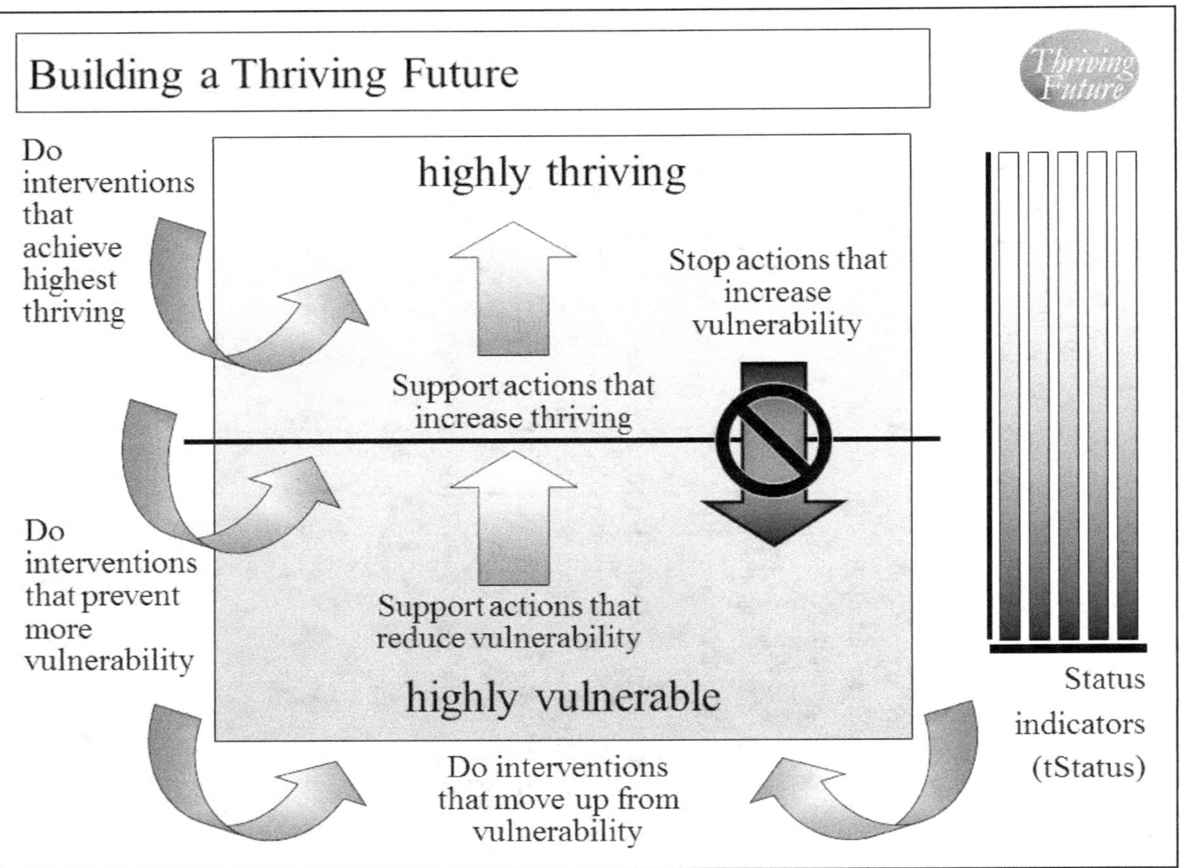

Figure 9.1. Building and Sustaining a Thriving Future.

With what result?

When successful, all of us, current and future, should be performing well. Be well-off (financially). Be well nourished (food and drink). Be well housed. Be well protected (exposures, crime). Be well educated. Be physically and mentally well (people). Personally grow/develop well. Be physically well (Earth, plants, animals, environment). Live within good habitat. Not be vulnerable. Produce personal and public goods. Live within a stable, positive climate. Be sustained.

But it is more than just people surviving and thriving. The Earth upon which we depend should be surviving and thriving.

When successful, we and all future generations achieve the surviving and thriving future for all forever, to the maximum extent possible. At this time in human history when we desire to thrive, when we need to survive, when our future is most endangered, and when we are most capable, the *Thrive!* **Endeavor**, all of us together, can and must build, achieve and sustain a thriving future for all forever.

Appendix: *Thrive!* Next Generation Toolkit
Strategy, policy and tools for creating and sustaining large, positive change and building a thriving future.

If we are to achieve a better future, we need "next generation" strategies for solving large problems and creating and sustaining positive, large and timely change. We need them to build and sustain a thriving future. *Thrive!* (including *via*Future and the supportive *via)* strategies, models and tools are "next generation" strategy.[129],[130]

Thirty years of experience at the national and local levels strongly suggests that most current policy and strategy models are too limited in scope for addressing today's problems and wholly inadequate for succeeding with a much more challenging future. No single strategy, model or tool by itself will help us do all this. However, a "next generation" strategic framework coupled with a core set of "next generation" strategies, models and tools together can help. The core set and system of supportive models addresses persons, systems, motivation, ability, behavior, performance and its improvement, process measures, and, most importantly, positive outcomes and improved status.

---

[129] *via*Future (path and means to the future) is the term used in other settings for the underlying strategies, models and tools for the next generation toolkit.
The *via* name is used because its definition is "by way of, through the medium or agency of, or by means of."

[130] You might also want to use *Thrive!* - **Building a Thriving Future**, the previous book, which provides greater depth on strategy and tools and is available via www.Amazon.com or as free download from www.ThrivingFuture.org.

Why *Thrive!* Next Generation Framework And Supportive Strategies

Going back to what it means to be "next generation", here is how they match up to the need.

1) First, they focus on individual "persons" -- individuals with unique abilities, motivation, and behaviors uniquely affected by and affecting their "environment." "Person" aspects are addressed by the Behavioral Effectiveness Model (BEM) and the "Person-centered Model". They have been used to help improve health and health care.

2) Second, they are designed to be more effective at addressing issue areas, especially large, complex ones. Large, complex issue areas (e.g., health) have been addressed with them.

3) Third, they are designed to effectively handle the cross-cutting issues of a highly interactive and interdependent world. Cross-cutting issue areas, including health and vulnerability, have been explored with the full *via* strategy core set.

4) Fourth, they are designed to tackle issues as a system (e.g. a health system) interacting with other systems and within larger systems (e.g. communities, nations, broader areas). Systems (personal health, health care delivery systems, and public health) have been addressed with the full *via* strategy core set, including the "system" models.

5) Fifth, they are designed to effectively handle "whole" systems, including whole communities, whole nations, and whole broader areas. Systems have been addressed (e.g., health system for America in context of America and the world) or explored (e.g., vulnerability, community, a nation) with the full *via* strategy core set.

6) Sixth, they are designed to effectively handle the future in terms of sustaining whatever progress we make and adjusting to a changing future. Sustainable, future-adaptive systems have been addressed (e.g., personal health, large health care delivery systems) or explored (e.g., vulnerability, community, nation) with the full *via*

strategy core set, including the predictive aspects of the core set's models.

What Is The *Thrive!* Strategy Core Set And How Does It Work In Supporting *Thrive!*

The overall strategy and strategy core set is explored here along with three areas of potential application:
- Health, a large, complex, individual issue area, where it has already been applied.
- Vulnerability, a large complex cross-cutting issue area, where it is being explored to develop coordinated strategy and policy.
- Whole communities, whole nations and whole broader areas where it is being explored to develop coordinated strategy and policy.

What does the strategy core set include? As shown in Table A.1, the core set includes the overall Strategy, the Performance Improvement Model, the *via* Model, the Behavioral Effectiveness Model (BEM), the Person Model, the Population Model, the System(s) Model, the Strategy Model, and the Status Model. The overall core set and the supportive components can be applied to a single issue area, cross-cutting issue areas, and whole non-geographic populations, communities, nations and broader areas. Though this paper focuses on their use as a set, each can be used independently as well.

Overall Thrive! Strategy and Strategy Core Set.

What is it? As displayed in Figure A.1 and detailed in Table A.1, the overall strategy core set is to effectively use the strategy core set as a set of integrated, coordinated components to produce the necessary knowledge and an effective overall strategy with supportive strategies. By using the full core set, we can better identify and understand the targeted system (e.g., community, nation), decide what we want to achieve on a sustained basis, understand and select the target behaviors, design and select what interventions we need, and develop the overall strategy and supportive strategies to achieve the desired state. [Table A.1 and Figure A.1.]

Table A.1: *Thrive!* Strategy Core Set and Applicable Issue Levels and Scope			
	Issue Level and Scope		
Strategy Core Set	Single Issue Area (E.g. Health)	Cross-cutting Issue Areas (E.g. Vulnerability)	Whole Community, Nation, Broader Areas
Overall Strategy	X	X	X
System(s) Model, Including "Ideal" Systems	X	X	X
Performance Improvement Model	X	X	X
via Model	X	X	X
Behavioral Effectiveness Model (BEM)	X	X	X
Person Model (applying BEM over individual person's time & life stages)	X	X	X
Population Model (applying BEM over multiple persons' time & life stages)	X	X	X
Strategy Model (strategies & interventions)	X	X	X
Status Model	X	X	X

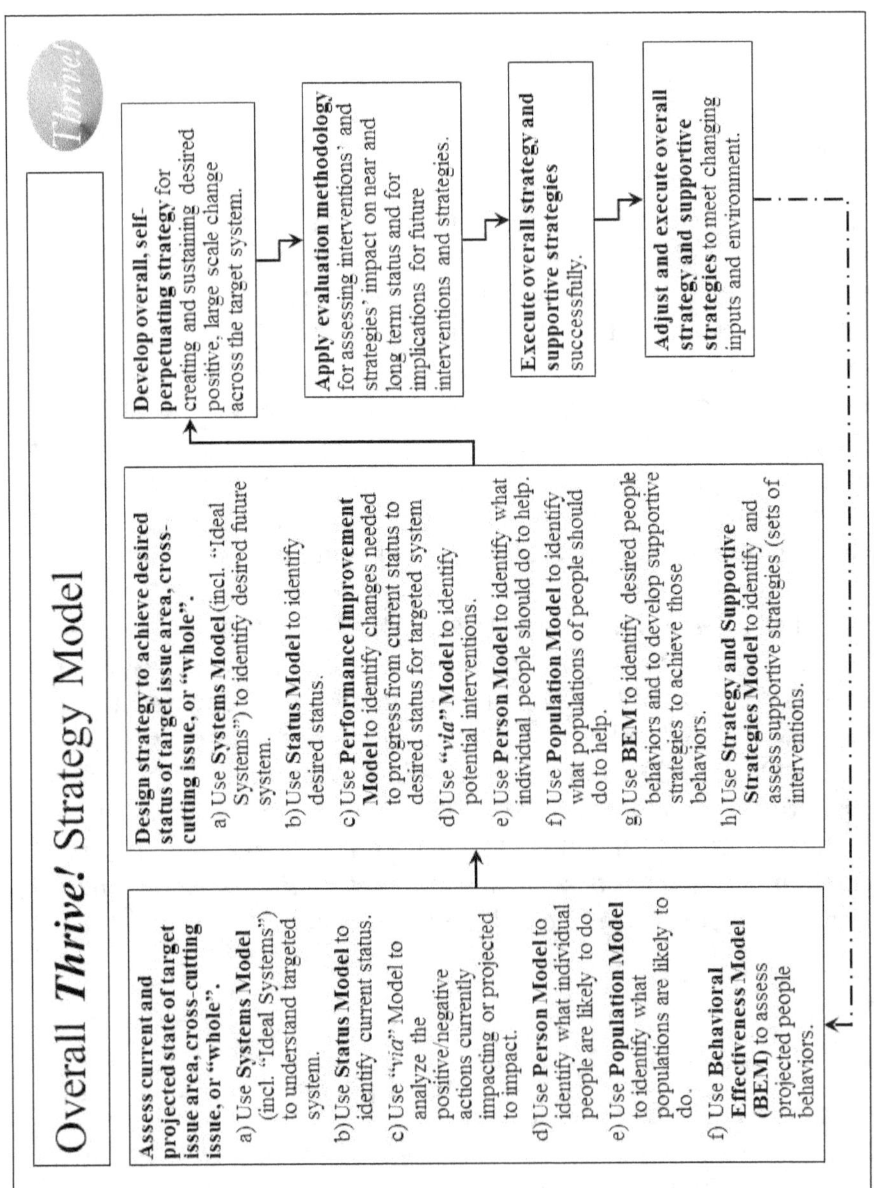

Figure A.1. Overall *Thrive!* Strategy Model.

How does it work? It works through the systematic application of the core set by people who have both the motivation and the ability to help create and sustain positive, large and timely change.

Though the steps in Table A.2 imply their sequential application that is not always the case. Step 1 is important in our understanding what is the current system, its status, its projected actions, and its projected people and population behaviors. Step 1c helps us organize that thinking of how we might get from the current situation to the desired status for the targeted system. Step 2 helps us work through what needs to be changed and how we might make that change. Step 3 pulls all this together to help us create and execute the overall strategy and supportive strategies. Step 4 is to make sure we evaluate how we are doing and provide input for changes in strategy. Step 5 focuses on the successful execution of the overall strategy and supportive strategies. Step 6 makes sure we understand that strategy is not static and needs to adjust to unanticipated input and environmental changes, and the strategy needs to be executed successfully on an ongoing basis.

How has it been used and helped? The *Thrive!* strategy core set has been used for several large scale changes, including systems such as the $15+ billion Military Health System (Department of Defense), the $1+ billion Health*e*Vet VistA health information system (Veterans Health Administration), the draft Strategic and Operational Plan for the $500+ billion Centers for Medicare and Medicaid Services, a potential strategy for reducing vulnerability for communities and nations, and a potential strategy for Building a Healthy America (over 1/6th of the U.S. economy).

Table A.2. Overall *Thrive!* Strategy - Creating and Sustaining Positive, Large Change

The overall strategy for creating and sustaining positive, large change is as follows:

1. Assess current and projected state of target issue area, cross-cutting issue, or "whole".
   a. Use Systems Model (including Ideal Systems) to understand targeted system (e.g. health system, community, nation, broader area) today.
   b. Use Status Model to identify current status for "whole" (e.g., community, nation, broader areas), issue areas (e.g., health, education), or cross-cutting issue area (e.g., vulnerability, climate, habitat) targeted for positive, large scale change.
   c. Use via Model to analyze positive/negative actions currently impacting or projected to impact issue, cross-cutting issue, or "whole".
   d. Use Person Model to identify what individual people are likely to do in future.
   e. Use Population Model to identify what populations are likely to do in future.
   f. Use Behavioral Effectiveness Model (BEM) to assess projected people behaviors.
2. Design strategy to achieve desired status for target issue area, cross-cutting issue, or "whole".
   a. Use Systems Model (incl. "Ideal Systems") to identify desired future system state.
   b. Use Status Model to identify desired status for targeted system.
   c. Use Performance Improvement Model to identify changes, including behavior, needed to progress from current status and achieve desired status for targeted system.
   d. Use via Model to identify potential interventions for creating and sustaining desired positive, large scale change.
   e. Use Person Model to identify what individual people should do to help achieve the desired positive, large scale change.
   f. Use Population Model to identify what populations of people should do to help achieve the desired positive, large scale change.
   g. Use BEM to identify ability, motivation and desired behaviors that help achieve desired change and to develop supportive strategies to achieve desired behaviors.
   h. Use Strategy and Supportive Strategies Model to identify and assess and organize supportive strategies (sets of interventions) for creating/sustaining desired change.

> 3. With above inputs, develop overall, self-perpetuating strategy for creating and sustaining desired positive, large scale change across target system.
> 4. Apply evaluation methodology for assessing strategies/interventions impact on near and long term status and implications for future interventions/strategies.
> 5. Execute overall strategy and supportive strategies successfully.
> 6. Adjust and execute overall strategy and supportive strategies to meet changing inputs and environment.

In 2006, the Centers for Medicare and Medicaid Services (CMS) used the combination for drafting a strategic and operational plan for 2007-12. Essentially, the whole strategy was used, working with the CMS staff, to develop a strategic plan covering six years for the $500+ billion agency and its programs. The desired health status and outcome measures were identified. The "ideal" system was identified. The performance improvement model was developed as the framework. Evaluation measures were developed. The strategy addressed "person", "population" and behavioral issues and how to address them. The end result was a comprehensive draft strategic and operational plan that was developed with the staff. The plan remains available for future CMS use.

An important example of the combination's use in the early 2000s, was to create and sustain positive change to the Veterans Health Administration (VHA) health information system, a nationwide system covering over 1000 sites of care and with an annual budget of over $1 billion. The desired change was to build upon and expand the capability of VHA's existing VistA health information system by creating a sustainable next generation system named Health*e*Vet VistA. The new system was approved by VHA, the Department of Veterans Affairs and the Office of Management and budget and received increased funding of about $125 million annually. Much of the new system is already in place and operating successfully.

The *Thrive!* strategy core set is being explored on the cross-cutting issue of vulnerability. Here it is being used to create a potential strategy for minimizing vulnerability and maximizing thriving for a whole population (e.g., community, nation). The resulting strategy addresses the system of a community or a nation. It establishes the desired status as minimized vulnerability and maximized thriving and includes a set of measures for that status. It uses the full core set to lay out the performance improvement framework, to analyze and design interventions, to determine how best to address both an individual person and whole populations over time, to develop the behavioral interventions, and to design the overall strategy and supportive strategies.

The combination has also been used to design a **Health_ePeople** strategy to improve health and health care across America. The same design has applicability in communities, states, and other nations.

The combination's application to whole communities, nations and broader areas is also being explored as a total system interacting with other systems.. In this case, the focus is on the whole population and its individual whole persons. It also addresses animals, plants and other natural resources in the context of the community, nation or broader area. The full range of significant issue areas within the target community, nation or broader area is explored, including their interaction and interdependency. Status indicators to assess current and desired future state are being developed. The intended result is an overall, sustainable, executable strategy for improving the status of a community, a nation or a broader area.

Performance Improvement Model.

What is it? The Performance Improvement Model lays out the process by which a desired performance or status (e.g. minimized vulnerability and maximized thriving, high health status, sustainable and good human and animal habitat, sustainable energy) is set and compared to the current status. Based on that, a strategy is developed that makes the necessary changes to achieve the desired performance or status. [See Figure A.2.]

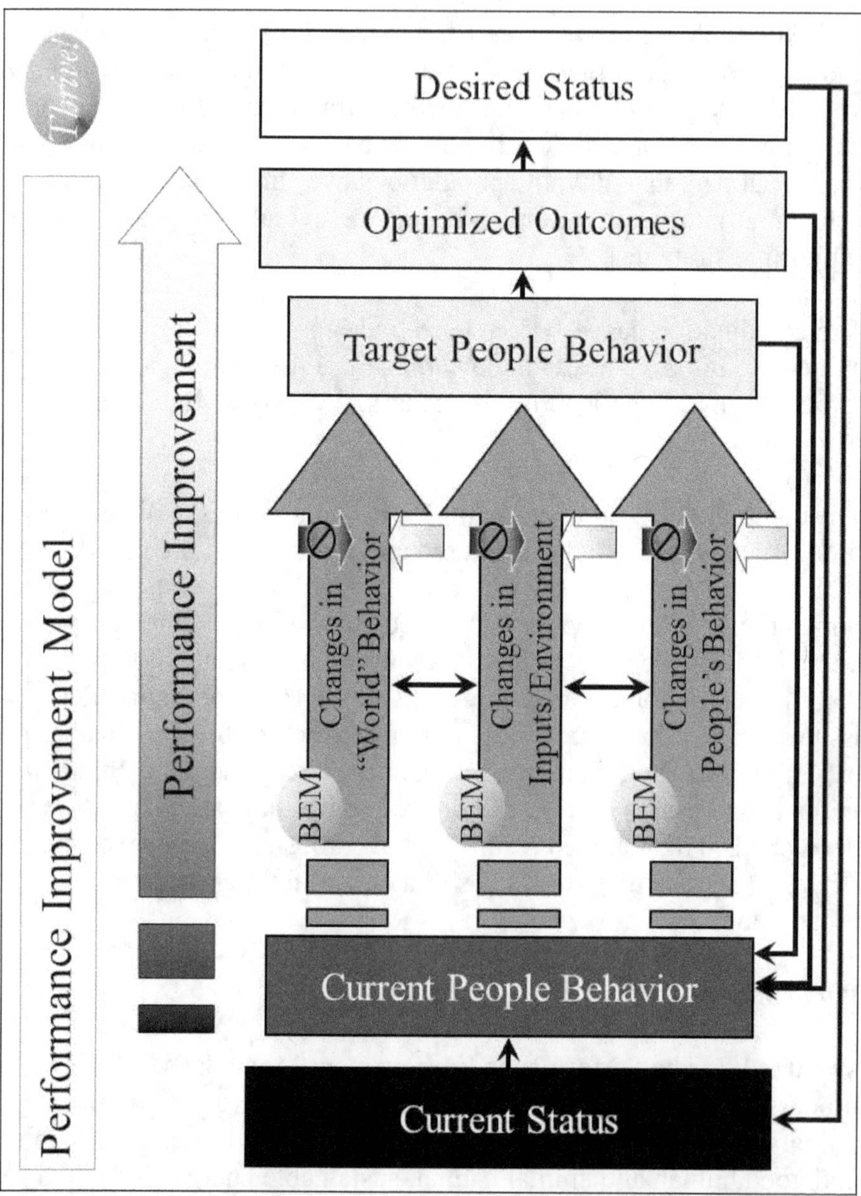

Figure A.2. Performance Improvement Model - Strategies for Improving Performance to Achieve Desired Status.

How does it work? Based on an understanding of the system that is to be improved and its current status or performance level, a desired level of status or performance is chosen. The model is designed to help determine what it will take to achieve that performance or status level. [See Table A.3.]

How has it been used and helped? The Performance Improvement Model's primary use to date has been for improving health care quality, outcomes and status. Its potential use is being explored in creating an overall strategy for reducing vulnerability and improving the status of a community, nation or broader area.

At the Centers for Medicare and Medicaid Services (CMS), the model was used in 2006 to design an overall strategy for national quality improvement for health care, including but not limited to care funded by Medicare and Medicaid. The desired outcome was health status based on the best knowledge on how much health status can be improved through health care. The current status was based on the best available information on current health status. The model helped identify what outcomes, properly optimized, could best produce the desired health status. Further, it helped identify what target people (persons, health care personnel) behaviors could best produce those optimized outcomes. The Person Model was used to understand how individual persons do and should behave over time. The Population Model was used to understand how populations do and should behave over time. The BEM Model was used to determine what interventions would likely produce the desired behavior change. The *via* Model was used to determine how to apply those interventions as a coordinated, ongoing strategy. These strategies and interventions were used to enhance the overall quality improvement program for CMS.

Table A.3. Performance Improvement Model – Strategies for Improving Performance to Achieve Desired Status

The overall strategy for improving performance is as follows:
1. Based on an understanding of the system that is to be improved, assess its current status or performance level.
2. Determine what should be the desired level of status or performance.
3. Assess what is the delta (difference) between those two levels.
4. Determine what outcomes need to be produced in order to achieve the desired level of status or performance.
5. Determine what people's current behaviors are.
6. Determine what people's target behaviors should be.
7. Assess what is the delta between those two sets of behavior and what behavior changes are desired.
8. Determine how "world", input/environment, and people behavior already occurring or projected to occur affect people behaviors. "World" behaviors are changes in people behaviors that are outside the system being changed. "Inputs/Environment" changes are non-people behaviors such as climate change, and plant and animal change.
9. Determine the set of strategies and interventions needed to change people behaviors by using other models, including the Behavioral Effectiveness Model (BEM), the *via* model, and the Person and Population models. These strategies and interventions may be applied to any or all of "world", input/environment and people behavior already occurring or projected to occur.
10. Measure the effect that these strategies and interventions are having on changing people's behavior, the outcomes and the status.
11. Feed the strategies and interventions into the Overall Strategy and Supporting Strategies.
12. Determine how changes in status, outcomes and behavior create a new level of "current" status, outcomes and behavior and rerun the Performance Improvement Model on an ongoing basis.

***via* Model.**

What is it? The *via* Model serves as a basic framework for interventions that improve the status of an issue area (e.g., health, vulnerability, environment) or a "whole" (e.g., a non-geographic population, a community, a nation, or a broader area). [See Figure A.3.]

How does it work? As detailed in Table A.4, the *via* Model includes what it is we want to achieve and avoid, how to work through interventions and actions that affect that achievement, and how to measure progress.

How has it been used and helped? The *via* Model's primary use to date has been for improving health care. Its potential use is being explored in creating an overall strategy for reducing vulnerability and improving the status of a community, nation or broader area.

The combination has also been used to design a **Health_ePeople** strategy to improve health and health care across America and beyond. The same design has applicability in communities, states, and other nations.

At the Centers for Medicare and Medicaid Services (CMS), the model was used in 2006 to design the draft CMS Strategic and Operational Plan for 2007-12. It assessed current and projected actions by CMS and others affecting health status. It identified new interventions to stop actions that lower health status and to support actions that increase high and low status. New interventions were also identified that directly help achieve high and highest health status, prevent lowering of health status and move up from low health status. These *via* Model interventions were then used to develop the draft overall Strategic and Operational Plan for CMS.

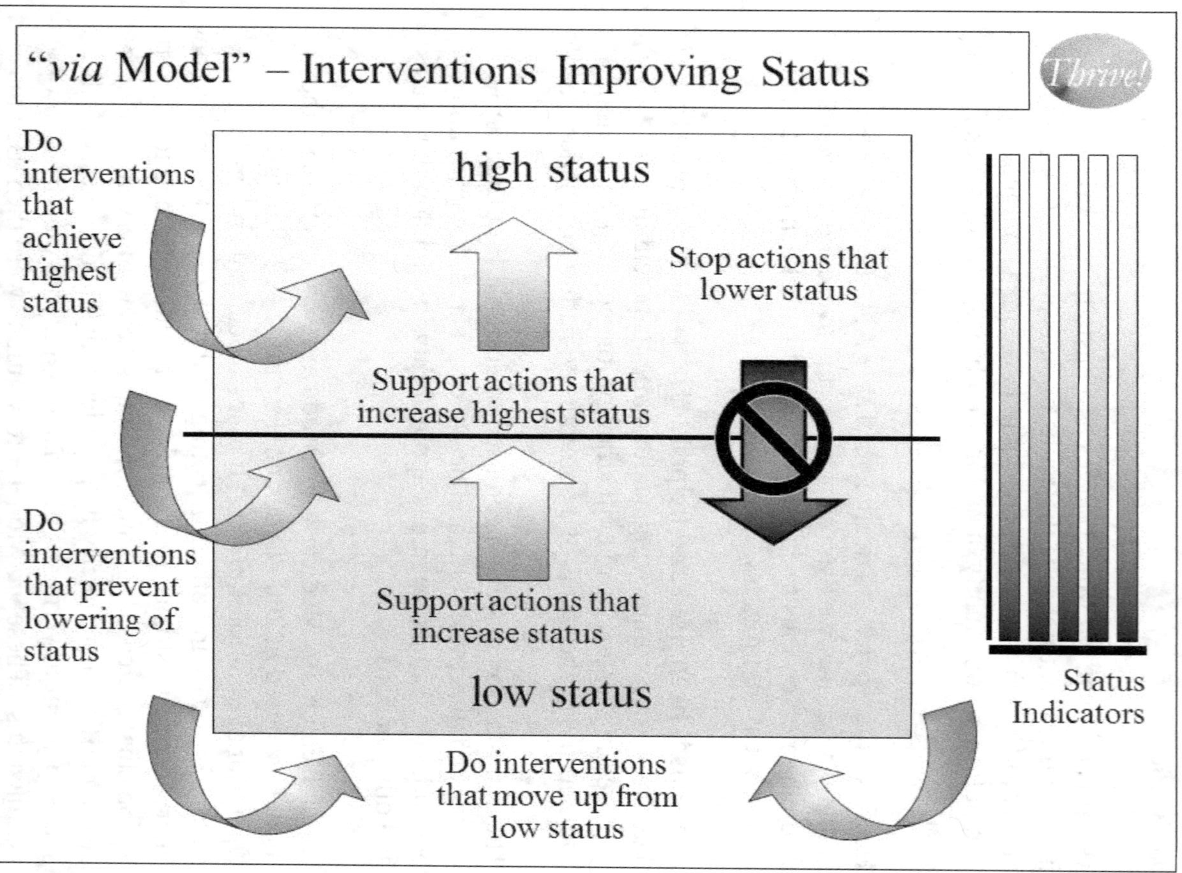

Figure A.3. "*via* Model" for Interventions Improving Status.

Table A.4. via Model - Interventions Improving Status

The via Model use for interventions improving status is as follows:

1. Decide what issue area or "whole" needs status improvement.
2. Decide what status indicators will be used to measure current and desired status.
3. Identify current and projected actions that affect status in one of the following ways:
   a. Actions that lower status.
   b. Actions that increase status for that portion above the mean or median.
   c. Actions that increase status for that portion below the mean or median.
4. Identify what new interventions that positively affect status in one of the following ways:
   a. Interventions that help achieve highest status, including supporting actions that further increase high or highest status.
   b. Interventions that help prevent lowering of status, including stopping actions that lower status.
   c. Interventions that help move up from low status, including supporting actions that increase status.
5. Measure the effect that the interventions are having on the current and projected actions and on the status indicators.
6. Feed the interventions into Overall Strategy and Supporting Strategies.

The model is being used on the cross-cutting issue of vulnerability. Here it is used to help create a proposed strategy for minimizing vulnerability and maximizing thriving for a whole population (e.g., a non-geographic population, a community, a nation). In this case, high status was "high thriving" and low status was "high vulnerability". An assessment has been done on what actions are already occurring or projected to occur that will affect vulnerability. The model is being used to determine what interventions could be used to reduce vulnerability and maximize thriving.

Preliminary work has also been done on using the model for non-geographic populations, communities, nations and broader areas. That work incorporates the work done on health and vulnerability into an expanded use applicable to whole communities, nations or broader areas. The focus is on a whole population and its whole persons, along with the respective animals, plants and other natural resources. It addresses the target area as a system with subsystems (e.g. issue areas like health, income, habitat, climate) and with interactions and interdependencies with other systems (i.e., other communities, nations, and broader areas).

Behavioral Effectiveness Model (BEM).

What is it? The Behavioral Effectiveness Model (BEM) is built upon several related models from expectancy theory, instrumentality theory, theory of reasoned action, contingency theory, system theory, social cognitive theory, behavioral theory, etc. that have been in use and refined over 30-40 years. A very detailed explanation of the BEM model and its use is provided in the Appendix: Behavioral Effectiveness Model (BEM). The *via* approach is built upon the premise that a person or a population's behavior is key to what creates and sustains positive change. [See Figure A.4.]

BEM's value lies in 1) being relatively parsimonious, 2) incorporating key aspects of other behavioral models, 3) being "computable" (i.e., it can use databases (personal and environmental characteristics, desired behaviors and tailored interventions)), 4) tailoring applicability to more than one person simultaneously by using individual characteristics and desired behavior(s) and 5) using evidence-based interventions that can be tailored to those characteristics and the desired behavior.

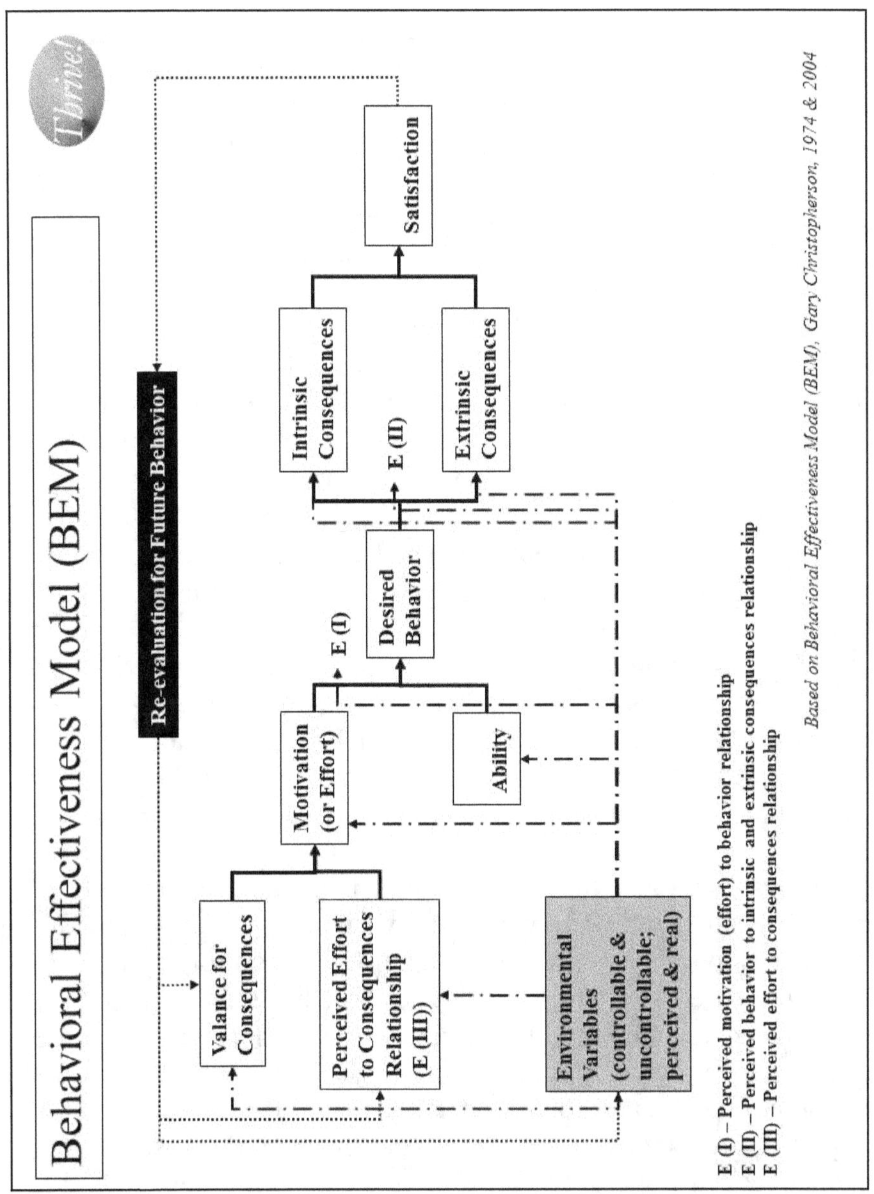

Figure A.4. "Behavioral Effectiveness Model (BEM) - Improving Personal Behavior/Performance

How does it work? As shown in Table A.5, the BEM model is designed to 1) apply interventions that help achieve the desired target behavior, 2) learn more about the person or population involved, 3) learn more about interventions and 4) learn more about the "system" in which intervention are used. It can also be used for prediction, analysis and program development and evaluation. The model can be applied to 1) an individual person, 2) populations whose characteristics are sufficiently the same, and/or 3) populations of individuals for which each individual gets a personalized and tailored intervention. The model can be linked to a database so that it can use and produce information and support personalized and tailored interventions:

- For any number of individuals and over any period of time
- For one-time behaviors and behavior over time
- For change in a single behavior and multiple behaviors.

How has it been used and helped?   The Behavioral Effectiveness Model's primary use to date has been for improving health. Its potential use is being explored in creating an overall strategy for reducing vulnerability and improving the status of a non-geographic population, a community, a nation or a broader area.

Its earliest use was in the middle 1970's, helping develop a high blood pressure control program in Milwaukee, Wisconsin. The desired behavior was adherence to methods for controlling high blood pressure. These methods could be medication use and/or life style change (e.g., diet, exercise, stress reduction). Through the use of BEM, the program was better able to get people to get their blood pressures checked and controlled and to determine the likely success of particular methods with a specific person and with persons with similar characteristics. The blood pressure control program was seen as a national model for community blood pressure control.

**Table A.5. "Behavioral Effectiveness Model (BEM)" –
Improving Personal Behavior/Performance**

The BEM Model use for achieving desired behavior is as follows:
1. Identify the person or population whose behavior is targeted.
2. Decide what is the desired behavior or behaviors. Note that some behavior is one-time and some is recurring.
3. Assess motivation in terms of its current and future characteristics.
4. Assess ability in terms of its current and future characteristics.
5. Assess environmental variables, both controllable and uncontrollable and both perceived and real.
6. Assess how motivation, ability and environmental variables are likely to affect future behavior without further intervention.
7. Assess what are likely to be the intrinsic (internal to the person or population) and extrinsic (external to the person or population) consequences of projected behavior and what is likely to be the person or population's satisfaction.
8. Assess how consequences and satisfaction are likely to affect future behavior
9. Assess how projected behavior, without further intervention, matches to desired behavior.
10. Assess what interventions will best move projected behavior to desired behavior for the near and long term.
11. Apply the interventions and assess their effect.
12. Adjust the interventions as needed over time and based on result.
13. Feed the interventions into the Overall Strategy and Supporting Strategies.

BEM is also being used on the cross-cutting issue of vulnerability. Here it is being used to help identify what behaviors are associated with vulnerability and thriving. It helps identify what ability and motivational factors are and would be determinants of vulnerability and thriving behavior as well as establishing what interventions to use to reduce such vulnerability and maximize thriving.

With respect to communities, nations or broader areas, BEM is used for addressing the full breadth of issue areas and of people, animals/plants, and other natural resources. Here it helps identify what behaviors are associated with the relevant status indicators. It helps identify what ability and motivational factors are and would be determinants of improving status. The model determines what interventions could improve the motivation and ability factors and, as a result, improve status. Based on these, a strategy is being created for improving status for a whole population, in this case America as a whole.

Person Model.

What is it? The Person Model helps us to understand that each person goes through several life stages depending on how long they live. If status (e.g. health, income, performance) is to be improved, it is seldom a one-time intervention and generally should be done across the life span. As a result, the Person Model works by applying the Behavioral Effectiveness Model over an individual person's time and life stages. [See Figure A.5.]

How does it work? The Person Model, with BEM as the underlying model, recognizes that each person is different at the beginning, throughout the life stages, and near the end. For status to be improved, the strategy needs to be both specific to each person across the life span and effective for all persons across the life span. [See Table A.6.]

How has it been used and helped? To date, the Person Model's primary use has been for improving health. Its potential use is being explored for creating an overall strategy for reducing vulnerability and improving the status of a community, nation or broader area.

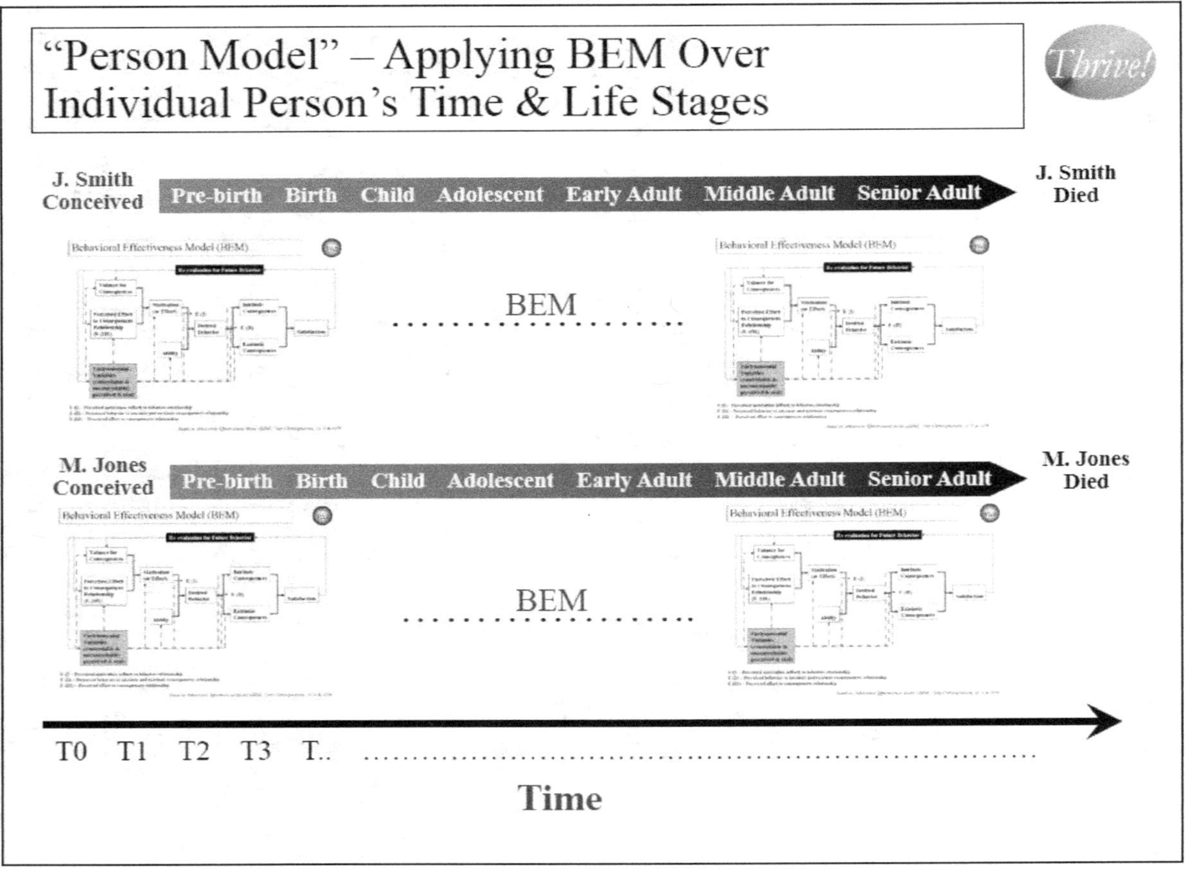

Figure A.5. "Person Model" – Applying BEM Over Each Person's Time and Life Stages.

Table A.6. Person Model – Applying BEM Over Each Person's Time and Life Stages

The Person Model use for achieving desired behavior is as follows:
1. Identify the person or population whose behavior is targeted.
2. Decide what is the time frame or life stage(s) to be addressed. The preferred time frame is the whole life.
3. Decide what is the desired behavior or behaviors over time and through life stages.
4. Apply BEM model as a recurring model (running the model as many times as necessary) adjusting to changes in motivation, ability and environmental variables.
5. Assess what interventions will best move projected behavior to desired behavior for the covered time and life stage(s).
6. Apply the interventions and assess their effect on an ongoing basis.
7. Adjust the interventions as needed over time and based on result.
8. Feed the interventions into the Overall Strategy and Supporting Strategies.

The model has been used to design the **Health*e*People** strategy to improve health and health care across America. The same design has applicability in communities, states, and other nations.
Its earliest use was in the middle 1970s to develop a high blood pressure control program in Milwaukee, Wisconsin. The desired behavior was adherence to a protocol for controlling high blood pressure over the person's remaining life. Through the use of the Person Model, the program was better able to understand how to match the intervention to time and different life stages. With respect to time, the interventions needed during the initial treatment were different than during the maintenance phase of treatment. With respect to life stages, interventions required refining for matching the behavioral determinants for a younger versus middle-age versus older persons. The blood pressure control program served as a model of community blood pressure control programs.

At the Centers for Medicare and Medicaid Services (CMS), the model was used in 2005 to enhance the overall strategy for national quality improvement for health care. The desired behavior was of health care providers over time and their careers. The model helped identify what target health care personnel behaviors, on an ongoing basis, could produce the best outcomes. Based on that, an approach was laid out using current and new interventions to improve health care provider behavior in a way that would produce improved outcomes and health status for the foreseeable future and over the health care providers' careers (life stages). These interventions were used to improve the overall quality improvement program for CMS.

The model was used in the early 2000s to create a new model called "person-centered health". [See Figure A.6.] The Person-Centered Health Model has been used to refine the programs of the Veterans Health Administration, including overall care, care in the community and the VHA health information system (electronic health record and personal health record systems). It was also used at the Centers for Medicare and Medicaid Services to help with the draft strategic and operational plan.

The Person Model is also being used on the cross-cutting issue of vulnerability. Since vulnerability is relevant over a person's whole life span and changes through the life stages, the model helps identify what ability and motivational factors, over time and across life stages, would be determinants of vulnerability and thriving behavior. It recognizes that reducing vulnerability prior to birth is very different than doing so for an adolescent or for a senior adult. Some factors (e.g. financial and cognitive ability) carry across a person's life and can help lower vulnerability throughout a person's life. Some factors (e.g. ability reduced by Alzheimer's disease or low birth weight) always or most likely occur at a specific life stage.

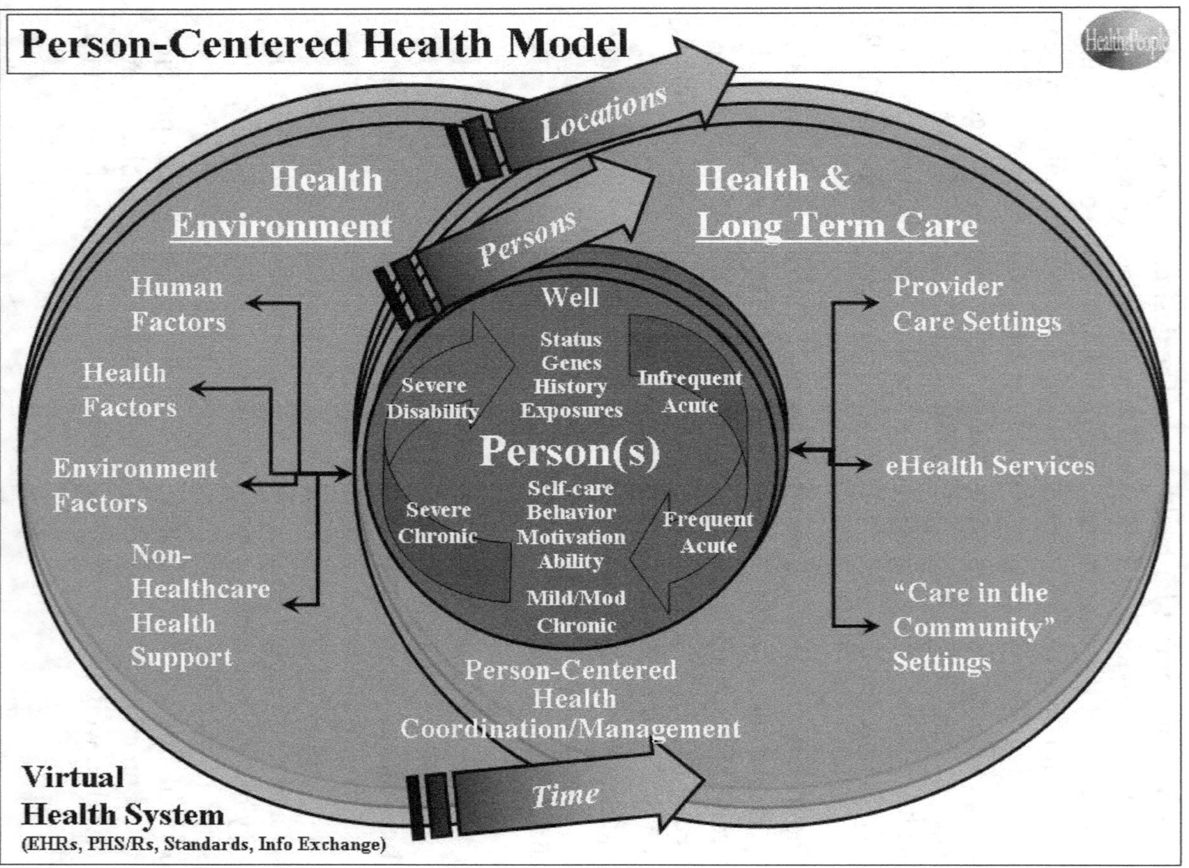

Figure A.6. Person-Centered Health Model.

Population Model.

What is it?   The Population Model addresses status from the perspective of what is happening at any point in time and the effect on a diverse or non-diverse population. Again, BEM is the underlying model for adjusting strategy to address points in time across persons and their life stages. This model also applies to other differences (e.g., racial, ethnic, income, vulnerability) in the target population [See Figure A.7.]

How does it work? The Population Model, with BEM as the underlying model, recognizes that strategy, at any point in time, must be both specific to each applicable person across the life span and effective across all persons across the life span. [See Table A.7.] Taking a time slice, the model recognizes that at any specific time, the target population likely includes persons from all different stages of life (pre-birth, birth, child, adolescent, early adult, middle adult and senior adult). At that time, each person has different status levels, different factors affecting status, and different responses to endeavors at improving status. This can be seen in how major disasters (e.g., tsunamis, earthquakes, disease outbreaks, crop failures, and drought) affect people differently. This can be seen in how program interventions (e.g. education, housing programs, financial assistance, health insurance programs, heating assistance, taxes) affect people differently.

How has it been used and helped? The Population Model's primary use to date has been for improving health. Its potential use is being explored for creating an overall strategy for reducing vulnerability and improving the status of a community, nation or broader area.

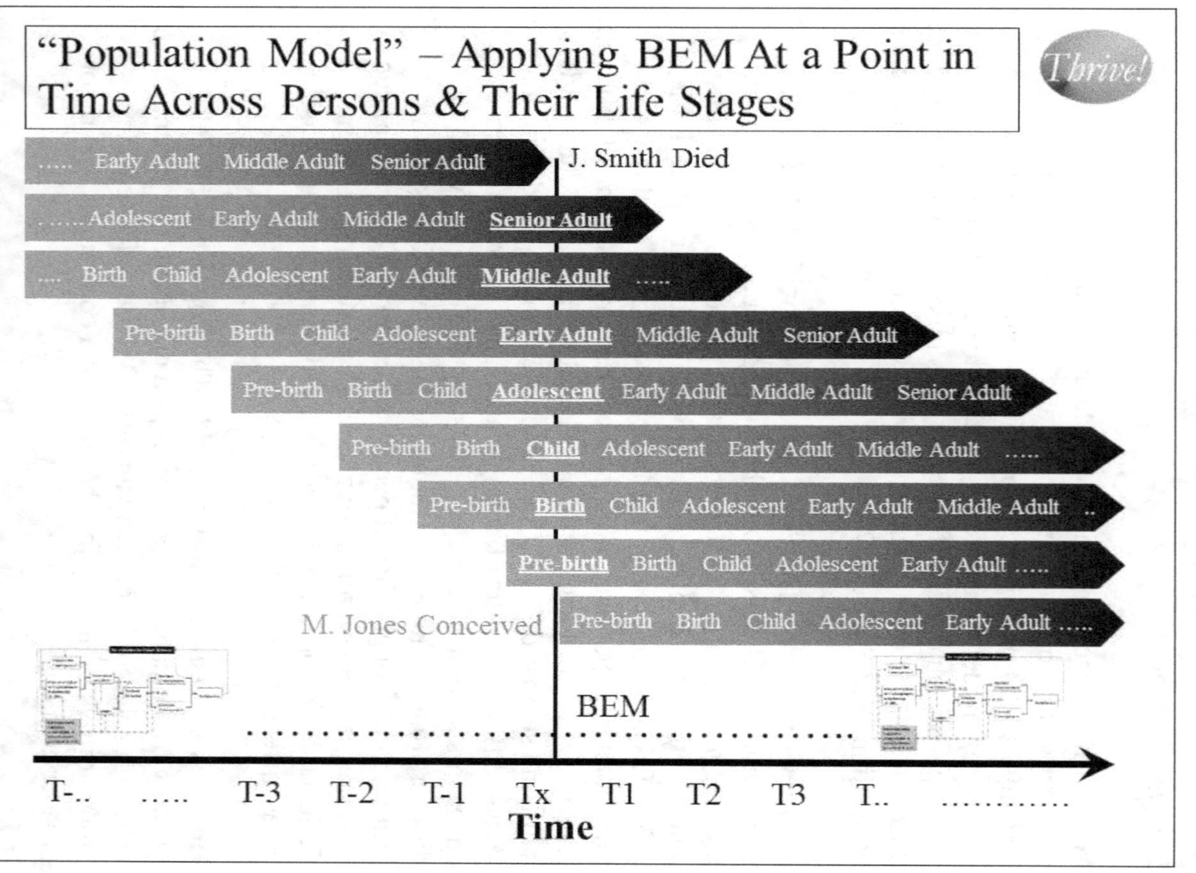

Figure A.7. "Population Model" – Applying BEM at a Point in Time Across Persons and Their Life Stages

---

Table A.7. Population Model – Applying BEM at a Point in Time Across Persons and Their Life Stages

The Population Model use for achieving desired behavior is as follows:
1. Identify the population whose behavior is targeted.
2. Decide what are the point(s) in time and life stage(s) to be addressed.
3. Decide what is the desired behavior or behaviors at different points in time across persons and their life stages.
4. Apply the BEM model across time and across populations and their life stages taking into account their differing motivation, ability and environmental variables.
5. Assess what interventions will best move projected behavior to desired behavior across time and across populations and their life stages.
6. Apply the interventions and assess their effect on a population on an ongoing basis.
7. Adjust the interventions as needed over time and based on result.
8. Feed the interventions into the Overall Strategy and Supporting Strategies.

At the Centers for Medicare and Medicaid Services (CMS), the model was used in 2006 to design the draft CMS Strategic and Operational Plan for 2007-12. It was used to address CMS's disparate beneficiary population and the timing and design of program interventions. The plan was designed to address the needs of both younger and older Medicaid beneficiaries, beneficiaries with disabilities, and healthier and severely ill Medicare beneficiaries. It also addressed the populations that are pre-Medicaid and pre-Medicare. The plan recognized that over time, these populations change as new age cohorts moved into the program. These Population Model interventions were then used to develop the draft overall Strategic and Operational Plan for CMS.

For the DoD Military Health System (MHS), the model was used in the 1990s to work with pre-military, active service, Guard and Reserve, veterans, retirees and their families. All are the responsibility of the MHS. Key points in time greatly affect how the health programs work and their effect. Earlier wars (and their effects) such as the two World Wars and the Korean War are very different than the Vietnam War than the first Iraq War, as well as the second Iraq War and then the Afghanistan operations. They are all likely to be different than future wars and other military actions. All of these factors were built into the overall strategy for the future Military Health System that was re-engineered to improve performance, adopted as a force health protection program, and was made more flexible to adjust to different futures.

The model has also been used to design a **Health*e*People** strategy to improve health and health care across America. The same design has applicability in communities, states, and other nations.

The Population Model is also being used on the cross-cutting issue of vulnerability. Since vulnerability is relevant at different points across a person's life stages, it is used to help identify what ability and motivational factors at those different points are most likely determinants of vulnerability and thriving behavior. For example, applying new policies on financial assistance or taxes over the next twelve months will have very different effects across the population of persons. If the intent of the new policies is reducing financial vulnerability across the U.S. population, then they must be modeled, at a minimum, against each subpopulation and, preferably, against each "person". The more desirable policies are those that both reduce vulnerability most for the most vulnerable and substantially reduce vulnerability for all persons. The most desirable policies are the ones that do this and continue the positive effect as the population moves through time (i.e., sustainable, reduced vulnerability for all people). As indicated earlier, the overall strategy has not been used to date, but is ready for application.

System(s) Model (Including "Ideal" Systems).

What is it? The System(s) Model views the world as a system of systems. When a strategy is being designed, it is important to determine what the target system is, what larger system it is part of, what its subsystems are, and what other systems it relates to. A system can be a community, a nation, or a broader area. It can be an issue area system such a health system, an education system, or an ecological system. The Ideal Systems Model, developed by people such as industrial engineers (e.g. Gerald Nadler) decades ago, is another key model for looking at how well a system could perform and how to achieve the highest performance for that system. [See Figure A.8.]

How does it work? For endeavors to improve status to be successful and sustainable, the strategy and its execution need to be systematic and positively change a system (a whole community, a whole nation or a whole broader area) of systems (e.g., health, education, employment/income, housing, habitat, climate) on a sustained basis. [See Table A.8.]

In a systems model, there is recognition that systems are "living". They change internally, impact other systems and are impacted by other systems. Systems are part of other systems and they have subsystems themselves. They are usually complex. They often overlap with other systems. They interact with other systems, sometimes fairly predictably and sometimes not. They often have permeable borders that are not always understood or constant. They may be nearly infinite in number. Often we apply an artificial construct to them to help us understand and work with them. Some systems are formal constructs (e.g., the British National Health Service system, the Kaiser Permanente system, the Military Health System, the veterans health system) and some are informal constructs (e.g. the American "health system"). They may be or appear to be "chaotic" or "ordered". They may be or appear to be "real".

To positively change a system (e.g. the American "health system") on a sustained basis, we need to understand the impact that existing and future systems will have on each person's or a population's status. We need to understand the impact of systems that we create, change or delete will have on other systems and, ultimately, on each person's status.

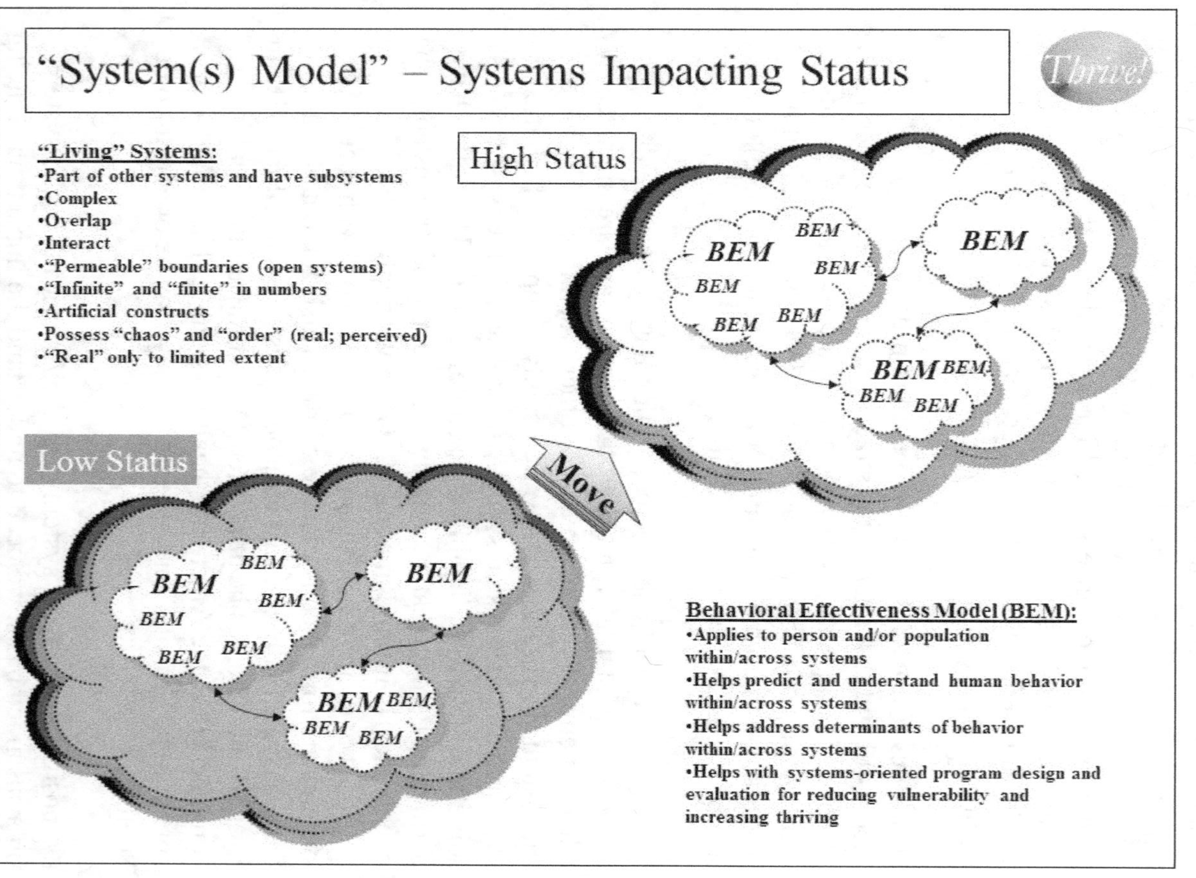

Figure A.8. Systems Model – Systems Impacting Status

Table A.8. Systems Model – Systems Impacting Status

The Systems Model use for achieving desired status is as follows:
1. Identify the target system within which status is to be improved.
2. Identify other systems that are related and might either be impacted or have an impact.
3. Identify the status (lower than desired) for the current system and key characteristics of the current system.
4. Identify the desired status and characteristics for the future system using the Ideal Systems Model.
5. Identify the key behaviors in the current systems and what they need to be in the future system.
6. Determine what changes need to be made to the current system to move it to the desired system.
7. Assess what interventions will best change the current system into the desired future system.
8. Apply the interventions and assess their effect on behavior change and on status.
9. Adjust the interventions as needed over time and based on result.
10. Feed the interventions into the Overall Strategy and Supporting Strategies.

Within "human" systems are real people (individual persons, populations of persons) and organizations (made up of persons) whose behaviors collectively help determine the behavior of the system. The Behavioral Effectiveness Model (BEM) helps us understand the behaviors and their determinants (ability, motivation, environmental factors) on an individual level and on a population of individuals level. In the systems model used here, there is recognition that moving from low status to high status requires moving individual behavior on a massive scale if it is a large system like the American "health system". This movement includes the persons we want to move to higher status and the persons that help or hinder that movement.

As shown in Figure A.9, the Ideal Systems Model helps determine the desired system. It starts out by assessing the current system. It then sets what is the theoretical ideal system assuming there are no costs or constraints preventing us from reaching that system. The theoretical ideal is a guide but is not reachable in the real world for the foreseeable future. Then the model helps us think through the options between the current system and the theoretical ideal system. The ultimate ideal system is one which imposes no constrains but is not yet feasible due to the "means" not yet being available. The feasible ideal system is one where the constraints are removed or reduced and the "means" are available. Finally, the recommended system is the best given the constraints and available means and is on the glide path to the ultimate ideal. The *via* Model helps design and assess these different systems.

How has it been used and helped? The primary use of the System Model (this adapted version) to date has been for improving health. Its potential use is being explored in creating an overall strategy for reducing vulnerability and improving the status of a community, nation or broader area.

One of its earliest uses was in the late 1970s to design and execute an inner city health system for Milwaukee, Wisconsin. The result was a new public/private multi-clinic system providing preventive services, primary care, maternal and infant care, mental health care, dental care, and social services for the community poorest and highest risk people. The total system also included hospital services from public and private hospitals. The system operated successfully for over 30 years and has been viewed as a successful model for improving inner city health care.

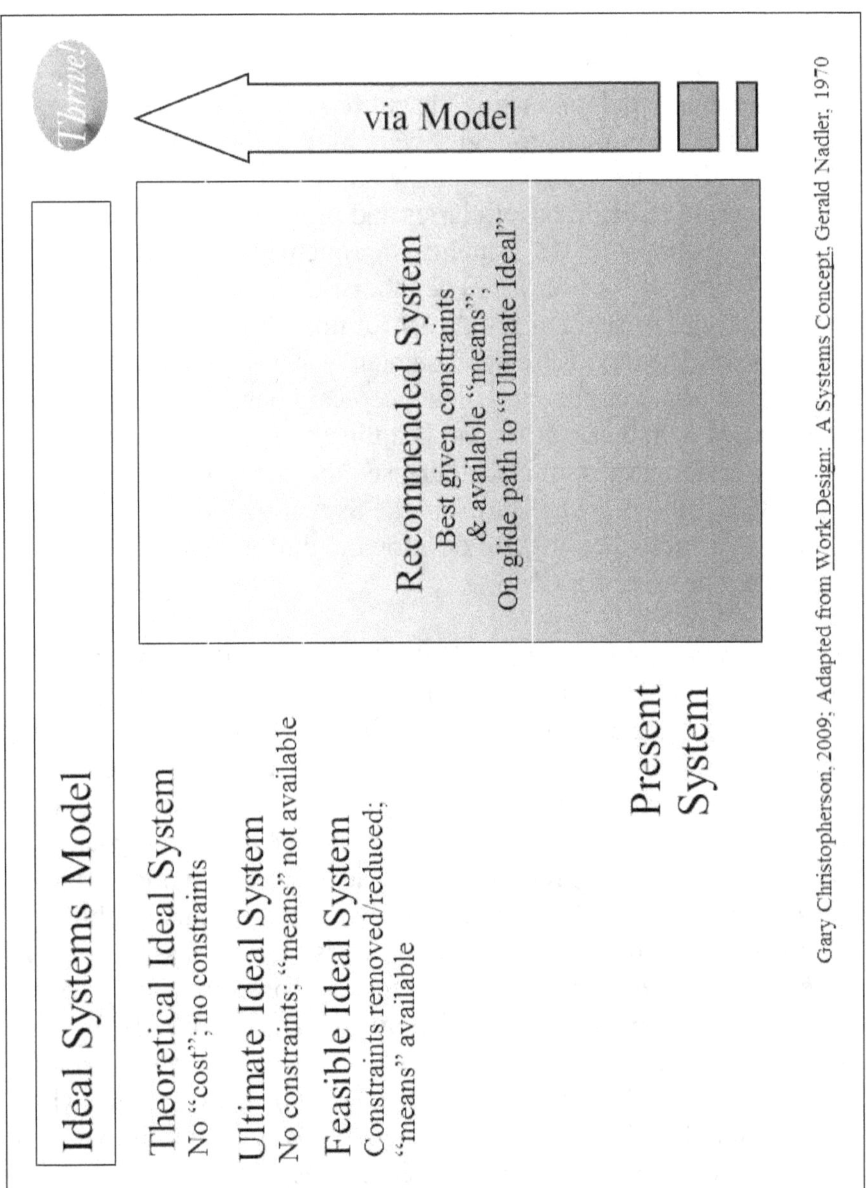

Figure A.9. Ideal Systems Model

At the Centers for Medicare and Medicaid Services (CMS), the Systems Model was used in 2006 to design the draft CMS Strategic and Operational Plan for 2007-12. Rather than approaching the plan as a program by program plan or a CMS only plan, the whole

American "health system" was used as the framework. The plan was designed using the Ideal Systems Model to improve health across the total American population using the entire American "health system". The CMS plan strategies were built on how best to move to high health status by using both CMS programs focused on Medicare and Medicaid beneficiaries and programs with broader scope. For example, CMS's quality improvement program has impact far beyond care for CMS beneficiaries. Similarly, CMS' payment programs serve as the driver for non-CMS payment programs (e.g. health insurers). The plan was designed to address the needs of both younger and older Medicaid beneficiaries, beneficiaries with disabilities, and healthier and severely ill Medicare beneficiaries. It also addressed the populations that are pre-Medicaid and pre-Medicare. These Systems Model interventions were then used to develop the draft overall strategic and operational plan for CMS.

For the Department of Defense (DoD) Military Health System (MHS), the model was used in the middle 1990s to work with full set of DoD health-related programs. The Military Health System was treated as a system that encompassed health care for 1) service members when not engaged in military action, 2) service members (including the Guard and Reserve) when engaged in military action, and 3) family members, retirees, Guard and Reserve in non-active status, veterans served by other providers (e.g., Veterans Health Administration and private providers). It also encompassed preventive services for service members, and force health protection (including protective tools when deployed). The overall MHS strategy was built using the Ideal Systems Model coupled with other "futures" models. It included the health of all of these people. The strategy included all the services needed to protect and improve their health. It included working with other entities, including the Veterans Health Administration and the Centers for Disease Control. All of this was built into the overall strategy for the future Military Health System that was re-engineered, adopted a force health protection program, was more effective and efficient, and was more flexible to adjust to different futures.

The model has also been used to design a **Health*e*People** strategy to improve health and health care across America. The same design has applicability in communities, states, and other nations.

The Systems Model is also being used on the cross-cutting issue of vulnerability. Since vulnerability is both personal and heavily affected by the "system" in which people live, the model is the best way to address both. Similar to what is shown in Figure A.8, the idea is to move from low status (high vulnerability and low thriving) to high status (low vulnerability and high thriving). To best accomplish that, the Systems Model is being used to address the whole system (e.g. the United States) but has its impact on the person level. The Ideal System Model is used to determine what overall strategy would not only minimize vulnerability and maximize thriving at a point in time but to do it on a sustained basis. The strategy identifies what status measures would be relevant at the system-wide level and at the individual person level. It identifies what interventions and actions would both reduce vulnerability most for the most vulnerable and reduce vulnerability substantially for all persons. The Ideal Systems Model is being used to ensure the strategy is one that does this in both the near and long term.

The model's application is being explored for whole communities, nations and broader areas where these are treated as total systems interacting with other systems outside. Building an appropriate set of status indicators is a critical step given the breadth of such systems and the need to assess current and desired future status. The focus is on the whole human population (as well as its individual whole persons), and on animals, plants and natural resources within the targeted community, nation or broader area. The full range of significant issue areas within the target community, nation or broader areas is explored, including their interaction and interdependency. The Ideal Systems model is used to both set the vision and design the recommended systems for now and for the future. The intended result is an overall, sustainable, executable strategy for improving the status of a community, a nation or a broader area.

Strategy Model.

What is it?   The Strategy Model builds on the above groundwork and brings this all together to develop and execute stainable, effective strategies for improving status. It includes the model for building the strategies as well as the framework into which the strategies fit. The model includes both the overall strategy and supportive strategies and the actual interventions supporting the strategies.   [See Figure A.10.]

How does it work? The model brings together all the previous information into an overall strategy and supportive strategies to improve status (e.g. health, income, vulnerability, habitat, climate). [See Table A.9.]

How has it been used and helped?   The Strategy Model's primary use to date has been for improving health. Its potential use for creating an overall strategy for reducing vulnerability and improving the status of a community, nation or broader area is being explored.

At the Centers for Medicare and Medicaid Services (CMS), the Strategy Model was used in 2006 to design the draft CMS Strategic and Operational Plan for 2007-12. The result of that endeavor was a plan similar to what is shown in Figure A.11. For each of the supportive strategies, a set of specific interventions were developed to make the plan fully operational. With respect to quality improvement for CMS, a more in-depth strategy was developed using the Strategy Model.

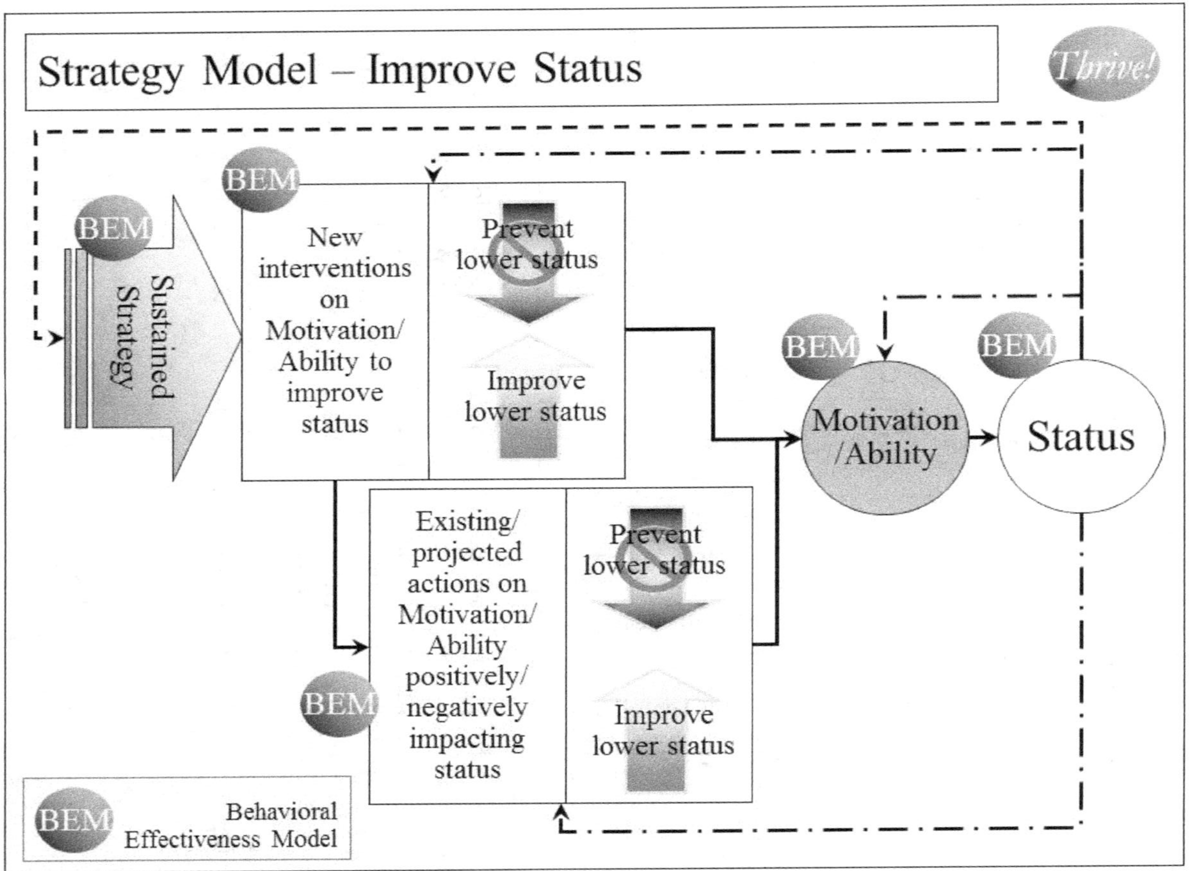

Figure A.10. "Strategy Model" – Improve Status

Table A.9. Strategy Model – Improve Status

The Strategy Model use for achieving desired status incorporates previous work from the other models and input and is as follows:

1. Load the desired status and the associated indicators.
2. Load the optimized outcomes that will best produce high status.
3. Load the target behaviors that will best produce the optimized outcomes.
4. Use pathways to connect how the supportive strategies will best produce the target behavior. The pathways are customized to the issue area or "whole".
5. Identify the specific supportive strategies that, working through the pathways will best produce the target behaviors.
6. Execute the strategy and its supportive strategies effectively.
7. Assess the progress on improving status. Assess the effectiveness of the strategy and its supportive strategies.
8. Revise strategy and supportive strategies as needed to be effective and sustained over time.

The model is being used on the overall American health system. It is being used to try to answer how could we "achieve a healthy America" using an enhanced whole American health system. With many similarities to the CMS Plan, the strategy model helps create a strategy, **Health_ePeople**, but with the larger scope of all Americans, all payers and all health providers.

The Strategy Model is also being used on the cross-cutting issue of vulnerability.

Similarly, it is being used to build an overall strategic approach, **Thriving Future**, addressing whole communities, nations and broader areas.

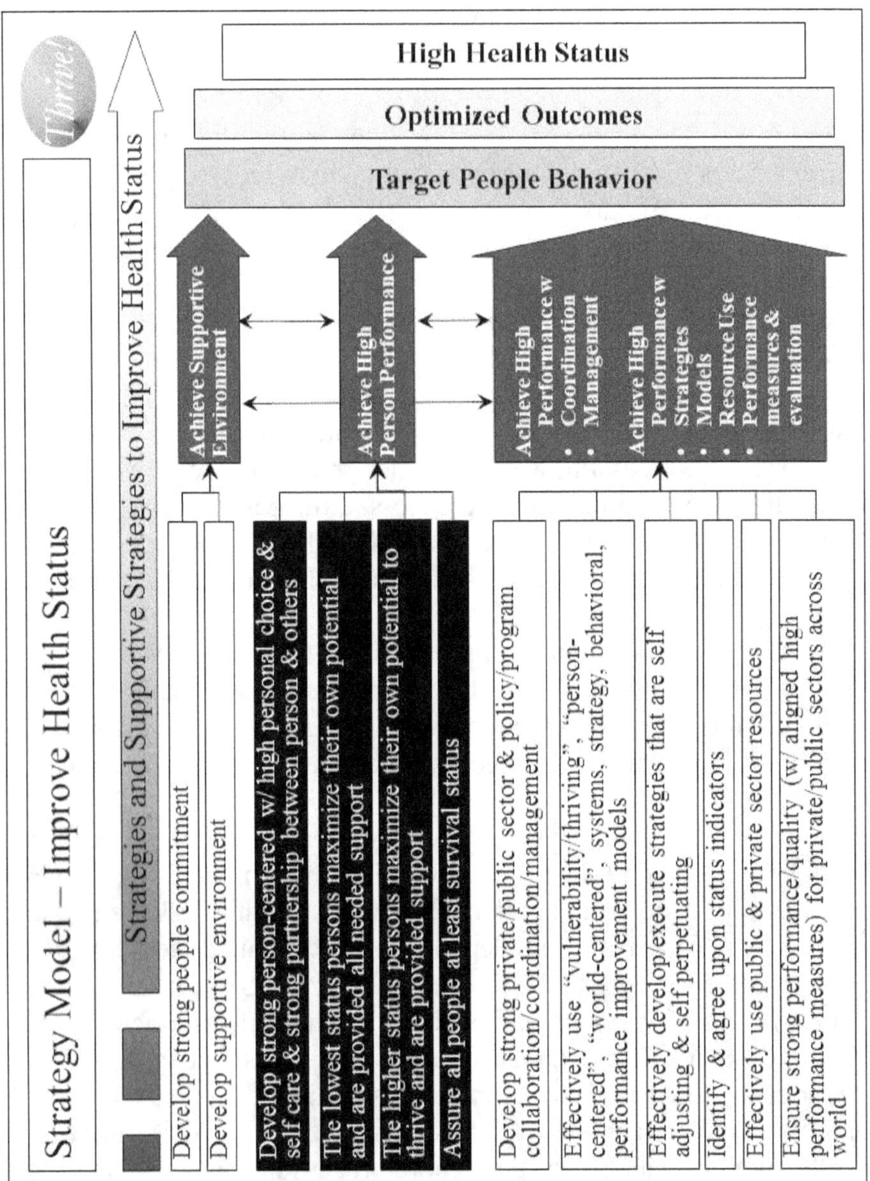

Figure A.11. Strategy Model – Improve Health [and Functional] Status

Status Model.

What is it?   The Status Model is used to identify the desired and current status for "whole" systems (e.g., a non-geographic population, a community, a nation, a broader area), issue areas (e.g., health, education) or cross-cutting issue areas (e.g., vulnerability, climate, habitat) that are targeted for positive, large scale change. It also includes the status indicators and their supportive measures such as those shown in Figure A.12.

How does it work? For endeavors to create and sustain positive systems to be successful, we need to determine how we are doing today, how we are doing as we progress to the desired system and how we are doing when we achieve and work to sustain the desired system. The Status Model helps do that as shown in Table A.10.

How has it been used and helped?   The Status Model's primary use has been for improving health. Its potential use is being explored in creating an overall strategy for reducing vulnerability and improving the status of a community, nation or broader area.

In both the draft CMS Strategic and Operational Plan (2006) and the work being done on how to "achieve a healthy America", the model's applications are similar. Both include status indicators that apply across America. Both depend on more detailed measures to support and add depth to the indicators. The CMS approach focused a bit more on CMS beneficiaries but did include all Americans. The "healthy America" approach uses status indicators that apply to all Americans. The health status indicators address the person's ability and motivation to achieve high health status. The same is true for health care providers. These are more process indicators. The status indicators include outcomes of various treatments and other health interventions. The status indicators go further and include what most consider as "health status" indicators such as low morbidity and mortality, high quality of life, high satisfaction, and low future risk for adverse events. Current status is assessed as well as the negative gap between the desired future high health status and current lower health status.

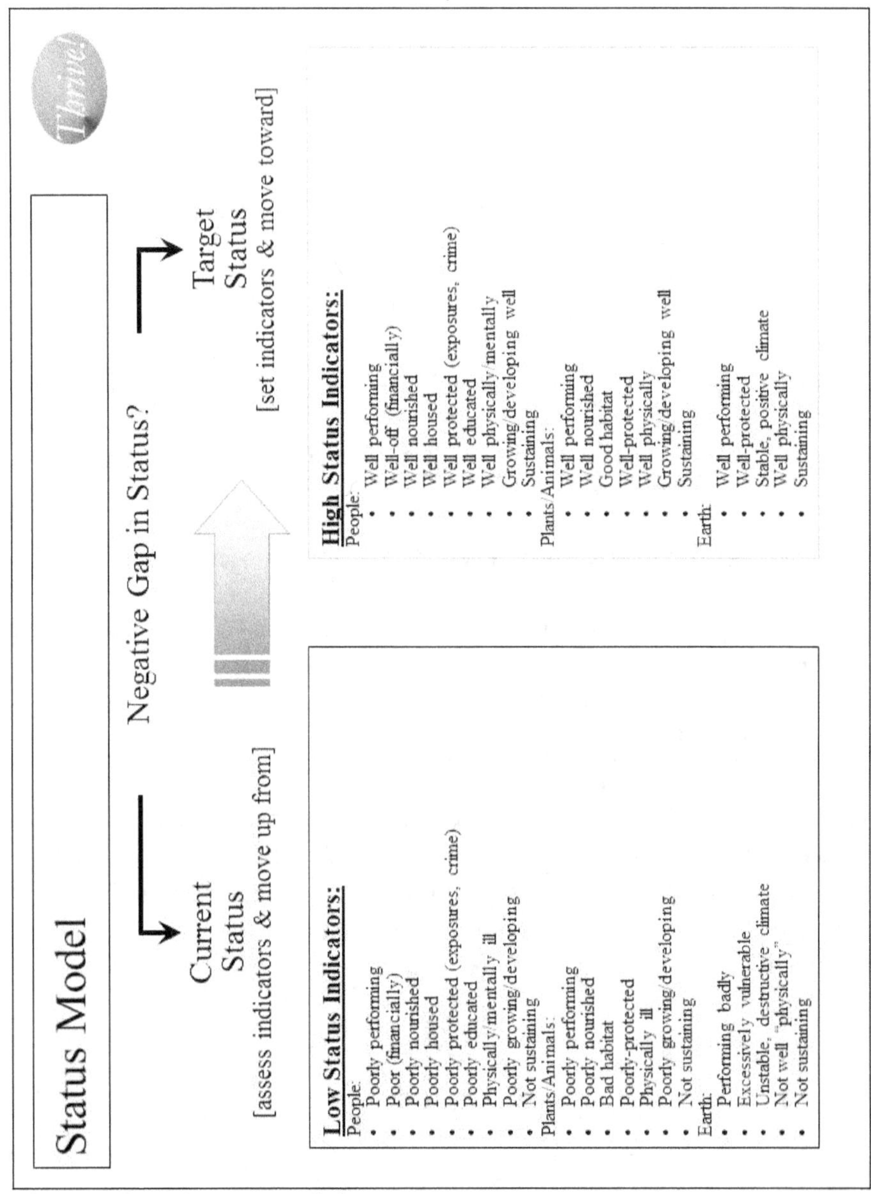

Figure A.12. Status Model

Table A.10. Status Model

The Status Model is as follows:
- Determine what is the issue area, cross-cutting area or "whole" system for which the strategy is targeted and status indicators are needed.
- Decide how high, in general, is the desired status. Is it optimal?   If not, how close can we get to optimal?
- Identify all of the indicators that, as a set, indicate the desired high status. These are the "Target Status" set of indicators.
- Decide what each indicator's level should be to match the desired high status.
- Decide what each indicator's level is to describe low status.
- To the extent needed, identify more detailed measures for each indicator.
- Assess the "Current Status", i.e., the current level of indicators for the target population.
- Assess the "Negative Gap" between the current status and the desired target status. This is the gap to be closed with the overall strategy.
- Execute the status model effectively and measure progress.
- Assess the effectiveness of the status indicators.
- Revise status indicators, individually and as a set, as needed to be effective.

The model is being used on the overall American health and to answer what is a "healthy America". With similarities to the CMS Plan, the status model helps support a strategy, **Health_ePeople**, with the larger scope of all Americans and all health providers. [See Figure A.13.]

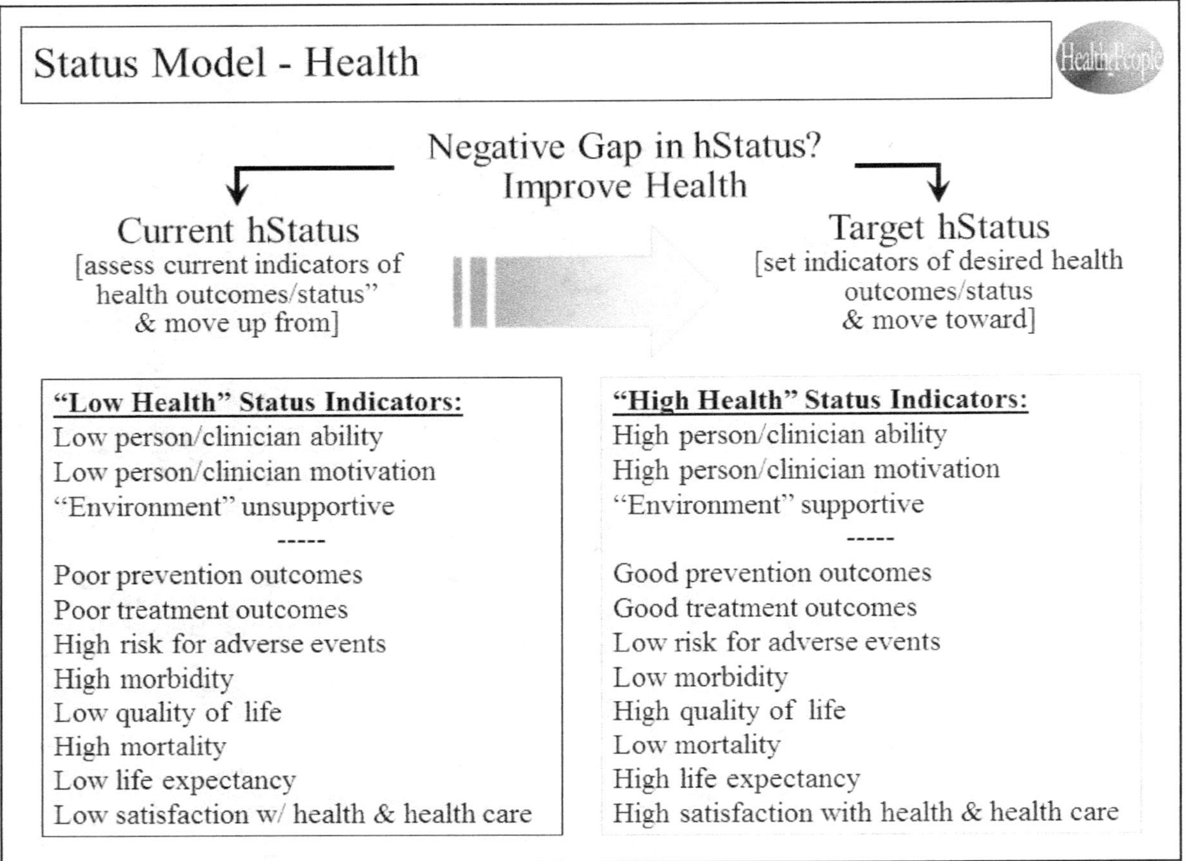

Figure A.13. Status Model - Health

For the broader work on communities, nations and broader areas, the full set of status indicators is very large but can be grouped into high level categories with supportive measures. They should encompass all the significant indicators covering the full breadth of the target area. On the highest level, they must be meaningful enough to provide guidance on improving the whole target area as a whole system. They must be supported by clearly defined measures that can be measured by data that is available into the future. Further, the status indicators must be flexible enough to adjust to changing future conditions. With these status indicators, a strategy can be developed and its progress assessed.

The Path Ahead

Potential "next generation" models do exist for strategy at system (issue area, community, nation, broader area) and person levels. As proposed here, one such model is the *Thrive!* **Next Generation Toolkit** - a core set and system of supportive models addressing persons, systems, motivation, ability, behavior, performance and its improvement, process measures, and, most importantly, positive outcomes and improved status. While parts of the strategy can be used independently, they have more power and are more likely to produce the best results when used as a full set.

The path ahead offers many opportunities, as outlined above, to tackle large, complex issue areas, cross-cutting issues and whole communities and nations. Already late, now is the time to aggressively use "next generation" strategies for solving large problems and creating and sustaining positive, large scale change and a surviving and thriving future for all forever, to the maximum extent possible.